Successful COBOL Upgrades

Highlights and Programming Techniques

Young Chae
Steven Rogers

Wiley Computer Publishing

John Wiley & Sons, Inc.
NEW YORK · CHICHESTER · WEINHEIM · BRISBANE · SINGAPORE · TORONTO

*To the memory of my loving parents,
Dongsun and Soran Chae.*

–Y. C.

To my wife, Terri Rogers.

–S. R.

Designations used by companies to distinguish their products are often claimed as trademarks. In all instances where John Wiley & Sons, Inc., is aware of a claim, the product names appear in initial capital or ALL CAPITAL LETTERS. Readers, however, should contact the appropriate companies for more complete information regarding trademarks and registration.

This book is printed on acid-free paper. ∞

Copyright © by Young Chae and Steven Rogers. All rights reserved.

Published by John Wiley & Sons, Inc.

Published simultaneously in Canada.

No part of this publication may be reproduced, stored in a retrieval system or transmitted in any form or by any means, electronic, mechanical, photocopying, recording, scanning or otherwise, except as permitted under Sections 107 or 108 of the 1976 United States Copyright Act, without either the prior written permission of the Publisher, or authorization through payment of the appropriate per-copy fee to the Copyright Clearance Center, 222 Rosewood Drive, Danvers, MA 01923, (978) 750-8400, fax (978) 750-4744. Requests to the Publisher for permission should be addressed to the Permissions Department, John Wiley & Sons, Inc., 605 Third Avenue, New York, NY, 10158-0012, (212) 850-6011, fax: (212) 850-6008, e-mail: PERMREQ@WILEY.COM.

This publication is designed to provide accurate and authoritative information in regard to the subject matter covered. It is sold with the understanding that the publisher is not engaged in professional services. If professional advice or other expert assistance is required, the services of a competent professional person should be sought.

Library of Congress Cataloging-in-Publication Data:
Chae, Young, 1939-
   Successful COBOL upgrades : highlights and programming techniques
  / Young Chae, Steven Rogers.
  p.   cm.
    "Wiley computer publishing."
    Includes index.
    ISBN 0-471-33011-6 (pbk. : alk. paper)
    1. COBOL (Computer program language) I. Rogers, Steven, 1961-
. II. Title.
QA76.73.C25C47 1999
005.13'3—dc21   99-17181
                                                                       CIP

Printed in the United States of America.

10 9 8 7 6 5 4 3 2 1

TABLE OF CONTENTS

Acknowledgments vi
Preface vii
Introduction: Why Should You Upgrade COBOL? viii
    The Future of the Mainframe viii
    What's So Good about COBOL? ix
    The History of COBOL Enhancements xi
    ANSI Standards xiii
    IBM's Language Environment (LE) xiv
    PC COBOL xvi
    Year 2000 Conversion xvi
    Experiences with COBOL Upgrades xxii
    COBOL Upgrades by Migration Path and Metrics xxiii
    The Future of COBOL Programming xxv
    Change Management xxviii
    Three Options for Your COBOL Upgrade xxix

Part I: Manually Upgrading COBOL 1

Chapter 1: Successful Manual Upgrades 3
    1.1 VS COBOL II: Unsupported Features 3
    1.2 Organizing the Project 5
    1.3 OS/VS COBOL Update Issues 8
    1.4 Reserved Words 12
    1.5 Determining Language Level(s) 22
    1.6 Upgrading OS/VS COBOL to VS COBOL II 23
    1.7 Migrating from OS/VS COBOL to VS COBOL II 53
    1.8 Conclusion 55

Chapter 2: Report Writer, ISAM, BDAM, and Communications ... 57
    2.1 Report Writer Conversion Options and Issues 57
    2.2 ISAM Conversion Options and Issues 59
    2.3 ISAM Extraction 62
    2.4 BDAM Conversion Issues 62
    2.5 Communications 66
    2.6 Conclusion 66

Chapter 3: Upgrading CICS Manually or Using a Tool (CCCA) 69
    3.1 Manually Converting CICS 69
    3.2 Using CCCA to Convert CICS 80
    3.3 Converting CICS Statements 81
    3.4 Conclusion 83

Chapter 4: Upgrading VS COBOL II to COBOL/370 Manually 85
    4.1 Introduction 85
    4.2 COBOL Language Elements Converted to
        COBOL for MVS & VM 88
    4.3 Migrating from COBOL II to COBOL for MVS 96
    4.4 Conclusion 98

Part II: Upgrading COBOL Using a Tool 99

Chapter 5: Tool-Based COBOL Upgrades 101
    5.1 Selecting a Tool 102
    5.2 The Conversion Process with CCCA 106
    5.3 Running CCCA for Upgrading OS/VS COBOL
        to VS COBOL II 119
    5.4 COBOL Language Elements Converted to VS COBOL II .. 121
    5.5 VSAM Problem with CCCA 155
    5.6 Conclusion 155

**Chapter 6: Upgrading OS/VS COBOL to
VS COBOL/370 Using CCCA** 157
    6.1 Ideal Migration Path 157
    6.2 COBOL Language Elements Converted to COBOL/370 ... 158
    6.3 CCCA Conversions 189
    6.4 Conclusion 198

Chapter 7: Upgrading VS COBOL II to COBOL/370 Using CCCA . . . 199
    7.1 Language Elements Converted to COBOL/370. 199
    7.2 Language Elements Converted to COBOL/370
        from VS COBOL II 200
    7.3 Migrating from VS COBOL II to COBOL/370 211
    7.4 Conclusion 219

Part III: Outsourcing the Upgrade 221

Chapter 8: The Factory Approach 223
    8.1 The Factory Process 223
    8.2 Factory Traits 224
    8.3 Finding the Right Partner 227
    8.4 Conclusion 228

Appendix A: COBOL Language Level Comparison 229

**Appendix B: A More Advanced Conversion
               and Compile Reporting Sample**. 243

Appendix C: Sample Compile Jobs 247

Appendix D: Comparing CCCA, Version 2.0 and Version 2.1 259

Appendix E: Run-time Issues with CCCA 2.0 271

About the Authors 279

Index 280

ACKNOWLEDGEMENTS

Ever since the authors started working as computer programmers in 1969 and 1979, it has been always their dream to write a book on computer programming. Our sincerest thanks to the people working with John Wiley & Sons, Inc.: Marjorie Spencer, Margaret Hendrey, Gerrie Cho, and Sheck Cho.

The authors wish to acknowledge the assistance of the employees of Ernst & Young, LLP (E&Y) in the preparation of this book. E&Y employees provided ideas, valuable information, and excellent comments on the subject of successful COBOL upgrades. Without such assistance, this book would have been much more difficult to write. Special thanks go to Terry Young, the director of E&Y's Accelerated Conversion Center (ACC), who approved the writing of this book. Special thanks also go to Gary Sabia, Trung To, Brad Kimball, and Alan Arnold, who provided ideas, encouragement, and other valuable information.

The authors also wish to acknowledge the assistance of the employees of IBM Corporation in the preparation of this book. Special thanks go to Jennifer D. Goff, the program administrator of IBM's Copyright, Intellectual Property Law Department in Armonk, New York, who provided us with written permission to use documentation from IBM's CCCA, Release 2.0 and CCCA, Release 2.1. We are also grateful to Brad Bocking of the CCCA, Release 2.0 Support department of IBM Global Services, Australia, for going through our list of problems and queries and addressing each of them separately. We would also like to thank Bob Folosio of IBM Languages Technical Support, Santa Teresa Lab, Santa Teresa, California, for supporting the authors on CCCA issues.

Young would like to give special thanks to his wife, Myoung, for her encouragement, support, criticisms, and concern as we completed this manuscript. He is also grateful to his son and daughter for their assistance reviewing the manuscript.

PREFACE

COBOL is not dead. Any company that has recently undergone any form of Year 2000 review of its core applications knows just how alive and invaluable COBOL programs still are. Your COBOL programs may not be pretty, they may not have been well cared for through an organized source management utility, but day in, day out, they worked for you. They managed your finances, processed your claims, printed your checks, and rarely complained about their tasks. But now they need a facelift, a little care to keep them healthy and active for the next ten to twenty years.

COBOL has never been dead. In fact, it has become more robust, shed many of its outdated features, and is ready to move into the twenty-first century. For anyone who will be involved in a COBOL upgrade project, this book will provide practical advice, technical hints, and perhaps dispel a few errant upgrade myths (e.g., it only takes a recompile to get from COBOL II to COBOL for MVS). The authors have been actively involved in many COBOL upgrades since joining Ernst & Young's Year 2000 conversion factory, the Accelerated Conversion Center (ACC), in 1996. Many companies used the Y2K problem as an opportunity to give a facelift to their code, and the ACC was there to upgrade from COBOL/68 to COBOL/74, COBOL II to COBOL for MVS, or anything in between. The lessons we learned from these efforts are in this book, which will cover everything from how to upgrade your code manually to upgrading using a tool, specifically IBM's COBOL upgrade utility, CCCA (Release 2.0).

We call it knowledge sharing. You call it reading a manual. In either case, let's get started.

INTRODUCTION

Why Should You Upgrade COBOL?

The Future of the Mainframe

We all know that the mainframe isn't going to disappear. With $5 trillion invested in legacy business systems globally, mainframe applications remain the lifeblood of the world's leading companies. Stable and tirelessly reliable, mainframe-based systems continue to run mission-critical business processes across many industries. In fact, it's been estimated that over 70 percent of all corporate data is stored and processed on mainframe computers. Mainframes excel wherever there is a need for high security, rock-solid reliability, or immense processing capacity. The mainframe market may not be growing as it once was, but at an estimated $17 billion worldwide, it is too big for anyone to ignore.

Recently, IBM announced the fifth generation of its System 390 mainframe, which effectively closed the performance gap with Hitachi's bipolar-based Skyline machines. But, more importantly, IBM also outlined a series of initiatives aimed at winning the deployment of new off-the-shelf applications on System 390. These include enterprise resource planning (ERP) programs, like SAP's R/3 backoffice suite, Oracle financial applications, and PeopleSoft's manufacturing and human resources software.

IBM has also made a pitch for electronic commerce (or "e-commerce") and has taken steps to make the venerable 390 architecture play better in a networked world.

Mainframes have become smaller and less expensive, but at $100,000 for an entry-level machine and up to several million dollars at the high end, they clearly cost more than PC-based servers. Nevertheless, because one mainframe can do the work of several servers, with considerable savings in reduced management and support, the total cost of ownership of a 390-class machine is competitive. As companies begin offering online transactions (e-commerce), the traditional virtues of the mainframe—security and high throughput—become attractive. By altering the System 390 so it can understand the communication rules of the Internet, IBM has made the machine a powerful Web server.

IBM's DB/2 is also probably the most secure place you can keep your data. One advantage of mainframes is that there is effectively no limit to how big the systems can become. Many 390s can be joined to function as one giant mainframe. The year 2000 and European currency (Euro dollar) issues are only increasing the demands on these systems. Even as UNIX and NT servers make inroads, mainframes continue to do the heavy lifting in most large corporations.

Mainframes are coming back. "Big iron is cheaper, more reliable, and more secure than UNIX or NT platforms," say many returning mainframe users. The mainframe, once the backbone of many enterprises, is regaining momentum. Mainframes provide better price, performance, and return on investment than UNIX and Windows NT systems, while delivering proven security, scalability, and reliable centralized management. And your COBOL applications are doing the heavy lifting on the mainframe machines.

What's So Good about COBOL?

COBOL is the most important programming language for business applications. There is no language that is more widely used than COBOL on the mainframe. COBOL is designed specifically for the large-volume data processing typical of commercial applications such as payroll, inventory, and accounting.

There are more lines of COBOL out there than any other language. Several billions lines of COBOL are still in use today. On December 6, 1995, the Great COBOL Debate, sponsored by IBM, took place at the Jacob K. Javits Center, in conjunction with the DBExpo show. According to Dave McFarland, founder and director of the COBOL Foundation, there are about thirty million man-years of COBOL code running the world. This is a sizable collection of work! COBOL is available on many platforms, which allows for portability. As a result, your programs will compile on a variety of different machines with very few changes needed to the actual code (aside from differing I/O environments).

There are thousands of third-party products that have been developed to aid the COBOL programmer in the critical areas of testing, debugging, application analysis, production support, and code reuse. In addition:

- COBOL is capable of handling a wide range of processing volumes.
- COBOL is the number-two language for developing client/server applications.
- Because of the advantages it offers in the development of business applications, COBOL is still frequently used worldwide for business applications (it's the lingua franca of business IT).
- COBOL applications are so feature-rich and are doing such an excellent job performing mission-critical applications that users don't really want to retire them.
- COBOL programs are relatively easy to develop, use, and maintain.

COBOL is a high-level, English-like language that, when used correctly, can resemble a well-structured novel with appendices, cross-reference tables, chapters, footnotes, and paragraphs. Accordingly, its greatest strength is the ease with which it adapts to almost all business-related applications.

Unlike other languages, COBOL is self-documenting, and even nontechnical people have been known to learn COBOL within a few weeks and become productive without understanding the internal architecture of the operating environment. More importantly, when the original programmer decides to leave, a replacement can be trained on the application and will be able to carry on with ease because of COBOL's readability.

COBOL is still the most portable language. COBOL users can transport their applications to many different hardware platforms without recompiling the source code. This important feature provides insurance against hardware obsolescence. The users' hardware investment retains its value. It is possible to upgrade to a new platform without changing a single line of code. For the developer providing systems on multiple platforms, this portability means they only have to maintain one set of source code, which significantly reduces maintenance costs. For the past thirty-five years, COBOL has been taught in colleges, universities, and trade schools worldwide. There are an estimated three million COBOL programmers employed today.

The History of COBOL Enhancements

COBOL has survived and flourished in great part due to its dynamic nature. As processing needs changed, COBOL changed. When a new database became en vogue, language developers for COBOL supported it. In Table I.1 we present a history of great moments in COBOL history.

Table I.1 A History of COBOL Events

YEAR	CATEGORY	ENHANCEMENTS OR SPECIAL EVENT
1959	COBOL was originated.	
1968	COBOL was revised.	ANSI 68 OS/VS COBOL language level (01). IBM product number is 5734-CB2.
1968–73	ISAM	Index Sequential Access Method (ISAM) was IBM's software for indexed files.
1973	VSAM	IBM provided Virtual Storage Access Method (VSAM) in 1973 as a replacement for ISAM.
1974	COBOL was revised a second time.	OS/VS COBOL language level (02) is COBOL 1974. IBM product number is 5740-CB1.
1980–85	COBOL was again revised.	
1984	VS COBOL II (Release 1.0) was issued by IBM, marking the beginning of the new standard in IBM COBOL. The compiler name is IGYCRTL.	The following features of OS/VS COBOL were eliminated: READY TRACE, EXHIBIT, EXAMINE, CURRENT-DATE, TRANSFORM, ON REMARKS, Report Writer, exponentiation, floating-point data, complex OCCURS DEPENDING ON data items, TALLY, and APPLY WRITE-ONLY. IBM product number is 5668-958.
1986	CCCA, Release 1.0,	COBOL and CICS/VS Command

continues

Table I.1 *(Continued)*

YEAR	CATEGORY	ENHANCEMENTS OR SPECIAL EVENT
	was made available by IBM.	Level Conversion Aid. (Program offering—Release 1.0)
1986	VS COBOL II, Release 2.0, was made available by IBM.	Exponentiation, floating-point data, complex OCCURS DEPENDING ON data items, TALLY, APPLY WRITE-ONLY features of OS/VS COBOL were reinstated by VS COBOL II (Release 2).
		The 1974 ANSI COBOL standard (except Report Writer, Communications Feature, and level 2 of the debug module) had been supported by VS COBOL II (Release 2).
		Some of the 1985 ANSI COBOL features (EVALUATE, INITIALIZE, and the in-line PERFORM) had been included on VS COBOL II (Release 2).
1987	Support for ISAM is dropped.	IBM dropped CICS support for ISAM.
		IBM also dropped all COBOL language support for ISAM in VS COBOL II.
1988	VS COBOL II, Release 3.0, was made available by IBM.	Multiple PROCEDURE DIVISIONs and seven levels of subscripts and indexes could be coded. Files and data could be externally shared among many programs. Many other changes to support 1985 ANSI COBOL standard had been incorporated in VS COBOL II (Release 3.0).
1990	VS COBOL II, Release 3.1, was made available by IBM.	VS COBOL II (Release 3.1) allowed programs running under VM/SP 6 to support those VS COBOL II functions that were only available when running under MVS.
1992	OS/VS COBOL support is dropped.	OS/VS COBOL was withdrawn from IBM's marketing.
1992	VS COBOL II, Release 4.0, was made available by IBM.	IBM product number is 5668-958.
1994	COBOL/370 Version 1, Release 1.0	In July, 1994, COBOL/370, Version 1, Release 1.0, compiler was shipped to customers by IBM.
		IBM product number is 5688-197 (Release 1.0).
		Intrinsic function provides the capability to reference a data item whose value is derived automatically at the time of reference during the execution of the object program. The examples are as follows:
		ANNUITY, CURRENT-DATE, DATE-OF-INTEGER,

YEAR	CATEGORY	ENHANCEMENTS OR SPECIAL EVENT
		MAX, MEAN, MIN, PRESENT-VALUE, SQRT, SUM, WHEN-COMPILED, and so on.
1994	OS/VS COBOL support is dropped.	OS/VS COBOL was withdrawn from IBM's service.
1994	CCCA, Release 1.6	Support for CCCA, Release 1.6, ceased in November 1994.
1995	COBOL for MVS & VM	In 1995, COBOL for MVS & VM was made available by IBM.
		IBM product number is 5688-197 (Release 2.0).
1996	VS COBOL II V1.3.X	For VS COBOL II V1.3.X, marketing and service support was withdrawn from IBM's service.
1997	VS COBOL II V1.4.0	Marketing support was withdrawn from IBM's service.
1997	VS COBOL II	IBM announced its withdrawal of support for VS COBOL II.
1998	CCCA, Release 2.1, was made available by IBM.	CCCA for OS/390 and MVS & VM was made available with Version 2, Release 1.0. MLE (millennium language extension) and DATE FORMAT conversion is added.
2001	VS COBOL II V1.4.0	For VS COBOL II V1.4.0, service support will be withdrawn from IBM's service.

ANSI Standards

COBOL has established a track record for maintaining open standards. The ANSI standard for COBOL has been set since 1968. Every six to ten years the standards for COBOL have been extended to meet the requirements of the current computing environment. See Table I.2. The ANSI standard committee played a big role in upgrades for COBOL.

Object-oriented language, OO COBOL, is an extension to the COBOL language. It will be included in the new standard COBOL 97. OO COBOL supports the transition from traditional programming style to object-oriented development techniques. With the growing availability of OO COBOL compilers the amount of OO COBOL code will also increase.

Table I.2 History of ANSI Standard and IBM COBOL Enhancements

YEAR	ANSI STANDARD	IBM COBOL ENHANCEMENTS
1968	ANSI 68	OS/VS COBOL language level (01). IBM product number is 5734-CB2.
1974	ANSI 74	OS/VS COBOL language level (02). IBM product number is 5740-CB1.
1984	ANSI 74	VS COBOL II (Release 1.0). IBM product number is 5668-958.
1986	ANSI 74	VS COBOL II (Release 2.0).
1988	ANSI 85	VS COBOL II (Release 3.0).
1990	ANSI 85	VS COBOL II (Release 3.1).
1992	ANSI 85	VS COBOL II (Release 4.0). IBM product number is 5668-958.
1994	ANSI 85	COBOL/370, Version 1, Release 1.0. IBM product number is 5688-197 (Release 1.0).
1995	ANSI 85	COBOL for MVS & VM. IBM product number is 5688-197 (Release 2).

IBM's Language Environment (LE)

IBM's Language Environment (LE) was created to allow mixed-language applications to have a consistent method for accessing common, frequently used services. Building mixed-language applications is easier with LE-conforming routines because Language Environment establishes a consistent environment for all languages in the application. Both the compiler and run time for COBOL for MVS & VM require LE, and, as we will see, LE gives applications a number of useful functions (think of it as "COBOL for MVS & VM Plus").

Language Environment provides the base for future IBM language library enhancements in the MVS, VM, VSE, and OS/400 environments. Many system dependencies have been removed from LE-conforming language products. Because Language Environment provides a common library with services that you can call through a common callable interface, the behavior of your applications may be easier to predict. Language Environment's common library includes the following:

- Common services such as messages, date and time functions, math functions
- Application utilities
- System services
- Subsystem support

The language-specific portions of Language Environment provide language interfaces and specific services that are supported for each individual language. Language Environment is accessed through defined, common, calling conventions. LE establishes consistent condition handling for HLLs, debug tools, and assembler language routines. For languages with little or no condition handling function, like COBOL, LE provides a user-controlled method that was not available before for predictable, robust error recovery. LE condition handling honors single- and mixed-language semantics and is integrated with message-handling services to provide specific information about each condition.

This language-independent condition handler, unlike some existing HLL condition semantics, is stack frame–based and delivers predictable behavior at a given stack frame. Language Environment condition handling enables you to construct applications out of building blocks of modules and control which modules will handle certain conditions. Language Environment provides compatible support for existing HLL applications. For mixed-language applications (for example, COBOL, PL/I, however, relinking is required. Routines compiled with the new LE-conforming compilers can be mixed with old routines in an application. Thus, applications can be enhanced or maintained selectively, without recompiling the whole application when a change is made to a single routine.

LE also eliminates incompatibilities among language-specific run-time environments. Routines call one another within one common run-time environment, eliminating the need for initialization and the termination of a language-specific run-time environment with each call. This makes interlanguage communication (ILC) in mixed-language applications easier, more efficient, and more consistent.

This ILC capability also means that you can share and reuse code easily. You can write a service routine in the language of your choice—C/C++,

COBOL, PL/I, or Assembler—and allow that routine to be called from C/C++, COBOL, PL/I, or Assembler applications. Language Environment also provides a common dump for all conforming languages. The dump includes, in an easier-to-read format, a description of any relevant conditions and information on error location, variables, and storage.

With Language Environment and OpenEdition DCE application support, you can access host data and application logic in CICS and IMS from any DCE client in the network. You write the client code in C and the server code in C, COBOL, or PL/I to access code you already have.

PC COBOL

Many developers prefer to do COBOL maintenance on the PC using packages such as Micro Focus, Realia, or IBM's VisualAge COBOL because it is easier and, if implemented well, less costly than doing it directly on the mainframe. As such, programmers download the code from the mainframe to the PC, work on the code, and then upload to the mainframe. They want to use COBOL on the PC to increase programmer productivity and reduce testing/debugging time.

COBOL programmers want portability and to be able to develop and run software on open systems and client/server architectures with graphical user interface (GUI) front ends and ease of use features associated with graphical environments. They want to build windows into character-based (non-GUI) applications, including menu bars and drop-down menus; list boxes; check boxes; and support for the use of a mouse, including editing features such as highlighting, erasing, and replacing selected text. PC-based COBOL helps them with these features and many others.

Year 2000 Conversion

There is not much time left until the year 2000! The approach of that date has forced the IT industry to confront the largest software maintenance job ever. Without some code changes, date-sensitive legacy computer systems will crash on or before January 1, 2000, if they cannot interpret dates with two-digit year values correctly.

The Year 2000 conversion for COBOL programs is an immense undertaking. More than 200 billion lines of COBOL code are in use today, with billions more being added every year. Companies will spend millions of dollars so they can successfully enter the next millennium. Today, an entire IT industry exists solely for the purpose of assisting organizations in dealing with this important issue. You can rest assured that COBOL will make a successful transition into the next century.

The following list shows the timeline for a typical COBOL upgrade in a Y2K remediation project. Many IT organizations would like to update their existing COBOL application systems at the same time they do their Y2K conversion because this takes advantage of the test environments that are generally constructed for completing Y2K testing. Which should you do first? Do you perform the language upgrade first and then perform the Y2K remediation, or should you do it the other way around? Our experience in these combined efforts has shown that it is preferable to complete them in the following order:

- Perform baseline testing with existing code.
- Perform COBOL upgrades.
- Execute Y2K conversion.
- Conduct remediated code testing.

You will conduct the testing only once after the two conversions are completed. This approach will save testing resources: MIPS, DASD (direct access storage device), and staff costs. Consider that when you do a COBOL upgrade and then test the result first and then complete the Y2K conversion and then test the results a second time, the time and cost for both conversions simply doubles. The goal of both conversions is *not* to change the application's functionality. Rather, its goal is only to change its ability to process with Y2K dates and within the newest, maintained operating environments, so the testing should look for the same results in both instances. You should perform the COBOL upgrade first, however, because you are likely to change field names, copybook structures, and other COBOL statements during this conversion. Your Y2K conversion, which should focus on date, year, and century fields, should use these new names, structures, and statements.

Table I.3 shows a typical schedule of Y2K conversion tasks for a typical application of five hundred COBOL programs and the sequence of operations to accomplish both COBOL upgrades and Y2K conversion simultaneously and efficiently. The schedule shown in Table I.3 assumes you will perform the language upgrade manually (tools are also available—more on them later in this book beginning in Chapter 3), but will use a utility to make your code Y2K-ready. Some tasks may be done simultaneously if you have the resources available. The plan in Table I.3 assumes that adequate technical resources and personnel who are knowledgeable about the application are available for both efforts.

Table I.3 Y2K Conversion Tasks Timetable

CONVERSION TIMELINE	CONVERSION TASK
Week 1	**COBOL Upgrades** During this week, if there are any COBOL programming language upgrades to be performed, you should begin the original source code and copybooks upgrade. You need to identify the correct source and copybook modules and exclude obsolete modules from the process. **Build a Test Environment** If a test environment does not exist, you need to construct a separate test environment containing appropriate databases and transaction environments. It should be as identical to the production environment (production like—don't forget user-exits!) as possible and as isolated from the production environment as possible. This helps isolate problems. If your test environment remains connected to your production environment, it becomes more difficult to narrow down where anomalies originate. You also need to begin deciding what you are going to test. Ideally, Y2K testing only involves testing those programs that are date-impacted. You need to identify business transactions that are impacted by dates and develop tests that will exercise these programs.
Week 2	**Date Identification—Updating the Date/Year/Century Field Filters** Subject matter experts (SMEs) should identify any potential date/year patterns (patterns other than typical YYMMDD, XX-DATE, etc.) and definitions (how are your dates defined? Any unusual types such as PIC S9(7)V9?) that might otherwise be missed. COBOL upgrades continue.
Week 3	**Build Repository and Produce Inventory Reports** A series of survey jobs are run to build the source repositories and identify missing inventory (source/load) elements. Y2K tools scan JCL to look for other procs, programs, and loads. Y2K tools scan programs for other programs and copybooks and then scan copybooks for other copybooks. Your conversion team uses these reports to identify missing elements or modules that may be in nonproduction libraries. COBOL upgrades continue.

CONVERSION TIMELINE	CONVERSION TASK
Week 4	**Complete COBOL Upgrade and Check Compiles** Once upgrades are completed, verify that all newly upgraded programs are compiling cleanly (now is also a good time to implement a policy of clean-compiles for production-bound code). This is an important step toward establishing a clean-room approach to source management. Move this code into your Y2K libraries. The impact should be minimal for the Y2K work completed so far since you shouldn't have changed date field names or formats. **Y2K Production of Dates in Indexes Report and External Sorts** The Dates in Indexes and External Sorts reports locate two-digit years involved in database indexing and sequencing. Uncorrected two-digit years in indexes or sorts will cause data to be returned in an incorrect order during processing once Y2K dates are introduced into the data. This may require that SMEs, including DBAs, review and respond. During this week, the Dates in Indexes report is generated and produced. If a file or database contains a two-digit year, processing (retrieving) records will not function properly after the year 2000 because of the function indexes play in a database. Indexes cause records to be sorted in a particular order (ascending or descending) based upon keys/indexes. If a database features a two-digit year (standalone or as part of a date field) it will not sort properly (as 00 suddenly comes before 99). The solution is either to expand the database to be fully four digits or to code a workaround. Expansion involves dropping the existing key with a two-digit year and writing programs or utilities to add a 19 (or 20) to a newly added century field for the now four-digit year key field and then reinserting the records. Then the programs and copybooks need to be changed to reflect a four-digit field. Expanding a database, if it is necessary, occurs later on in the process, however. **JCL:** Should there be any dates in batch sorts (sorted by SyncSort or DFSORT) that involve two-digit years, then these too require some form of correction (most sort packages today feature built-in window routines). Please note that your organization may not use SyncSort or DFSORT. While these are the most common sort utilities, other utilities including homegrown ones do exist. The most process-intensive method would be to expand the two-digit years to four-digit years, to sort, and then to shrink down again so any subsequent file reads are unaffected. The processing to perform this, however, is likely to have a serious impact on the time it takes to run the job and to expand, sort, and shrink the data. A better method is to use the data window feature built into the current releases of SyncSort and DFSORT. Just as we build windows to interpret the century bytes for application programs, SyncSort and DFSORT feature window routines to interpret centuries around two-digit year fields in data files.

(continues)

Table I.3 Continued

CONVERSION TIMELINE	CONVERSION TASK
	Other issues in JCL, while rarer, include date data used in SYSIN cards. If you have chosen an expansion methodology (expanding all fields to have four-digit years) you will need to find and expand in-stream dates as well.
Week 5	**Production of Other Y2K Issues Reports**
	The other Y2K issues reports are used to identify Y2K problem areas that fall outside of the standard calculate/conditional two-digit year problems. These are Y2K problems that are likely to require either input from the organization SMEs or approval from the organization for the recommended fix. These reports need to be individually examined to now produce the corresponding analysis reports. These analysis reports document the elements of the raw reports that are, in fact, Y2K sensitive.
	These reports should identify where your applications have incorrect leap year processing; dates or years that process data involving all zeros, all nines, or other company-specific delimiters (010101, 99365, 010100, etc.); the locations of zero suppression masks for dates (to avoid printing blanks in 2000); and internal sorts that use two-digit years.
	Baseline Tests
	Now you should begin testing the functionality you began identifying in Week 1 by capturing the output of jobs and screens. Later, in regression tests, you will compare these baseline results against your converted code test results.
Weeks 6, 7, 8, 9	**Y2K Code Remediation**
	During the next four weeks, the actual remediation, or *fixing*, of the code occurs. This is completed either using a Y2K tool or through manual (editing) efforts.
	Manual Remediation
	Year 2000 fixes applied manually (through an editor) should follow the company's coding standards and techniques.
	Refreshed Code
	Refreshed code means that some additional changes have been made by the application owners, and these changes need to be included to make sure the process is operating on the latest version.
Week 10	**Compiles**
	Converted code now should be compiled to verify that syntactically correct code has been produced.

CONVERSION TIMELINE	CONVERSION TASK
Week 11	**TQM of Converted Code** Quality needs to be a part of every step of this process. Care must be taken to implement standard: - Comments - Code fixes - Copybooks - Documentation along the way **Code Corrections and Additions** Were there any changes made to the code to get it to run through your Y2K tool? Now is the time to undo them. **Complete Baseline Testing** Baseline testing should complete this week. If the machine resources are available, a separate Y2K environment should be established so any reruns of baseline can occur independent of the Y2K environment.
Weeks 12–24	At this point, the conversion team shifts focus from conversion to anomaly support and is responsible for correcting (debugging) implemented or missed fixes in the converted code. **Complete Integration Testing** Integration testing ensures your batch jobs complete all steps and your online tests finish all screens. However, you need not be concerned with verifying the accuracy of the tests, just that they complete. This is where you should identify the majority of your anomalies, including your COBOL upgrade errors. **Complete Regression Testing** Regression tests compare the baseline results to make sure that nonheader data remains accurate. Tests must complete in the identical way as baseline tests. **Complete Simulation Tests** System clock dates and data in files and databases are reset to important Y2K dates (this process is known as "aging"). Important dates will vary, but they often include dates in 1999, 2000, March of 2000 (to check leap year), 2001, and sometimes beyond.

Are there any Year 2000–related benefits to upgrading a particular programming language from an older version to the most current? Table I.4 provides a list of the known and current information on this subject.

Table I.4 Year 2000 Benefits of Upgrading to the Most Current Version of COBOL

LANGUAGE	VERSION	YEAR 2000 NOTE
COBOL	OS/VS	No longer supported. No Y2K support.
VS COBOL II	Non-LE	No Y2K (four-digit year) support. No future support planned.
COBOL for MVS (or COBOL/370)	LE	Intrinsic date functions. Four-digit year system dates. Ability to call PL/I programs under LE. May be able to use IBM's MLE (Millennium Language Extension, a compiler-based windowing technique that adjusts two-digit year date fields that are specifically identified by a new field type called 'DATE').

Experiences with COBOL Upgrades

Way back in 1972–78, Young Chae had an opportunity to convert old COBOL F programs to new ANS COBOL programs using IBM's LCP (Language Conversion Program) tool. At that time, the COBOL upgrade process was relatively simple, in that the tool converted almost all of the programs automatically.

Between June 1997 and September 1998, both authors converted almost 6,107 COBOL programs, including the following:

- OS/VS COBOL to VS COBOL II (4,362)
- OS/VS COBOL to VS COBOL/370 (599)
- VS COBOL II to COBOL/370 (1,146)

These types of COBOL upgrades are much more complex and difficult than the ones converted in the 1970s from old COBOL F programs to ANS COBOL. We also discovered, unfortunately, that the present-day tools can't convert all the old COBOL programs automatically, hence we needed to convert an extensive number of the COBOL programs manually. And when we started work on one particular Year 2000 conversion project in May 1997, the client saw the benefits of performing both the COBOL upgrade and Y2K conversion of their applications simultaneously. They wanted us to do it, and we were tasked with finding the best way to do it. With a little research, we chose to implement IBM's COBOL and CICS/VS Command Level Conversion Aid (which we will also refer to as CCCA, Release 2.0) This was in keeping with the Y2K factory's direction to automate all conversion activities as much as possible.

As with any other software tool product line, there are many other COBOL upgrade tools available. We have tried to present the various requirements of the tasks you will need to complete and how well a conversion tool will enhance the process, though it can still be completed manually. When we first started on this task, we spent many hours learning how to most effectively use the tool in a team environment. Without any duplication of effort we were able to break the work into manageable components and successfully execute the conversions of those thousands of COBOL programs. The ideas and effort we put in during that time has all gone into this book—and we are still converting those old COBOL programs of our clients. Once you have studied our processes and adapted them, like us you will also see a significant reduction in the hours needed to finish the job and yet still retain a maximum level of accuracy. If you don't have thousands of programs to convert and don't need to use a tool, you will still find value in the processes and information we provide in the rest of this book.

COBOL Upgrades by Migration Path and Metrics

Over the past four decades, IBM developed the following three COBOL products for the MVS & VM mainframe:

- OS/VS COBOL
- VS COBOL II
- COBOL for MVS & VM (originally known as COBOL/370)

OS/VS COBOL was withdrawn from IBM's marketing efforts in June 1992 and withdrawn from service in June 1994. Depending on which product you are currently using and how you want to migrate, there are three possible migration paths:

1. OS/VS COBOL to COBOL for MVS & VM
2. OS/VS COBOL to VS COBOL II
3. VS COBOL II to COBOL for MVS & VM

The metrics summary given in Table I.5 is an abridged yet helpful synopsis (compare your own company's COBOL inventory) that encapsulates

Table I.5 Migration Paths and Number of Upgraded Programs

MIGRATION PATHS	NUMBER OF COBOL PROGRAMS THE AUTHORS UPGRADED
OS/VS COBOL to COBOL for MVS & VM	599
OS/VS COBOL to VS COBOL II	4,362
VS COBOL II to COBOL for MVS & VM	1,146
TOTAL	6,107

our migration paths with the number of COBOL programs we have upgraded as of October 1998. The metrics shown in Tables I.5, I.6, and I.7 should give you some idea of the Herculean task we have accomplished.

Table I.6 Tracking of Converted Programs, Part 1

DATE STARTED	DATE ENDED	OS/VS COBOL TO VS COBOL II	VS COBOL II TO COBOL/370	OS/VS COBOL TO COBOL/370	TOTAL NUMBER OF PROGRAMS
5/19/97	6/15/97	364			364
6/6/97	7/11/97	85			85
6/22/97	6/27/97	208			208
7/14/97	11/12/97		284	336	620
9/8/97	9/26/97	362			362
9/23/97	10/13/98	431			431
10/18/97	1/23/98	75	10	189	274
11/8/97	11/30/97	864			864
12/17/97	1/3/98	22			22
1/26/98	2/1/98	32			32
2/16/98	3/29/98	305			305
2/19/98	3/5/98		245	74	319
3/1/98	6/19/98	395	298		693
3/26/98	7/8/98	220	309		529
4/13/98	5/28/98	434			434
5/28/98	7/9/98	191			191
5/29/98	6/16/98	56			56
6/2/98	7/1/98	302			302
6/29/98	6/23/98	16			16
TOTAL		4,362	1,146	599	6,107

Table I.7 Tracking of Converted Programs, Part 2

DATE STARTED	DATE ENDED	TOTAL NUMBER OF PROGRAMS	NUMBER OF CICS PROGRAMS	NUMBER OF DB/2 PROGRAMS	NUMBER OF ADABAS PROGRAMS
5/19/97	6/15/97	364			
6/6/97	7/11/97	85	17	0	36
6/22/97	6/27/97	208	10	15	
7/14/97	11/12/97	620	0	60	
9/8/97	9/26/97	362	0	0	301
9/23/97	10/13/98	431	0	0	
10/18/97	1/23/98	274	4	3	
11/8/97	11/30/97	864			
12/17/97	1/3/98	22	0	0	
1/26/98	2/1/98	32	3	1	10
2/16/98	3/29/98	305	3	0	
2/19/98	3/5/98	319	0	87	
3/1/98	6/19/98	693	0	159	
3/26/98	7/8/98	529	446		
4/13/98	5/28/98	434	40	1	161
5/28/98	7/9/98	191	27	0	80
5/29/98	6/16/98	56	5	2	14
6/2/98	7/1/98	302	58	1	101
6/29/98	6/23/98	16	7	1	7
TOTAL		6,107	700	330	710

There are many different reasons why COBOL upgrading is both a very interesting and a challenging task. Two of the primary reasons your company should want to upgrade your COBOL code is *to determine and manage your actual active inventory of programs and to bring your valuable mainframe applications up to current supported standards.*

Future of COBOL Programming

Technology consulting companies estimate the worldwide cost of Year 2000 conversion at $300 billion to $600 billion (Gartner Group), based on the overwhelming size of the effort and the late start made by most governments and business. The calculation of the U.S. federal government's portion of the bill: $30 billion. Qualified COBOL programmers now demand annual salaries of $100,000 to $200,000—and the price is going up. IT managers predict that the $1,200 daily rate for qualified COBOL consultants is likely to double soon.

People have been saying for years that COBOL is dead. Most colleges, universities, and trade schools no longer teach COBOL. But, recently, some have begun teaching it again. Also, many young people pick it up at job sites where it is still used. And many retired programmers are going back to work, lured by the premiums being offered for their services. Rather than getting caught up in the bidding wars, some companies are trying to stay out of the mainframe skills market altogether. One insurance company we know of, for example, is encouraging non-IT employees who want to change jobs to apply for slots in a recently reinstated in-house COBOL training program. This insurance company dropped its COBOL training in the mid-1980s when client/server skills became the priority but decided to restart the program this spring because of the increasing contracting fees.

Other companies never stopped COBOL training but are now trying to encourage more non-IT employees to take advantage of the programs. There's also outside help available to create fluent COBOL programmers. Training firms and universities offer intensive, short-term COBOL training programs to people who have an aptitude for computing but don't necessarily have prior mainframe experience. Some consulting firms are taking a similar tack by starting a COBOL training program specifically designed to draw people from nontechnology careers into the mainframe profession. Ideal candidates for the eight-week certificate program have strong backgrounds in math, languages, or music and are experienced workers who are looking for a career change. The challenge they usually face, however, is adapting not to COBOL but to the application's I/O environments (CICS, IMS, DB/2, VSAM, etc.). If your company is hoping to train non-IT professionals, don't forget to include these subjects as well.

It may be ironic, it may be irritating, but after years of being taken for granted and treated as a technological dinosaur by all the UNIX programmers, client/server programmers, and Web site developers, COBOL programmers are finally getting some respect. Many young people, who are learning COBOL at job sites, are searching for good COBOL books now, especially a good COBOL upgrade book. Since IT organizations will spend approximately $600 billion (worldwide) to resolve their Y2K problem, it seems unlikely that firms will toss away their newly renovated mainframe-based and COBOL-based application systems immediately after the year 2000. Since these organizations need to maintain and enhance these application systems, they will need COBOL programmers and ideally those who can provide version upgrading as well.

After their Y2K conversion projects are over, many IT organizations will face the following decisions:

- Should we modernize the existing COBOL applications that we could not improve during our Y2K renovation efforts? Or:
- Should we scrap the existing COBOL applications that we could not improve during Y2K in favor of entirely new advanced systems?

Both options have their own pros and cons. But if you convert your COBOL applications to another language, *you may lose your COBOL programmers and the knowledge of the application that they carry with them.* We have seen many companies that had downsized their IT staffs struggle through Y2K because they did not have enough resources knowledgeable about their applications. It was not that they didn't have enough programmers, just not enough people who knew the users and the business purpose of the applications.

There are basically four options for modernizing "legacy" applications written in COBOL:

- Reengineer the business process.
- Rewrite the COBOL applications that you could not touch during Y2K in a newer, Web-enabled language.
- Replace the COBOL application that you could not touch during Y2K with purchased software.
- Modernize the COBOL applications that you could not touch during Y2K to give the desired capabilities (almost a facelift).

The reengineering option carries the highest costs, lead times, and business risk because reengineering involves a change to the culture of the organization. The costs of rewriting applications in other languages would most likely be as expensive an effort as developing the original application (because you would have to take time to design, code, test, and implement in parallel). In addition, there will be a major cost for replacing and/or training the programmers in the new language(s). By replacing applications with purchased software packages, the organization incurs implementation costs as well as the cost of the package. The total can be staggering.

While organizations with applications written in earlier versions of COBOL can still function, we are seeing an increasing trend toward moving applications to newer and later technologies, such as COBOL for MVS, that support Web-based front ends and other e-business constructs. IBM has dubbed this process *application mining*, which allows application owners to quickly reuse existing applications and personnel to develop GUI front-end Web applications (see Figure I.1).

Modernizing a COBOL application to last another ten years can often be the option with the least cost, minimum lead time, and minimum business risk. For some versions of COBOL, modernizing to a COBOL that supports an open system, client/server configuration might take relatively little time and effort. For other versions and/or applications, the effort may be significant, perhaps at best involving *the use of conversion tools*. Next, we will describe how to choose the method that best suits your organization.

Change Management

Before you embark on your upgrade project, remember to document your Change Management procedures. That is, ask yourself how will you address changes to code made during the upgrade process. In other

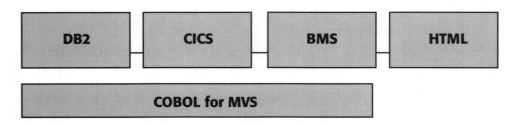

Figure I.1 Example of a Web-based front-end application.

words, suppose you upgrade one thousand programs, and you expect it to take you two months manually and four months if you include testing. What happens to any code changes (production fixes, regulatory mandates) that you make? You certainly aren't making the upgrade changes each night and reimplementing the upgraded code. So you need to decide how to manage these deltas.

These are your three options:

1. Freeze all code changes during the entire upgrade and testing process. This is the best option but is only practical if you have absolutely no changes. Otherwise, it is impractical.

2. Freeze the code only during regression tests (you have to freeze at some point). For the rest of the period, agree to take a refresh (deltas), such as before integration tests. Only re-upgrade changed programs. Take another refresh right before regression tests. If your application is especially volatile, you may need to wait for a more calm period.

3. Freeze the code only during regression tests (again, you need to freeze at some point). For the code that had changed, use a merge tool to merge the deltas with the upgraded code. If the changes do not impact the upgrade, you will not have to re-upgrade.

Three Options for Your COBOL Upgrade

Because original investments in COBOL tend to be large, your organization should carefully consider the three following options for upgrading existing COBOL applications. You may have business systems written across different versions of COBOL, where multiple compilers are maintained (for example, OS/VS COBOL and COBOL II). In that case, some departments may have experience with COBOL upgrades. There is no time like the present to upgrade when you consider the substantial savings to be gained from eliminating older compilers, especially when they are under maintenance contracts. Consider each of the following options for the COBOL upgrade task:

1. Do it manually, using internal staff and resources (including contractors).

2. Do it yourself with a purchased or leased conversion tool.

3. Hire a consultant with a factory approach (using their own tool suite and resources).

You should address each of the following cost concerns when deciding how to proceed with your own COBOL upgrades:

- Conversion labor costs
- Conversion management costs
- Conversion administrative costs
- Conversion tool costs (if tools are used)
- Conversion implementation times
- The availability of qualified COBOL programmers for the upgrade project
- Business risks due to COBOL upgrade (list the pros and cons: What are the risks of not upgrading, as well the risks of upgrading?)
- Training costs and time to learn new tools
- Training costs and time to learn differences between old COBOL and new COBOL
- The availability of experienced project managers
- The availability of computer resources for COBOL upgrade
- The availability of technical infrastructure group resources (networks, systems programmers, and DBAs)
- Configuration management to manage inventory and refreshed codes during your COBOL upgrade project

After considering this list of evaluation criteria, you will need to assign relative weights (values) to each of the items. Table I.8 will provide you with information on how to address the evaluation criteria. It is based on the following assumptions:

1. Your company will upgrade one thousand COBOL programs on the mainframe (not a PC environment, hence there are MIPS and DASD costs, plus tool costs based upon the size of the CPU).
2. Your company's average labor cost (including fringe benefits) for a COBOL programmer is $110 per hour.
3. If your company chooses to convert using your own technical personnel, with a tool, an employee needs an average of 40 hours training for a new conversion tool.
4. If your company chooses to do it manually, an employee needs an average of forty hours training for language differences.

5. The costs do not include time for test design, creating the test environment, testing, resolving anomalies, or implementation.

Manual Upgrade, Internal Resources

This option may carry the highest costs, longest lead times, and greatest business risk because of the possibility of human errors. If in-house staff are not experts in this area, they will require training to learn the differences between old and new COBOL. Of course, you can reduce costs by implementing more efficient education for programmers (using this book, for example) and by writing a few automated utilities yourself to speed the process (such as removing REMARKS sections). This option is discussed in Chapter 1, "Successful Manual Upgrades."

Automated Upgrade, Internal Resources

The cost of an in-house conversion using a tool is determined by the price of the tool, the implementation time, and programmer training costs. Note that you may be able to negotiate training as part of the tool purchase price. The cost effectiveness of conversion with a tool will improve with experience. However, the lessons learned from previous upgrade projects must be passed along to improve the overall efficiency of the project. Efficiency will also improve if you have or hire resources who have used the conversion tool before or have gone through several conversions elsewhere. In Part 2 we will examine in detail using a tool for the conversion.

Table I.8 Cost Estimating Table for COBOL Upgrades

CATEGORY	HOURS	LABOR COSTS	TOOL COSTS	TOOL TRAINING COSTS	LANGUAGE DIFFERENCES TRAINING COST	PROJECT MANAGE COSTS	SYSTEM USAGE COST	TECHNICAL INFRA STRUCTURE COST	INVENTORY REFRESHED	TOTAL COST
Manually	2,800	$308,000			$44,000	$11,000	$3,000	$11,000	$11,000	$388,000
With a tool	1,400	$154,000	$30,000	$4,400	$ 4,400	$11,000	$6,000	$11,000	$11,000	$231,800
Factory		$2,200				$11,000				approx. $180,000-$300,000

Outsourced Factory Upgrade

Hiring a consulting firm with a factory approach may be the option with the lowest cost, minimum lead time, and minimum business risk. On the positive side, hiring outside specialists to do a COBOL upgrade may boost morale since the conversion may seem like a tedious task to in-house COBOL programmers. However, in many cases an organization will not allow proprietary code to travel outside their four walls. If you do outsource, be sure to insist on physical and electronic security. On the negative side, your programmer may miss a valuable opportunity to learn the differences between old COBOL and new COBOL by not executing the upgrade in house. You will also need to include your own time to package the code for delivery as well as expenses for visiting the factory site.

An experienced COBOL upgrade factory may be able to compress project duration, assist with computer resources, and reduce conversion costs for your company. The factory should house the information technology and human resources required to execute different upgrade projects. These resources include computing hardware (CPU, DASD), utilities, references, personnel, and all of the necessary supporting infrastructure (networks, technical support).

The factory should fulfill resource requirements that cannot realistically be met by your company's on-site capabilities. Examine their methodology. Do they utilize a repeatable process? How many programs and from what level to what level have they previously converted? Have they been involved in the testing aspects of the upgrade effort? If so, a factory may help compress the duration of the project.

In the next three parts of this book we will describe the challenges, requirements, technical specifications, and the lessons we have learned for each of the three upgrade approaches we have described here: a manual in-house upgrade, upgrades using a tool, and hiring a consultant to do your upgrade using a factory approach.

PART ONE

Manually Upgrading COBOL

In Part 1, we will discuss how to upgrade your COBOL programs internally and manually (with our help, of course). We'll begin with a little education on some of the issues that lie between the various levels of COBOL that have become available.

We'll then follow that with a high-level view of how to manage your COBOL upgrade, illustrating the various phases of upgrading and what the major upgrade activities are. We will also give you some idea of the amount of resources and time you will need to complete your upgrade project.

Then, step by step, we'll discuss the technical specifications for upgrading from level to level:

1. Converting COBOL Language Elements to VS COBOL II from OS/VS COBOL
2. Converting COBOL Language Elements to COBOL/370 from OS/VS COBOL
3. Converting COBOL Language Elements to COBOL/370 from VS COBOL II

CHAPTER 1

Successful Manual Upgrades

Manually upgrading your applications means using the old-fashioned brute-force method, otherwise known as editing. If you have the programmers available and the time necessary to do the job, manually upgrading your code will allow your team to become reacquainted with their code and learn about the issues inherent in language upgrades.

1.1 VS COBOL II: Unsupported Features

Several environment items that had been widely used in OS/VS COBOL were discontinued when COBOL II was released. Much of this code has never been upgraded only because of these discontinued elements. These include the following:

- ISAM (Index Sequential Access Method files)
- Report Writer (a collection of shorthand commands for generating and organizing report layouts)
- BDAM (Basic Direct Access Method file format)
- Remarks Section
- CURRENT-DATE
- TIME-OF-DAY

- TRANSFORM
- EXAMINE
- ON
- READY TRACE or EXHIBIT
- Flow Option, Verb Count
- COMMUNICATIONS SECTION

Later in this book we'll look at what to do with obsolete or discontinued elements such as Report Writer. You can't fully upgrade until you either convert these elements or purchase software (precompilers) that convert them for you. Later, in Chapter 2, we'll discuss IBM's conversion tool CCCA and tell you what CCCA does automatedly for these elements as well.

COBOL II didn't just remove items, however; IBM also added the following features:

- New compiler messages and codes
- New compiler options
- FILLER is optional
- New "PROCESS" statement
- New TITLE statement
- New user return codes and fdump option
- FD simplification
- WORKING STORAGE simplifications
- PROCEDURE DIVISION simplifications
- NOT AT END
- NOT INVALID KEY
- INITIALIZE VERB
- Enhancements to PERFORM
- IF/ELSE
- EVALUATE
- SET
- ENDIF
- TABLE improvements
- Numeric-handling differences

- User-defined data classes
- Character-handling enhancements
- VSAM changes
- Use SORT without sections
- COBTEST batch mode debugging
- Interactive COBTEST

Now let's discuss how to organize your project from start to finish.

1.2 Organizing the Project

The project will require most, if not all, of the following organizational elements:

- The upgrade is in line with the corporate technology direction/strategy (without being facetious, we're of course assuming there is one).
- Executive sponsorship.
- Budget allocations and/or ROI are completed that identify the costs of upgrading along with the benefits (migration to newer technologies, Web-enablement possibilities, removal of older compiler maintenance, enhanced maintenance, supported technologies, and so on).
- A goal. Is the project intended just to get rid of the old compiler? Reduce production anomalies (try not to add a whole series of functional additions during this project unless mandatory; this causes configuration management problems).
- Committed, allocated resources.
- A project manager.
- A team manager.
- Regular capabilities for sharing lessons learned (either through regular meetings, like a once-a-week technical session for one hour [in addition to the regular training] or by creating an internal Web site to distribute lessons learned). It must be current and easily updatable.
- A *project plan* that has, at least, milestones, phases, and tasks (see the sample in Section 1.2.1). Team members should be aware of dependencies in the upgrade project—that is, how their task may affect others. They should also be accountable for meeting deadlines.

- Communications methods to report status (status reports, metrics capturing for progress).
- Risk management (What can go wrong? How will you deal with it?), including contingency plans (What if we don't implement on time?).

1.2.1 Sample Project Plan

The following is a simplified version of our own initial project plan.

COBOL Conversion Summary Workplan

Phase 1: Install New Compiler
Tasks:
- Install your new compiler and/or Language Environment (LE).
- Verify install.
- Update compile procs in the upgrade environment.
- Develop (agree upon) upgrade standards.
- Publish (and be prepared to enforce) upgrade standards (see Section 1.2.2 for examples of standards).
- Allocate access authority to team members.

Phase 2: Determine Inventory
Tasks:
- Migrate production source to upgrade libraries.
- Migrate copybooks to upgrade libraries.
- Migrate JCL and procs to upgrade libraries.
- Compile using old compiler to verify accurate inventory.

Phase 3: Identify Special Migration Issues
Tasks:
- Identify Report Writer code (if any).
- Choose Report Writer strategy (more on this later).
- Identify ISAM files.
- Identify BDAM files.
- Identify environmental upgrades (for example, CICS 2.1 to CICS 4.1).
- Determine specific language levels each program is currently executing under.

Phase 4: Create Test Environment
Tasks:
- Create test regions.
- Move production executables to test region.
- Move test databases to test regions.
- Identify tests to compare upgrade against later (online transactions, batch jobs).

1.2.2 Standards Examples

You will need to establish upgrade standards early, and you should enforce them throughout the upgrade project's life span.

Commenting. Do you want to leave obsolete code in place and comment it out? Or do you want to remove it altogether? (We recommend leaving it in place and commenting it out. This maintains a history of the changes. If you move to a clean-room environment, you may want to delete the obsolete code at that time.)

- **Determine frequency of backups in tests (control points).**
- **Execute test scripts/jobs.**
- **Capture output.**
- **QA output to ensure completeness.**
- **Determine comparison methods (tools or utilities to compare results).**
   - **Phase 5: Allocate Tasks**
      - **Tasks:**
- **Break application into manageable components.**
- **Allocate components to programmers.**
- **Set completion dates (update project plan).**
- **Determine configuration management techniques (to deal with any modifications made to code while the language upgrades are progressing, since you'll be modifying copies of production code, not the production code itself).**
   - **Phase 6: Upgrade Programs**
      - **Tasks:**
- **Following standards, edit (upgrade) code.**
- **Compile upgraded code using new compiler.**
- **QA upgrades for adherence to standards.**
- **Test upgraded programs in test region.**
- **Convert any necessary files.**
- **Compare results.**
- **Document anomalies (errors).**
- **Correct anomalies.**
- **Retest.**
- **Schedule move into production over weekend.**
   - **Phase 7: Move into Production**
      - **Tasks:**
- **Develop contingency plans.**
- **Convert files.**
- **Implement new code.**
- **Report on results.**

Do you want to comment each change made to the upgrade code, such as when you change file lengths or field names? (We recommend that you don't here, as you will probably change many field names, and this could get very confusing in the code.)

Field names that require changes. Occasionally, you will have to change a field name because it has become a reserve word after it was first used in OS/VS. What will your standard be for changing the name? Some tools append the language level (for example, -74, -68) to the field name.

File changes. Agree on what you will do with obsolete files (such as ISAM or BDAM). You may want to convert them to VSAM, flat files, or migrate to a database (IMS, DB/2, etc.). Establish the criteria (size, type, etc.) that impact your processing, and document what should be done about the files and how to convert them.

1.3 OS/VS COBOL Update Issues

IBM has permanently removed the support in OS/VS COBOL for some common language elements (see Table 1.1). We will provide more details on how to upgrade these elements in Chapter 3. Appendix A contains a complete list that compares OS/VS and COBOL II language elements. In Section 1.6 we discuss how to handle the conditions you will face when upgrading OS/VS COBOL to VS COBOL II.

Table 1.1 OS/VS COBOL Commands No Longer Supported

NONSUPPORTED LANGUAGE ELEMENTS	NOTE
ACCEPT MESSAGE COUNT statement	This is a Communications statement. The Communications module is not supported by the target languages, and there is nothing with which it can be replaced.
ACTUAL KEY	The ACTUAL KEY clause should be for a BDAM file. ACTUAL KEY is replaced by RELATIVE KEY. Programs using BDAM files should be converted to programs using VSAM/RRDS (Relative Record Data Set) files. This can be done by using the VSAM utility program IDCAMS. The ACTUAL KEY is flagged if the new organization for the file is not RELATIVE.
APPLY CORE-INDEX	This is an ISAM file clause-handling clause. It needs to be removed from the program.
APPLY KEY	It has been removed from VS COBOL II.

NONSUPPORTED LANGUAGE ELEMENTS	NOTE
APPLY RECORD-OVERFLOW	The APPLY RECORD-OVERFLOW clause in the IO-CONTROL paragraph should be removed from the program.
APPLY REORG-CRITERIA	This is an ISAM file clause-handling clause. It needs to be removed from the program.
Basic Direct Access Method (BDAM) files	Programs using BDAM files should be converted to programs using VSAM/RRDS files. This can be done by using the VSAM utility program IDCAMS. Some tools convert the file definitions, but you must update the key algorithms manually.
CURRENT-DATE	Whenever CURRENT-DATE is referenced in the program, it should be replaced by code that contains the date from the system and puts it in the format of the CURRENT-DATE register.
DISABLE	This is a Communications statement. The Communications module is not supported by the target languages, and there is nothing with which it can be replaced. Most tools will flag it as requiring attention.
ENABLE	This is a Communications statement. The Communications module is not supported by the target languages, and there is nothing with which it can be replaced. Most upgrading tools will flag it as requiring attention.
Index Sequential Access Method (ISAM) files	You should convert to Key-Sequenced Data Set (KSDS) Virtual Storage Access Method (VSAM) files using IDCAMS. Some upgrade utility tools will convert the file definition and I/O statements for ISAM files. However, you will need to convert the file itself.
NOMINAL KEY clause	You should convert this to the Virtual Storage Access Method (VSAM) file convention.
NOTE	It is removed from VS COBOL II. Some upgrade tools will simply comment this out. You can do the same.
ON statement	It was removed from VS COBOL II. This statement needs to be converted.
RECEIVE	This is a Communications statement. The Communications module is not supported by the target languages, and there is nothing with which it can be replaced.
REMARKS	VS COBOL II does not support this statement, which was typically used at the beginning of a program to code a paragraph or more of program description. It can be replaced by the regular * in column 7 for comments.

continues

Table 1.1 *(Continued)*

NONSUPPORTED LANGUAGE ELEMENTS	NOTE
SEEK	This is a BDAM file-handling statement. The statement should be removed from the program. Programs using BDAM files should be converted to programs using VSAM/RRDS files. This can be done by using the VSAM utility program IDCAMS.
SEND	This is a Communications statement. The Communications module is not supported by the target languages, and there is nothing with which it can be replaced.
TIME-OF-DAY	Whenever TIME-OF-DAY is referenced in the program, it needs to be replaced by code that contains the date from the system and puts it in the format of the TIME-OF-DAY register.
TRACK-AREA	The clause needs to be simply removed from the program.
TRACK-LIMIT	The clause needs to be simply removed from the program.
TRANSFORM	Transform needs to be changed to inspect.

1.3.1 Detecting Other COBOL II Issues

The purpose of Table 1.2 is to suggest ways to identify other, not-so-obvious, problematic OS/VS issues before you start your upgrade. We had problems in tests with these elements, so you probably will too.

Table 1.2 OS/VS Problematic Elements

RECORD LENGTH DIFFERENCE BETWEEN JCL AND COBOL SOURCE	
Detected by:	Scanning file record lengths inside the COBOL source and JCL and/or procs.
Reason:	Record Length is different between JCL and COBOL source. This was allowed under OS/VS but will cause ABENDs in execution under COBOL II.
Corrective Actions:	Someone needs to determine which length is correct (unless it is obvious) and adjust accordingly. This may be more difficult

Successful Manual Upgrades

than you imagine. Often, there are varying file lengths between programs, and you may not know which copybook to use. These issues usually require a little investigation. Watch for these programs while you conduct tests after COBOL conversion. This will help you resolve any problems related to opening and reading a file.

In addition, OS/VS COBOL allowed the DISP, LEAVE, REREAD, and REVERSED clauses in the OPEN statement; they are not supported in VS COBOL II.

QSAM FILE LENGTH RECORD ISSUES

Detected by:	Manually scanning using TSO/ISPF Option 3.1.4 SuperC scans for Recording Mode [IS] S. Similar to the file Record Length issue earlier in this table; QSAM file lengths were often a problem for us.
Reason:	The RECORDING MODE clause specifies the format of the physical records in QSAM file. Recording Mode S (Spanned) is very unique in the sense that the records may be either fixed or variable in length and may be larger than a block. Record Length is different between JCL and COBOL source.
Corrective Actions:	Prior to testing, review the SuperC report that lists all the programs that have discrepancies in the Record Length between JCL and COBOL source. If any discrepancy exists, watch out for those programs while you conduct tests after COBOL conversion and modify COBOL source as shown in the following example:

```
FD   TUCS-IN
       RECORDING MODE IS S
     BLOCK CONTAINS 0
       RECORD IS VARYING IN SIZE FROM 62 TO 526 CHARACTERS
         DEPENDING ON Y2K-IN-SIZE
     .

WORKING STORAGE SECTION.
  01   Y2K-IN-SIZE                    PIC 9(3) COMP-3.
```

The following coding was before modification:

```
005200 FD   TUCS-IN
005300        LABEL RECORDS ARE STANDARD
005400        RECORDING MODE IS S
005500        RECORD CONTAINS 168 CHARACTERS
005600        BLOCK CONTAINS 0
005700        DATA RECORD IS TUCS-INP.
005800 01   TUCS-INP                  PIC X(168).
```

continues

Table 1.2 *(Continued)*

REDEFINES CONTAINING COPYBOOK ISSUES	
Detected by:	Searches by CCCA and TSO/ISPF 1.4 SuperC for 'REDEFINES' and 'COPY'.

Reason:	`01 CHRTDATA   REDEFINES DUMMY-DATA-SEG PIC X(61).`
	`COPY CHRTDATA.`
	
	The problem is that even though the compiler accepted this coding with no errors, this did not work when we tested it.

Corrective Actions:	`COPY CHRTDATA REPLACING`
	`==CHRTDATA.==                          BY`
	`==CHRTDATA REDEFINES DUMMY-DATA-SEG.==.`
	
	A sequence of character strings and /or separators bounded by, but not including, pseudotext delimiters (= =) was used in the COPY . . . REPLACING phrase. Both characters of each pseudotext delimiter must appear on one line; however, character strings within pseudotext can be continued. We proved that this change worked when we tested it.

REPORT WRITER NO LONGER SUPPORTED BY COBOL II	
Detected by:	Search with SuperC for 'RD'.
Reason:	Report Writer not support by COBOL II.
Corrective Actions:	Rewrite entire program in language other than COBOL (FOCUS, DYL); change the Report Writer code to COBOL II code (which can be done manually by examining the code and implementing duplicate report functionality using standard COBOL II commands or by using a translation utility such as Prince Software's Translate R/W) or by purchasing IBM's Report Writer Precompiler, product 5798-DYR, which converts Report Writer code to standard COBOL calls prior to the compile step (has a list price of about $10,000). To maintain code using the precompiler, however, programmers still need to understand Report Writer. If you can upgrade your code out of Report Writer, you will probably have better success in maintaining the code, but it will definitely take longer to convert to COBOL II.

1.4 Reserved Words

In its various incarnations over the years, COBOL has featured various words that were reserved for specific functions and could not be used as field names. Depending on the version of COBOL, certain words may have slipped from the reserved list to the unreserved (available for field name usage), or vice versa, as shown in Table 1.3.

Table 1.3 COBOL Terms Changed between Reserved and Unreserved Status

LEGEND	
X	The word is reserved in the product.
-	The word is not reserved in the product. (This includes obsolete reserved words that are no longer flagged.)
CDW	The word is a COBOL/370 and COBOL for MVS & VM compiler-directing statement. If used as a user-defined word, it is flagged with a severe message.
COD	The word is a CODASYL reserved word not used by this compiler. If used, it is recognized as a user-defined word and flagged with an informational message.
SYS	The word is a word with specific meaning to the operating system. It can be used only in specific contexts within the program.
UNS	The word is a COBOL 1985 standard reserved word for a feature not supported by this compiler. If used in a program, it is recognized as a reserved word and flagged with a severe message.

RESERVED WORD	370	VSII	OS/VS	RESERVED WORD	370	VSII	OS/VS
ACCEPT	X	X	X	AREA	X	X	X
ACCESS	X	X	X	AREAS	X	X	X
ACTUAL	-	-	X	ARITHMETIC	COD	COD	-
ADD	X	X	X	ASCENDING	X	X	X
ADDRESS	X	X	X	ASSIGN	X	X	X
ADVANCING	X	X	X	AT	X	X	X
AFTER	X	X	X	AUTHOR	X	X	X
ALL	X	X	X	B-AND	COD	COD	-
ALPHABET	X	X	-	B-EXOR	COD	COD	-
ALPHABETIC	X	X	X	B-LESS	COD	COD	-
ALPHABETIC-LOWER	X	X	-	B-NOT	COD	COD	-
ALPHABETIC-UPPER	X	X	-	B-OR	COD	COD	-
ALPHANUMERIC	X	X	-	BASIS	CDW	CDW	X
ALPHANUMERIC-EDITED	X	X	-	BEFORE	X	X	X
ALSO	X	X	X	BEGINNING	X	X	X
ALTER	X	X	X	BINARY	X	X	-
ALTERNATE	X	X	X	BIT	COD	COD	-
AND	X	X	X	BITS	COD	COD	-
ANY	X	X	-	BLANK	X	X	X
APPLY	X	X	X	BLOCK	X	X	X
ARE	X	X	X	BOOLEAN	COD	COD	-

continues

Table 1.3 (Continued)

RESERVED WORD	370	VSII	OS/VS	RESERVED WORD	370	VSII	OS/VS
BOTTOM	X	X	X	COMP-8	COD	COD	-
BY	X	X	X	COMP-9	COD	COD	-
CALL	X	X	X	COMPUTATIONAL	X	X	X
CANCEL	X	X	X	COMPUTATIONAL-1	X	X	X
CBL	CDW	CDW	X	COMPUTATIONAL-2	X	X	X
CD	UNS	UNS	X	COMPUTATIONAL-3	X	X	X
CF	UNS	UNS	X	COMPUTATIONAL-4	X	X	X
CH	UNS	UNS	X	COMPUTATIONAL-5	COD	COD	-
CHANGED	-	-	X	COMPUTATIONAL-6	COD	COD	-
CHARACTER	X	X	X	COMPUTATIONAL-7	COD	COD	-
CHARACTERS	X	X	X	COMPUTATIONAL-8	COD	COD	-
CLASS	X	X	-	COMPUTATIONAL-9	COD	COD	-
CLASS-ID(R2)	X			COMPUTE	X	X	X
CLOCK-UNITS	UNS	UNS	-	CONFIGURATION	X	X	X
CLOSE	X	X	X	CONNECT	COD	COD	-
COBOL	X	X	-	CONSOLE	SYS	SYS	X
CODE	X	X	X	CONTAINED	COD	COD	-
CODE-SET	X	X	X	CONTAINS	X	X	X
COLLATING	X	X	X	CONTENT	X	X	-
COLUMN	UNS	UNS	X	CONTINUE	X	X	-
COM-REG	X	X	-	CONTROL	UNS	UNS	X
COMMA	X	X	X	CONTROLS	UNS	UNS	X
COMMIT	COD	COD	-	CONVERTING	X	X	-
COMMON	X	X	-	COPY	X	X	X
COMMUNICATION	UNS	UNS	X	CORR-INDEX	-	-	X
COMP	X	X	X	CORR	X	X	X
COMP-1	X	X	X	CORRESPONDING	X	X	X
COMP-2	X	X	X	COUNT	X	X	X
COMP-3	X	X	X	CSP	SYS	SYS	X
COMP-4	X	X	X	CURRENCY	X	X	X
COMP-5	COD	COD	-	CURRENT	COD	COD	-
COMP-6	COD	COD	-	CURRENT-DATE	-	-	X
COMP-7	COD	COD	-	C01	SYS	SYS	X

Successful Manual Upgrades

RESERVED WORD	370	VSII	OS/VS	RESERVED WORD	370	VSII	OS/VS
C02	SYS	SYS	X	DEBUG-SUB-3	X	X	X
C03	SYS	SYS	X	DEBUGGING	X	X	X
C04	SYS	SYS	X	DECIMAL-POINT	X	X	X
C05	SYS	SYS	X	DECLARATIVES	X	X	X
C06	SYS	SYS	X	DEFAULT	COD	COD	-
C07	SYS	SYS	X	DELETE	X	X	X
C08	SYS	SYS	X	DELIMITED	X	X	X
C09	SYS	SYS	X	DELIMITER	X	X	X
C10	SYS	SYS	X	DEPENDING	X	X	X
C11	SYS	SYS	X	DESCENDING	X	X	X
C12	SYS	SYS	X	DESTINATION	UNS	UNS	X
DATA	X	X	X	DETAIL	UNS	UNS	X
DATE	X	X	X	DISABLE	UNS	UNS	X
DATE-COMPILED	X	X	X	DISCONNECT	COD	COD	-
DATE-WRITTEN	X	X	X	DISP	-	-	X
DAY	X	X	X	DISPLAY	X	X	X
DAY-OF-WEEK	X	X	-	DISPLAY-ST	-	-	X
DB	COD	COD	-	DISPLAY-1	X	X	-
DB-ACCESS-CONTROL-KEY	COD	COD	-	DISPLAY-2	COD	COD	-
DB-DATA-NAME	COD	COD	-	DISPLAY-3	COD	COD	-
DB-EXCEPTION	COD	COD	-	DISPLAY-4	COD	COD	-
DB-RECORD-NAME	COD	COD	-	DISPLAY-5	COD	COD	-
DB-SET-NAME	COD	COD	-	DISPLAY-6	COD	COD	-
DB-STATUS	COD	COD	-	DISPLAY-7	COD	COD	-
DBCS	X	X	-	DISPLAY-8	COD	COD	-
DE	UNS	UNS	X	DISPLAY-9	COD	COD	-
DEBUG	-	-	X	DIVIDE	X	X	X
DEBUG-CONTENTS	X	X	X	DIVISION	X	X	X
DEBUG-ITEM	X	X	X	DOWN	X	X	X
DEBUG-LINE	X	X	X	DUPLICATE	COD	COD	-
DEBUG-NAME	X	X	X	DUPLICATES	X	X	X
DEBUG-SUB-1	X	X	X	DYNAMIC	X	X	X
DEBUG-SUB-2	X	X	X	EGCS	X	X	-

continues

Table 1.3 *(Continued)*

RESERVED WORD	370	VSII	OS/VS	RESERVED WORD	370	VSII	OS/VS
EGI	UNS	UNS	X	ENTER	X	X	X
EJECT	CDW	CDW	X	ENTRY	X	X	X
ELSE	X	X	X	ENVIRONMENT	X	X	X
EMI	UNS	UNS	X	EOP	X	X	X
EMPTY	COD	COD	-	EQUAL	X	X	X
ENABLE	UNS	UNS	X	EQUALS	COD	COD	-
END	X	X	X	ERASE	COD	COD	-
END-ADD	X	X	-	ERROR	X	X	X
END-CALL	X	X	-	ESI	UNS	UNS	X
END-COMPUTE	X	X	-	EVALUATE	X	X	-
END-DELETE	X	X	-	EVERY	X	X	X
END-DISABLE	COD	COD	-	EXACT	COD	COD	-
END-DIVIDE	X	X	-	EXAMINE	-	-	X
END-ENABLE	COD	COD	-	EXCEEDS	COD	COD	-
END-EVALUATE	X	X	-	EXCEPTION	X	X	X
END-IF	X	X	-	EXCLUSIVE	COD	COD	-
END-INVOKE(R2)	X			EXHIBIT	-	-	X
END-MULTIPLY	X	X	-	EXIT	X	X	X
END-OF-PAGE	X	X	X	EXTEND	X	X	X
END-PERFORM	X	X	-	EXTERNAL	X	X	-
END-READ	X	X	-	FALSE	X	X	-
END-RECEIVE	UNS	UNS	-	FD	X	X	X
END-RETURN	X	X	-	FETCH	COD	COD	-
END-REWRITE	X	X	-	FILE	X	X	X
END-SEARCH	X	X	-	FILE-CONTROL	X	X	X
END-SEND	COD	COD	-	FILE-LIMIT	-	-	X
END-START	X	X	-	FILE-LIMITS	-	-	X
END-STRING	X	X	-	FILLER	X	X	X
END-SUBTRACT	X	X	-	FINAL	UNS	UNS	X
END-TRANSCEIVE	COD	COD	-	FIND	COD	COD	-
END-UNSTRING	X	X	-	FINISH	COD	COD	-
END-WRITE	X	X	-	FIRST	X	X	X
ENDING	X	X	X	FOOTING	X	X	X

Successful Manual Upgrades

RESERVED WORD	370	VSII	OS/VS	RESERVED WORD	370	VSII	OS/VS
FOR	X	X	X	INDICATE	UNS	UNS	X
FORMAT	COD	COD	-	INHERITS(R2)	X		
FREE	COD	COD	-	INITIAL	X	X	X
FROM	X	X	X	INITIALIZE	X	X	X
FUNCTION	X	COD	-	INITIATE	UNS	UNS	X
GENERATE	UNS	UNS	X	INPUT	X	X	X
GET	COD	COD	-	INPUT-OUTPUT	X	X	X
GIVING	X	X	X	INSERT	CDW	CDW	X
GLOBAL	X	X	-	INSPECT	X	X	X
GO	X	X	X	INSTALLATION	X	X	X
GOBACK	X	X	X	INTO	X	X	X
GREATER	X	X	X	INVALID	X	X	X
GROUP	UNS	UNS	X	INVOKE(R2)	X		
HEADING	UNS	UNS	X	IS	X	X	X
HIGH-VALUE	X	X	X	JUST	X	X	X
HIGH-VALUES	X	X	X	JUSTIFIED	X	X	X
I-O	X	X	X	KANJI	X	X	-
I-O-CONTROL	X	X	X	KEEP	COD	COD	-
ID	X	X	X	KEY	X	X	X
IDENTIFICATION	X	X	X	LABEL	X	X	X
IF	X	X	X	LAST	UNS	UNS	X
IN	X	X	X	LD	COD	COD	-
INDEX	X	X	X	LEADING	X	X	X
INDEX-1	COD	COD	-	LEAVE	-	-	X
INDEX-2	COD	COD	-	LEFT	X	X	X
INDEX-3	COD	COD	-	LENGTH	X	X	X
INDEX-4	COD	COD	-	LESS	X	X	X
INDEX-5	COD	COD	-	LIMIT	UNS	UNS	X
INDEX-6	COD	COD	-	LIMITS	UNS	UNS	X
INDEX-7	COD	COD	-	LINAGE	X	X	X
INDEX-8	COD	COD	-	LINAGE-COUNTER	X	X	X
INDEX-9	COD	COD	-	LINE	X	X	X
INDEXED	X	X	X	LINE-COUNTER	UNS	UNS	X

continues

Table 1.3 *(Continued)*

RESERVED WORD	370	VSII	OS/VS	RESERVED WORD	370	VSII	OS/VS
LINES	X	X	X	NUMERIC	X	X	X
LINKAGE	X	X	X	NUMERIC-EDITED	X	X	-
LOCAL-STORAGE(R2)	X			OBJECT(R2)	X		
LOCALLY	COD	COD	-	OBJECT-COMPUTER	X	X	X
LOCK	X	X	X	OCCURS	X	X	X
LOW-VALUE	X	X	X	OF	X	X	X
LOW-VALUES	X	X	X	OFF	X	X	X
MEMBER	COD	COD	-	OMITTED	X	X	X
MEMORY	X	X	X	ON	X	X	X
MERGE	X	X	X	ONLY	COD	COD	-
MESSAGE	UNS	UNS	X	OPEN	X	X	X
METACLASS(R2)	X			OPTIONAL	X	X	X
METHOD(R2)	X			OR	X	X	X
METHOD-ID(R2)	X			ORDER	X	X	-
MODE	X	X	X	ORGANIZATION	X	X	X
MODIFY	COD	COD	-	OTHER	X	X	-
MODULES	X	X	X	OTHERWISE	-	-	X
MORE-LABELS	X	X	X	OUTPUT	X	X	X
MOVE	X	X	X	OVERFLOW	X	X	X
MULTIPLE	X	X	X	OVERRIDE(R2)	X		
MULTIPLY	X	X	X	OWNER	COD	COD	-
NAMED	-	-	X	PACKED-DECIMAL	X	X	-
NATIVE	X	X	X	PADDING	X	X	-
NEGATIVE	X	X	X	PAGE	X	X	X
NEXT	X	X	X	PAGE-COUNTER	UNS	UNS	X
NO	X	X	X	PARAGRAPH	COD	COD	-
NOMINAL	-	-	X	PASSWORD	X	X	X
NONE	COD	COD	-	PERFORM	X	X	X
NOT	X	X	X	PF	UNS	UNS	X
NOTE	-	-	X	PH	UNS	UNS	X
NULL	X	X	-	PIC	X	X	X
NULLS	X	X	-	PICTURE	X	X	X
NUMBER	UNS	UNS	X	PLUS	UNS	UNS	X

RESERVED WORD	370	VSII	OS/VS	RESERVED WORD	370	VSII	OS/VS
POINTER	X	X	X	REDEFINES	X	X	X
POSITION	X	X	X	REEL	X	X	X
POSITIONING	-	-	X	REFERENCE	X	X	-
POSITIVE	X	X	X	RELATION	COD	COD	-
PRESENT	COD	COD	-	RELATIVE	X	X	X
PRINT-SWITCH	-	-	X	RELEASE	X	X	X
PRINTING	UNS	UNS	-	RELOAD	X	X	X
PRIOR	COD	COD	-	REMAINDER	X	X	X
PROCEDURE	X	X	X	REMARKS	-	-	X
PROCEDURE-POINTER	X	-	-	REMOVAL	X	X	X
PROCEDURES	X	X	X	RENAMES	X	X	X
PROCEED	X	X	X	REORG-CRITERIA	-	-	X
PROCESSING	X	X	X	REPEATED	COD	COD	-
PROGRAM	X	X	X	REPLACE	X	X	-
PROGRAM-ID	X	X	X	REPLACING	X	X	X
PROTECTED	COD	COD	-	REPORT	UNS	UNS	X
PURGE	UNS	UNS	-	REPORTING	UNS	UNS	X
QUEUE	UNS	UNS	X	REPORTS	UNS	UNS	X
QUOTE	X	X	X	REPOSITORY(R2)	X		
QUOTES	X	X	X	REREAD	-	-	X
RANDOM	X	X	X	RERUN	X	X	X
RD	UNS	UNS	X	RESERVE	X	X	X
READ	X	X	X	RESET	-	-	X
READY	X	X	X	RETAINING	COD	COD	-
REALM	COD	COD	-	RETRIEVAL	COD	COD	-
RECEIVE	UNS	UNS	X	RETURN	X	X	X
RECONNECT	COD	COD	-	RETURNING(R2)	X		
RECORD	X	X	X	RETURN-CODE	X	X	X
RECORD-NAME	COD	COD	-	REVERSED	X	X	X
RECORD-OVERFLOW	-	-	X	REWIND	X	X	X
RECORDING	X	X	X	REWRITE	X	X	X
RECORDS	X	X	X	RF	UNS	UNS	X
RECURSIVE(R2)	X			RH	UNS	UNS	X

continues

Table 1.3 *(Continued)*

RESERVED WORD	370	VSII	OS/VS	RESERVED WORD	370	VSII	OS/VS
RIGHT	X	X	X	SKIP3	CDW	CDW	-
ROLLBACK	COD	COD	-	SORT	X	X	X
ROUNDED	X	X	X	SORT-CONTROL	X	X	-
RUN	X	X	X	SORT-CORE-SIZE	X	X	X
SAME	X	X	X	SORT-FILE-SIZE	X	X	X
SD	X	X	X	SORT-MERGE	X	X	X
SEARCH	X	X	X	SORT-MESSAGE	X	X	X
SECTION	X	X	X	SORT-MODE-SIZE	X	X	X
SECURITY	X	X	X	SORT-RETURN	X	X	X
SEEK	-	-	X	SOURCE	UNS	UNS	X
SEGMENT	UNS	UNS	X	SOURCE-COMPUTER	X	X	X
SEGMENT-LIMIT	X	X	X	SPACE	X	X	X
SELECT	X	X	X	SPACES	X	X	X
SELECTIVE	-	-	X	SPECIAL-NAMES	X	X	X
SELF(R2)	X			STANDARD	X	X	X
SEND	UNS	UNS	X	STANDARD-1	X	X	X
SENTENCE	X	X	X	STANDARD-2	X	X	-
SEPARATE	X	X	X	STANDARD-3	COD	COD	-
SEQUENCE	X	X	X	STANDARD-4	COD	COD	-
SEQUENTIAL	X	X	X	START	X	X	X
SERVICE	X	X	X	STATUS	X	X	X
SESSION-ID	COD	COD	-	STOP	X	X	X
SET	X	X	X	STORE	COD	COD	X
SHARED	COD	COD	-	STRING	X	X	X
SHIFT-IN	X	X	-	SUB-QUEUE-1	UNS	UNS	X
SHIFT-OUT	X	X	-	SUB-QUEUE-2	UNS	UNS	X
SIGN	X	X	X	SUB-QUEUE-3	UNS	UNS	X
SIZE	X	X	X	SUB-SCHEMA	COD	COD	-
SKIP-1	-	-	X	SUBTRACT	X	X	X
SKIP-2	-	-	X	SUM	UNS	UNS	X
SKIP-3	-	-	X	SUPER(R2)	X		
SKIP1	CDW	CDW	-	SUPPRESS	X	X	X
SKIP2	CDW	CDW	-	SYMBOLIC	X	X	X

RESERVED WORD	370	VSII	OS/VS	RESERVED WORD	370	VSII	OS/VS
SYNC	X	X	X	TOTALED	-	-	X
SYNCHRONIZED	X	X	X	TOTALING	-	-	X
SYSIN	SYS	SYS	X	TRACE	X	X	X
SYSIPT	SYS	SYS	-	TRACK-AREA	-	-	X
SYSLIST	SYS	SYS	X	TRACK-LIMIT	-	-	X
SYSLST	SYS	SYS	-	TRACKS	-	-	X
SYSOUT	SYS	SYS	X	TRAILING	X	X	X
SYSPCH	SYS	SYS	-	TRANSCEIVE	COD	COD	-
SYSPUNCH	SYS	SYS	X	TRANSFORM	-	-	X
S01	SYS	SYS	X	TRUE	X	X	-
S02	SYS	SYS	X	TYPE	UNS	UNS	X
S03	SYS	SYS	-	UNEQUAL	COD	COD	-
S04	SYS	SYS	-	UNIT	X	X	X
S05	SYS	SYS	-	UNSTRING	X	X	X
TABLE	UNS	UNS	X	UNTIL	X	X	X
TALLY	X	X	X	UP	X	X	X
TALLYING	X	X	X	UPDATE	COD	COD	-
TAPE	X	X	X	UPON	X	X	X
TENANT	COD	COD	-	UPSI-0	SYS	SYS	X
TERMINAL	UNS	UNS	X	UPSI-1	SYS	SYS	X
TERMINATE	UNS	UNS	X	UPSI-2	SYS	SYS	X
TEST	X	X	-	UPSI-3	SYS	SYS	X
TEXT	UNS	UNS	X	UPSI-4	SYS	SYS	X
THAN	X	X	X	UPSI-5	SYS	SYS	X
THEN	X	X	X	UPSI-6	SYS	SYS	X
THROUGH	X	X	X	UPSI-7	SYS	SYS	X
THRU	X	X	X	USAGE	X	X	X
TIME	X	X	X	USAGE-MODE	COD	COD	-
TIME-OF-DAY	-	-	X	USE	X	X	X
TIMES	X	X	X	USING	X	X	X
TITLE	CDW	CDW	-	VALID	COD	COD	-
TO	X	X	X	VALIDATE	COD	COD	-
TOP	X	X	X	VALUE	X	X	X

continues

Table 1.3 *(Continued)*

RESERVED WORD	370	VSII	OS/VS	RESERVED WORD	370	VSII	OS/VS
VALUES	X	X	X	ZEROES	X	X	X
VARYING	X	X	X	ZEROS	X	X	X
WAIT	COD	COD	-	<	X	X	X
WHEN	X	X	X	<=	X	X	-
WHEN-COMPILED	X	X	X	+	X	X	X
WITH	X	X	X	*	X	X	X
WITHIN	COD	COD	-	**	X	X	X
WORDS	X	X	X	-	X	X	X
WORKING STORAGE	X	X	X	/	X	X	X
WRITE	X	X	X	>	X	X	X
WRITE-ONLY	X	X	X	>=	X	X	-
ZERO	X	X	X	=	X	X	X

Source: IBM.

1.5 Determining Language Level(s)

One of the most difficult tasks we faced during our COBOL upgrades was determining the language level(s) of input COBOL source programs so our tool could upgrade to the appropriate output COBOL target level. You will also want to know which language level you are dealing with in case you are dealing with an environment that has had multiple compilers over the years. It may also be a good idea to segregate the programs into different language-level libraries so programmers working on the conversion will be less confused by the different levels.

These are the possible COBOL source program language level(s):

1. DOS/VS COBOL: ANSI 68 standard
2. OS/VS COBOL LANGLVL(1): ANSI 68 standard
3. OS/VS COBOL LANGLVL(2): ANSI 74 standard
4. VS COBOL II Release 1.0, Release 1.1, or Release 2.0: ANSI 74 standard
5. VS COBOL II CMPR2 Release 3.0, Release 3.1, or Release 3.2: ANSI 74 standard

6. VS COBOL II NOCMPR2 Release 3.0, Release 3.1, or Release 3.2: ANSI 85 standard

One way to distinguish between OS/VS COBOL and VS COBOL II is to review the content of the Load program of the input source COBOL program. If the Load program contains 5740-CB1, then it is OS/VS COBOL. If the Load program contains 5668-958, then it is VS COBOL II.

Another way to determine this is to scan the appropriate reserved words using TSO/ISPF OPTION 3.14.

NOTE:
The difference between OS/VS COBOL LANGLVL(1): ANSI 68 standard and OS/VS COBOL LANGLVL(2): ANSI 74 standard is extremely important to CCCA, Release 2.0, in converting COBOL programs. The authors found that the easiest "eye catcher" to determine whether code is ANSI 68 or 74 level is to look at the COPY statements. If you see something like "01 A   COPY B.", then you can be pretty sure that the code is ANSI 68.

1.6 Upgrading OS/VS COBOL to VS COBOL II

OS/VS COBOL was withdrawn from IBM's marketing efforts in June of 1992 and withdrawn from IBM service in June of 1994. COBOL II is probably not long for support either.

Organizations with OS/VS COBOL who would like to migrate to LE (IBM's Language Environment) but who do not yet meet the standards for upgrading, must migrate to VS COBOL II first. After the IBM Language Environment for MVS & VM (currently supported compiler) prerequisites are met, then you could move to IBM COBOL for MVS & VM. So now, if you're convinced that you should upgrade from OS/VS to COBOL II and you've read the section on testing upgraded code, you're ready to begin conversion. Item by item, we'll take you through the commands you'll need to change and how to change them. Remember, reserved words in OS/VS may not be reserved words in COBOL II, and many of your field names in OS/VS may be reserved words now.

If your organization has a data dictionary, don't forget to update it. And be sure to establish renaming standards for those reserved words. Don't have multiple resources that are working on the application make field name changes without coordination.

1.6.1 Commands Requiring Updates

This section discusses the commands that need updating, presented in alphabetic order within Behaviors (how execution behaves) and Divisions (Identification, Environment, Data, and Procedure).

Behaviors

Will your code "behave" the same after upgrading? By this, we mean that the processing flow that you had come to expect in your preupgraded code may not be identical to the processing flow in your post-upgraded code. Why? Changes in commands and compiler options affect execution. You may have conditionals that tested true in OS/VS that no longer test true in COBOL II or COBOL for MVS. This is why regression tests are so important in upgrade projects. What follows in the remainder of this section are the issues we detected in compiling and regression test failures.

CBL Compiler Directing Statement Changes

OS/VS COBOL accepts the CBL statement only if you specify BATCH in the EXEC statement. VS COBOL II always accepts the CBL statement; however, the options you specify are subject to a set order of precedence. For additional information, see the *VS COBOL II Application Programming Guide for MVS and CMS* (IBM, Document Number SC26-4045-05, Program Number 5668-958, 5688-022, 5688-023, 6th ed., March 1993).

CMPR2 compiler option. Not only have a number of new features been added to Releases 3 and 4 of VS COBOL II, but there are a number of statements that execute differently between Release 2 and Release 3 (and 4) of VS COBOL II. The compiler option of CMPR2 has been added to Release 3 and 4 of VS COBOL II. When CMPR2 option is used, it allows a Release 2 program, without modification, to execute under Release 3 (and 4) and yield the same results. It is not a good idea to use CMPR2 as more than a temporary crutch since many new features of Release 3 (and 4) are not available to the program.

Under CMPR2, a data item with the symbol B in its PICTURE clause is an alphabetic data item. Under NOCMPR2, a data item with the symbol B in its PICTURE clause is an alphanumeric-edited item. Most functions do not pose a problem with this change. However, there are a few subtleties relating to the INITIALIZE, STRING, CALL and CANCEL verbs that you should watch for when migrating from CMPR2 to NOCMPR2.

If a program is compiled with the CMPR2 and FLAGMIG options, a migration message will appear for any alphabetic items that had been defined with the symbol B.

IGYDS1105-W

MIGR A PICTURE clause was found that consisted of the symbols A and B. This alphabetic item will be treated as an alphanumeric-edited item under the "NOCMPR2" compiler option (where "A" is alphabetic, and "B" is spaces). VS COBOL II makes a new distinction concerning edited fields. In the OS/VS COBOL, a PICTURE like the following example (FIELD-1) was considered since it consisted entirely of alphabetic characters separated by spaces (B):

```
01    GROUP-1.
10    FIELD-1 PICTURE A(3)BA(2)BA(4).
10        FIELD-2 PICTURE X(10).
10        FIELD-3 PICTURE 9(5).
```

This FIELD-1 in VS COBOL II (Release 3 and 4 NOCMPR2) is considered to be ALPHABETIC-EDITED.

INSPECT statement. The INSPECT statement is problematic if the PROGRAM COLLATING SEQUENCE established in the OBJECT COMPUTER paragraph identifies an alphabet that was defined with the ALSO clause to override the standard EBCDIC collating sequence. Under these circumstances, the statement will behave differently under the ANSI 85 standard. When coded, it affects the INSPECT, STRING, and UNSTRING statements. (It also affects nonnumeric keys in a MERGE or SORT when the COLLATING SEQUENCE is not specified in the SORT or MERGE statement). The PROGRAM COLLATING SEQUENCE affects nonnumeric comparisons.

In OS/VS COBOL it affects both explicitly coded conditions and implicitly performed conditions (those comparisons that the compiler deems necessary to perform) in INSPECT, STRING, and UNSTRING statements. In VS COBOL II, the PROGRAM COLLATING SEQUENCE only affects explicitly coded conditions in these statements.

PERFORM VARYING issue. The *problem* is that the processing of the PERFORM VARYING/AFTER statement in COBOL/370 may differ from OS/VS COBOL depending on usage. The rules for "PERFORM VARYING" have changed from OS/VS COBOL to COBOL/370. In OS/VS COBOL, in a PERFORM statement with the VARYING/AFTER phrase, two actions take place when an inner condition tests as TRUE:

1. The identifier/index associated with the inner condition is set to its current FROM value.
2. The identifier/index associated with the outer condition is augmented by its current BY value.

With such a PERFORM statement in COBOL/370, COBOL for MVS & VM, and COBOL/370, the following takes place when an inner condition tests as TRUE:

1. The identifier/index associated with the outer condition is augmented by its current BY value.
2. The identifier/index associated with the inner condition is set to its current FROM value.

The following example illustrates the differences in execution:

```
PERFORM ABC VARYING X FROM 1 BY 1 UNTIL X > 3
                AFTER Y FROM X BY 1 UNTIL Y > 3
```

In OS/VS COBOL, ABC is executed eight times with the following values:

```
X:  1  1  1  2  2  2  3  3
Y:  1  2  3  1  2  3  2  3
```

In COBOL/370, COBOL for MVS & VM, and COBOL/370, ABC is executed six times with the following values:

```
X:  1  1  1  2  2  3
Y:  1  2  3  2  3  3
```

PROGRAM COLLATING SEQUENCE clause changes. In OS/VS COBOL and in VS COBOL II with CMPR2, the collating sequence specified in the alphabet name of the PROGRAM COLLATING SEQUENCE clause is applied to comparisons implicitly performed during the execution of INSPECT, STRING, and UNSTRING statements.

In VS COBOL II with NOCMPR2, the collating sequence specified in alphabet name is no longer used for these implicit comparisons. If your OS/VS COBOL program depends upon such comparisons being made, you can compile the program under VS COBOL II, specifying the CMPR2 option. This gives results compatible with OS/VS COBOL. The element is affected by the VS COBOL II CMPR2/NOCMPR2 compiler option.

Segmentation Changes—PERFORM statement in independent segments. In OS/VS COBOL with LANGLVL(1), if a PERFORM statement in an independent segment refers to a permanent segment, the independent segment is initialized on each exit from the performed procedures. In OS/VS COBOL with LANGLVL(2), for a PERFORM statement in an independent segment that refers to a permanent segment, control is passed to the performed procedures only once for each execution of the PERFORM statement.

In VS COBOL II, the compiler does not perform overlay; therefore, the rules just given do not apply. If your program logic depends upon either of the OS/VS COBOL implementations of these segmentation rules, you must rewrite the program.

Source Language Debugging Changes

In both VS COBOL II and OS/VS COBOL, source language debugging can be done using the USE FOR DEBUGGING declarative. Valid operands are shown in Table 1.4. Operands that invalid for VS COBOL II must be removed from the OS/VS COBOL program. Use the COBTEST debugging tool to achieve the same debugging results.

STOP RUN statement. Under the ANSI 85 standard, control cannot flow beyond the last line of a called subprogram. The compiler generates an implicit EXIT PROGRAM at the end of each program. Under the ANSI 68

Table 1.4 Use for Debugging Declarative Valid Operands

VS COBOL II DEBUGGING OPERANDS	OS/VS COBOL DEBUGGING OPERANDS	PROCEDURES ARE EXECUTED IMMEDIATELY
procedure-name-1	procedure-name-1	Before each execution of the named procedure.
		After execution of an ALTER statement referring to the named procedure.
ALL	ALL PROCEDURE	Before the execution of every PROCEDURES nondebugging procedure in the outermost program.
		After the execution of every ALTER statement in the outermost program (except ALTER statements in declarative procedure).
(none)	file-name-n	See VS COBOL for OS/VS for a description.
(none)	ALL REFERENCES OF identifier-n	See VS COBOL for OS/VS for a description.
(none)	cd-name-1	See VS COBOL for OS/VS for a description.

and ANSI 74 standard control can flow beyond the last line of a called program. When this happens, the program ABENDs. The ANSI 68 and ANSI 74 standard behavior can be preserved under the ANSI 85 standard by adding, at the end of the program, a section with a call to an ABEND macro.

STRING statement. The statement should be examined if it has a receiving field with a PICTURE string that consists of As and Bs only. The ANSI 74 standard classes these fields as alphabetic, while the ANSI 85 standard classes them as alphanumeric-edited. You will have to make a change to the program because alphanumeric-edited receiving fields in the STRING statement are not permitted.

The statement should also be reviewed if the PROGRAM COLLATING SEQUENCE established in the OBJECT COMPUTER paragraph identifies an alphabet that was defined with the ALSO clause. Under these circumstances, the statement will behave differently under the ANSI 85 standard.

The following string statement is an example:

STRING identifier-1 DELIMITED BY identifier-2

INTO identifier-3 WITH POINTER identifier-4 . . .

where identifier-1 or identifier-2 is the same as identifier-3 or identifier-4

or where identifier-3 is the same as identifier-4

Subscripts out of range—changes in evaluation. VS COBOL II generates an E-level compiler error message if a literal subscript or index value is coded that is greater than the allowed maximum. This message is generated whether or not the SSRANGE option is specified. OS/VS COBOL does not generate an equivalent error message.

Identification Division

The language upgrade changes to the Identification Division section are predominantly cosmetic, but they will cause compiler errors if they are not handled.

AUTHOR paragraph. Obsolete. Should be commented out for VS COBOL II.

DATE-COMPILED/ DATE-WRITTEN paragraphs. Obsolete. Should be commented out for VS COBOL II.

WHEN-COMPILED special register. Both VS COBOL II and OS/VS COBOL support the use of the WHEN-COMPILED special register. The

Table 1.5 Data Format Differences for VS COBOL II and OS/VS COBOL Compilers

IN OS/VS COBOL, THE FORMAT IS:	IN VS COBOL II, THE FORMAT IS:
hh.mm.ssMMM DD, YYYY	MM/DD/YYhh.mm.ss
(hour.minute.secondMONTH DAY, YEAR)	(MONTH/DAY/YEARhour.minute.second)

rules for use of the special register are the same for both compilers. However, the format of the data differs.

Environment Division

Most of the changes to the Environment Division, where COBOL defines outside elements, affect the obsolescence of items:

APPLY CORE-INDEX clause. This is an ISAM clause and needs to be removed (not supported in COBOL II).

APPLY CYL-INDEX clause. This is an ISAM clause and needs to be removed (not supported in COBOL II).

APPLY CYL-OVERFLOW clause. This is an ISAM clause and needs to be removed (not supported in COBOL II).

APPLY EXTENDED-SEARCH clause. This is an ISAM clause and needs to be removed (not supported in COBOL II).

APPLY MASTER-INDEX clause. This is an ISAM clause and needs to be removed (not supported in COBOL II).

APPLY RECORD-OVERFLOW clause. This is an ISAM clause and needs to be removed (not supported in COBOL II).

APPLY REORG-CRITERIA clause. This is an ISAM clause, and needs to be removed (not supported in COBOL II).

APPLY WRITE-VERIFY clause. This is an ISAM clause and needs to be removed (not supported in COBOL II).

ASSIGN clause changes. VS COBOL II supports only the following format of the ASSIGN clause:

```
ASSIGN TO assignment-name
```

where assignment name can have the following forms:

```
QSAM Files                        [comments-][S-]name
VSAM Sequential Files             [comments-][AS]name
VSAM Indexed or Relative Files    [comments-]name
```

If your OS/VS COBOL program uses other formats of the ASSIGN clause or other forms of the assignment name, you must change them to conform to the VS COBOL II format.

BLOCK CONTAINS clause. No longer has a meaning for VSAM files in VS COBOL II. It should be removed.

FILE STATUS clause changes. In OS/VS COBOL and in VS COBOL II with CMPR2, the FILE STATUS clause defines a single status key, which contains a status key value after every I/O operation is completed. Those values may have changed.

In VS COBOL II, the FILE STATUS clause defines up to two status keys. (The second status key is valid for VSAM files; it contains the VSAM return code, function code, and feedback code.)

In addition, status key values for VS COBOL II have been changed. For the status key values for QSAM files, see Table 1.6; for VSAM files, see Table 1.7. If your OS/VS COBOL program uses status key values to determine the course of execution, you must either modify the program to use the new status key values or compile it with the CMPR2 compiler option. This element is affected by the VS COBOL II CMPR2/ NOCMPR2 compiler option.

Table 1.6 Status Key Values—QSAM Files

VS COBOL II RELEASE 4 STATUS KEYS	OS/VS COBOL STATUS KEYS	MEANING
00	00	Successful completion.
04	(undefined)	Wrong length record. Successful completion.
05	(undefined)	Optional file not present. Successful completion.
07	(undefined)	The I/O statement was successfully executed, but a reel function (FOR REMOVAL, REWIND, and so on) was specified, and the file is not on a reel/unit medium.
10	10	At END (no next logical record). Successful completion.
30	30	Permanent error.
34	34	Permanent error. File boundary violation.

VS COBOL II RELEASE 4 STATUS KEYS	OS/VS COBOL STATUS KEYS	MEANING
35	93 96	Nonoptional file not present.
37	93	Device type conflict.
38	92	OPEN attempted for file closed. WITH LOCK.
39	95	Conflict of fixed file attributes; OPEN fails.
41	92	OPEN attempted for a file in OPEN mode.
42	92	CLOSE attempted for a file not in OPEN mode.
43	92	REWRITE attempted when last I/O statement was not READ.
44	92	Attempt to rewrite a sequential file record with a record of a different size.
46	92	Sequential READ attempted with no valid next record.
47	92	READ attempted when file not in OPEN INPUT or I-O mode.
48	92	WRITE attempted when file not in OPEN OUTPUT, I-O, or EXTEND mode.
49	92	DELETE or REWRITE attempted when file not in OPEN I-O mode.
90	90	Other errors with no further information.
91	91	VSAM password failure.
91	91	VSAM password failure.
92	92	Logic error.
93	93	VSAM resource not available.
94	94	No file position indicator for VSAM sequential request.
95	95	Invalid or incomplete VSAM file information.
96	96	No file identification (No DD statement).

Table 1.7 Status Key Values—VSAM Files

VS COBOL II RELEASE 4 STATUS KEYS	OS/VS COBOL STATUS KEYS	MEANING
00	00	Successful completion.
02	02	Duplicate key, and DUPLICATES specified. Successful completion.
04	00	Wrong length record. Successful completion.
05	00	Optional file not present. Successful completion.
10	10	At END (no next logical record). Successful completion.
14	(undefined)	On sequential READ for relative file, size of relative record number too large for relative key.
20	20	Invalid key for a VSAM indexed or relative file.
21	21	Invalid key for a VSAM indexed or relative file; sequence error.
22	22	Invalid key for a VSAM indexed or relative file; duplicate key and duplicates not allowed.
23	23	Invalid key for a VSAM indexed or relative file; no record found.
24	24	Invalid key for a VSAM indexed or relative file; attempt to write beyond file boundaries VS COBOL II only: For a WRITE to a relative file, size of relative record number too large for relative key.
30	30	Permanent error.
35	93 96	Nonoptional file not present.
37	90	Attempt to open a file not on a mass storage device.
39	95	Conflict of fixed file attributes; OPEN fails.
41	92	OPEN attempted for a file in OPEN mode.
42	92	CLOSE attempted for a file not in OPEN mode.
43	92	REWRITE attempted when last I/O statement was not READ or DELETE.

VS COBOL II RELEASE 4 STATUS KEYS	OS/VS COBOL STATUS KEYS	MEANING
46	92	Sequential READ attempted with no valid next record.
47	92	READ attempted when file not in OPEN INPUT or I-O mode.
48	92	WRITE attempted when file not in OPEN OUTPUT, I-O, or EXTEND mode.
49	92	DELETE or REWRITE attempted when file not in OPEN I-O mode.
90	90	Other errors with no further information.
91	91	VSAM password failure.
93	93	VSAM resource not available.
94	94	Under CMPR2: No file position indicator for VSAM sequential request.
95	95	Invalid or incomplete VSAM file information.
96	96	No file identification (no DD statement for this VSAM file).
97	97	OPEN statement execution successful; file integrity verified.

OPEN EXTEND statement changes. In VS COBOL II, you can specify OPEN EXTEND for sequential, indexed, or relative files. To conform to the COBOL/85 standard, you must not specify OPEN EXTEND and the LINAGE clause for the same file. (However, an IBM extension allows you to specify both clauses for the same file.) If your program must conform to the COBOL/85 standard, you must remove any LINAGE clauses for OPEN EXTEND files.

REMARKS paragraph. It is removed from support in VS COBOL II. You should fully convert this statement by commenting it out with an asterisk (*) inserted in column 7 of the paragraph header and in all succeeding lines of the paragraph.

RESERVE clause changes. OS/VS COBOL supports the following formats of the FILE-CONTROL paragraph RESERVE clause:

- RESERVE NO ALTERNATE AREA
- RESERVE NO ALTERNATE AREAS

- RESERVE integer ALTERNATE AREA
- RESERVE integer ALTERNATE AREAS
- RESERVE integer AREA
- RESERVE integer AREAS

VS COBOL II supports only the following forms of the RESERVE clause:

RESERVE integer AREA

RESERVE integer AREAS

If your OS/VS COBOL program utilizes either the RESERVE integer ALTERNATE AREA or the RESERVE integer ALTERNATE AREAS format, you must specify the RESERVE clause with integer + 1 areas to get equivalent processing under VS COBOL II. That is, the following specifications are equivalent:

- OS/VS COBOL RESERVE 2 ALTERNATE AREAS
- VS COBOL II RESERVE 3 AREAS

Under OS/VS COBOL, the interpretation of the RESERVE integer AREAS format using the LANGLVL(1) compiler option differs from the interpretation of this format using LANGLVL(2). With LANGLVL(1), when you use the RESERVE integer AREA or RESERVE integer AREAS format you must specify the RESERVE clause with integer = 1 areas to get equivalent processing under VS COBOL. This modification is not necessary with LANGLVL(2).

SAME AREA clause. SAME AREA should be changed to SAME RECORD AREA.

SELECT OPTIONAL clause changes. In OS/VS COBOL with LANGLVL(1), the SELECT OPTIONAL clause of the File Control entry is treated as documentation. In OS/VS COBOL with LANGLVL(2) and in VS COBOL II, the SELECT OPTIONAL clause is required for sequentially organized input files that are not necessarily present when the object program runs.

Data Division

Upgrade changes to the Data Division, where data structures are defined, mostly affect copybook formats, where file structures are described.

B Symbol in PICTURE clause—changes in evaluation. In defining an alphabetic item, OS/VS COBOL and VS COBOL II with CMPR2 both accept the PICTURE symbols A and B. VS COBOL II NOCMPR2 accepts only the PICTURE symbol A. (A PICTURE that contains both symbols A and B defines an alphanumeric-edited item.) This can cause execution differences between OS/VS COBOL and VS.

COBOL II effects evaluations of the following:

- The class test
- The STRING statement

The element is affected by the VS COBOL II CMPR2/NOCMPR2 compiler option.

BLANK WHEN ZERO clause. OS/VS COBOL accepts the BLANK WHEN ZERO clause. It is obsolete and should be removed for VS COBOL II.

Copybook Issue 1

Problem:
OS/VS COBOL allows COPY statements with associated names; VS COBOL II does not. For example, examine the following copy member (PROGC01L):

```
01  PROGC01L.      05  RECORD-TYPE    PIC X.       05  CTL-LOC
PIC X(4).          05  SUB-LOC        PIC X(4).    05  JOB-NO
PIC X(4).          05  PLT-NO         PIC X(4).
```

The problem is that the following coding technique is valid in OS/VS COBOL but not valid in VS COBOL II:

```
01   1-SAVE-AREA    COPY    PROGC01L.
```

In this case, the 01 level element in the Copybook member (PROGC01L) is PROGC01L and is *not the same* as 1-SAVE-AREA, which is the 01 level field in the COPY statement.

Resolution :
The program was manually revised for VS COBOL II compiler as follows:

```
COPY  PROGC01L  REPLACING  PROGC01L   BY   1-SAVE-AREA.
```

The majority of problems we experienced were with this type of COPY statement.

COM-REG special register. COM-REG is obsolete in VS COBOL II, and all references should be removed.

COPY statement changes. OS/VS COBOL accepts COPY statements written to conform to the COBOL/74 standard and also to the ANSI COBOL/68 standard when the LANGLVL(1) compiler option is specified. VS COBOL II accepts COPY statements written to conform to the COBOL/85 standard and also those that conform to the COBOL/74 standard.

JUSTIFIED clause changes. Under OS/VS COBOL with LANGLVL(1), if a JUSTIFIED clause is specified together with a VALUE clause for a data description entry, the initial data is right justified. For example,

```
77  DATA-1 PIC X(9) JUSTIFIED VALUE "FIRST".
```

results in "FIRST" occupying the five rightmost character positions of DATA-1:

```
----FIRST
```

Copybook Issue 2

Problem:
OS/VS COBOL allows COPY statements with associated names; VS COBOL II does not. For example, examine the following copy member (PROGM16L):

```
01  PROGM16L.           05  FILLER      PIC X(12) VALUE 'CHART-
MAP***'.
```

The problem is that the following coding technique is valid in OS/VS COBOL but not valid in VS COBOL II.

```
01  PROGM16L    COPY   PROGM16L.
```

In this case, the 01 level element in the Copybook member (PROGM16L) is PROGM16L and is the *same* as PROGM16L, which is the 01 level field in the COPY statement.

Resolution:
The program was manually revised for VS COBOL II compiler as follows:

```
COPY   PROGM16L.
```

In VS COBOL II, as in OS/VS COBOL with LANGLVL(2), the JUSTIFIED clause does not affect the initial placement of the data within the data item. If a VALUE and JUSTIFIED clause are both specified for an alphabetic or alphanumeric item, the initial value is left justified within the data item. For example,

```
77   DATA-1 PIC X(9) JUSTIFIED VALUE "FIRST".
```

results in "FIRST" occupying the five leftmost character positions of DATA-1:

```
FIRST----
```

To achieve unchanged results in VS COBOL II and OS/VS COBOL LANGLVL(2), you can specify the literal value as occupying all nine character positions of DATA-1. For example,

```
77   DATA-1 PIC X(9) JUSTIFIED VALUE "    FIRST".
```

which right justifies the value in DATA-1:

```
----FIRST
```

OCCURS DEPENDING ON clause—ASCENDING/DESCENDING KEY option. OS/VS COBOL accepts a variable-length key in the ASCENDING/DESCENDING KEY option of the OCCURS DEPENDING ON clause as an IBM extension in OS/VS COBOL. In VS COBOL II, the ASCENDING/DESCENDING KEY phrase may not specify a variable-length key.

CURRENCY SIGN. VS COBOL II does not accept the / (slash) character or the = (equal) character in the CURRENCY SIGN clause.

CURRENT-DATE special register. The CURRENT-DATE register is not supported by VS COBOL II.

Whenever CURRENT-DATE is referenced in the program, it should be replaced by code that contains the date from the system and puts it in the format of the CURRENT-DATE register. The fields required for the reformatting should be placed in the WORKING STORAGE section. For CICS programs, the date may be retrieved from the system using an EXEC CICS ASKTIME statement. CICS Release 1.7 or later is required.

For non-CICS programs the ACCEPT . . . FROM DATE statement is used to obtain the date. For DOS/VS COBOL, there are two different formats for the CURRENT-DATE register.

OCCURS DEPENDING ON clause—value for receiving items changed. In OS/VS COBOL, the current value of the OCCURS DEPENDING ON (ODO) object is always used for both sending and receiving items. In VS COBOL II, for sending items, the current value of the ODO object is used. For receiving items:

1. If a group item contains both the subject and object of an ODO, the maximum length of the item is used.
2. If a receiving item containing an ODO is followed in the same record by a nonsubordinate data item, the actual length of the receiving item is used.

When the maximum length is used, it is not necessary to initialize the ODO object before the table receives data. For items whose length or location depend on the value of the ODO object, you need to set the object of the DEPENDING ON option in an OCCURS CLAUSE before using it in the USING phrase of a CALL statement. Under VS COBOL II, for any group item that contains the subject and object of the OCCURS DEPENDING ON clause, you do not need to set the object for the item when it is used in the USING BY REFERENCE phrase of the CALL statement. This is true even if the group is described by rule number two, just given. The following example illustrates these points:

```
       01  TABLE-GROUP-1
               05  ODO-KEY-1 PIC 99.
               05  TABLE-1 PIC X(9)
                   OCCURS 1 TO 50 TIMES DEPENDING ON ODO-KEY-1.
           01  ANOTHER-GROUP.
               05  TABLE-GROUP-2.
                   10  ODO-KEY-2 PIC 99.
                   10  TABLE-2 PIC X(9)
                       OCCURS 1 to 50 TIMES DEPENDING ON ODO-KEY-2.
               05  TRAILER-ITEM PIC X(200).
                       .
                       .
                       .
           PROCEDURE DIVISION.
                       .
                       .
                       .
               MOVE SEND-ITEM-1 TO TABLE-GROUP-1
                       .
                       .
```

```
MOVE ODO-KEY-X TO ODO-KEY-2
MOVE SEND-ITEM-2 TO TABLE-GROUP-2.
```

When TABLE-GROUP-1 is a receiving item, VS COBOL II reserves the maximum number of character positions for it (450 bytes for TABLE-1 plus 2 bytes for ODO-KEY-1). Therefore, you need not initialize the length of TABLE-1 before moving the SEND-ITEM-1 data into the table. However, a nonsubordinate TRAILER-ITEM follows TABLE-GROUP-2 in the record description. In this case, VS COBOL II uses the actual value in ODO-KEY-2 to calculate the length of TABLE-GROUP-2, and you must set ODO-KEY-2 to its valid current length before moving the SEND-ITEM-2 data into the group receiving item.

ORGANIZATION clause. For VSAM files, this clause should be removed.

REDEFINES clause in FD or SD entry. VS COBOL II does not permit REDEFINES clauses in FD or SD entries. Because they are superfluous, they should be removed.

SPECIAL-NAMES paragraph changes. In the SPECIAL-NAMES paragraph, there are migration considerations for the ALPHABET clause, the CURRENCY SIGN clause, and function names (environment names).

ALPHABET clause changes. In OS/VS COBOL, the keyword ALPHABET is not allowed in the ALPHABET clause. In VS COBOL II with NOCMPR2, the ALPHABET keyword is required. Also, in VS COBOL II with NOCMPR2, alphabet-name-1, which specifies a character code set or collating sequence, can additionally be specified as follows:

EBCDIC	For EBCDIC
STANDARD-2	For the international reference version of the ISO 7-bit code (identical to STANDARD-1, except for the symbol "$")

CURRENCY SIGN clause changes. OS/VS COBOL with LANGLVL(1) accepts the / (slash) character in the CURRENCY SIGN clause. OS/VS COBOL with LANGLVL(2) and VS COBOL II do not accept this character as valid. In addition, VS COBOL II (for programs that use DBCS data items) does not accept the character G. If these characters are present, you must remove them from the CURRENCY SIGN clause.

UPSI switches. OS/VS COBOL and VS COBOL II with CMPR2 allow references to UPSI switches and mnemonic names associated to UPSI. VS COBOL II with NOCMPR2 allows condition names only. In OS/VS

COBOL, the condition names can be qualified, but in VS COBOL II the condition names must be unique. For example, if a condition name is defined in the SPECIAL-NAMES paragraph, the following will result under OS/VS COBOL:

```
SPECIAL-NAMES.
              UPSI-0 IS MNUPO
                     .
                     .
              PROCEDURE DIVISION
                     .
                     .
                     .
              IF UPSI-0 = 1 ...
              IF MNUPO=0 ...
```

And under VS COBOL II:

```
SPECIAL-NAMES.
              UPSI-0 IS MNUPO
                ON STATUS IS UPSI-0-ON
                OFF STATUS IS UPSI-0-OFF
                     .
                     .
              PROCEDURE DIVISION
                     .
                     .
                     .
              IF UPSI-0-ON ...
              IF UPSI-0-OFF ...
```

This item is affected by the VS COBOL II CMPR2/NOCMPR2 compiler option.

VALUE clause condition names. For VALUE clause condition names, releases prior to Release 2.4 of OS/VS COBOL allow the initialization of an alphanumeric field with a numeric value. For example, consider the following:

```
01 FIELD-A PICTURE XX.
           88    LAST-YEAR    VALUE 87.
           88    THIS-YEAR    VALUE 88.
```

```
           88   NEXT-YEAR   VALUE 89.
```

VS COBOL II does not accept this language extension. Therefore, to correct the preceding example, you must code alphanumeric values in the VALUE clauses:

```
01 FIELD-A PICTURE XX.
   88   LAST-YEAR   VALUE "87".
   88   THIS-YEAR   VALUE "88".
   88   NEXT-YEAR   VALUE "89".
```

Procedure Division

The Procedure Division, where COBOL places its executable commands, generally constitutes the majority of the code and, as such, also constitutes the majority of the upgrade changes. In this section, we'll present the commands that have been altered and tell you what needs to change.

ALPHABETIC class changes. In OS/VS COBOL and in VS COBOL II with CMPR2, only uppercase letters and the space character are considered to be ALPHABETIC. In VS COBOL II with NOCMPR2, uppercase letters, lowercase letters, and the space character are considered to be ALPHABETIC. If your OS/VS COBOL program uses the ALPHABETIC class test, and the data tested consists of mixed uppercase and lowercase letters, there may be differences in execution results. In such cases, you can ensure identical results by substituting the VS COBOL II ALPHABETIC-UPPER class test for the OS/VS COBOL ALPHABETIC test. The element is affected by the VS COBOL II CMPR2/NOCMPR2 compiler option.

APPLY-WRITE ONLY clause restrictions removed. In OS/VS COBOL, when using the APPLY-WRITE ONLY clause, all WRITE statements must have FROM options. In addition, none of the subfields of the associated records may be referred to by procedure statements or be the object of the DEPENDING ON option in an OCCURS clause. In VS COBOL II these restrictions do not apply.

Arithmetic statement changes. VS COBOL II supports the following arithmetic items with enhanced accuracy:

- Definitions of floating-point data items
- Usage of floating-point literals
- Usage of exponentiation

Therefore, for arithmetic statements that contain these items, VS COBOL II may provide more accurate results than OS/VS COBOL. This means that as a result of this your regression test results may vary.

CALL Statement Changes. OS/VS COBOL accepts procedure names and file names in the USING option of the CALL statement. If there are no literal delimiters around the name of the called program, you should put it in quotation marks.

VS COBOL II CALL statements do not accept procedure names and only accept QSAM file names in the USING option. Therefore, you must remove the procedure names and make sure that file names used in the USING option of the CALL statement name QSAM physical sequential files. To convert OS/VS COBOL programs that call assembler programs passing procedure names, you need to rewrite the assembler routines. In OS/VS COBOL programs, assembler routines can be written to receive an address or a list of addresses from the paragraph name that was passed as a parameter. The assembler routines can then use this address to return to an alternate place in the main program if an error occurs. In VS COBOL II, code your assembler routines so that they return to the point of origin with an assigned number, such as zero. If an error occurs in the assembler program, this number can then be used to go to alternate places in the calling routine. For example,

```
OS/VS COBOL:
            CALL "ASMMOD" USING PARAMETER-1,
                                PARAGRAPH-1,
                                PARAGRAPH-2,
            NEXT STATEMENT.
            :
            PARAGRAPH-1.
            :
            :
            PARAGRAPH-2.


    VS COBOL II
        CALL "ASMMOD" USING PARAMETER-1,
                            PARAMETER-2.
        IF PARAMETER-2 NOT = 0
           GOTO PARAGRAPH-1,
                PARAGRAPH-2,
                DEPENDING ON PARAMETER-2.
```

In this example, you would modify the assembler program (ASMMOD) so it does not branch to an alternative location. Instead, it will pass back the number zero to the calling routine if there are no errors and will pass back a nonzero return value if an error occurred. The nonzero value would be used to determine which paragraph in the COBOL program will handle the error condition.

CLOSE WITH DISP /CLOSE . . .WITH POSITIONING statements. The WITH DISP and WITH POSITIONING options are obsolete in VS COBOL II and should be removed.

CLOSE . . . REEL/UNIT FOR REMOVAL statement. CLOSE . . . REEL/UNIT FOR REMOVAL are obsolete in VS COBOL II and should be removed.

Combined Abbreviated Relation Condition Changes. Three considerations affect combined abbreviated relation conditions:

1. NOT and logical operator/relational operator evaluation
2. Parenthesis evaluation
3. The optional word IS

All are described in the following three sections of this chapter.

NOT and Logical Operator/Relational Operator Evaluation. OS/VS COBOL with LANGLVL(1) accepts the use of NOT in combined abbreviated relation conditions as follows:

- When only the subject of the relation condition is implied, NOT is considered a logical operator. For example,

    ```
    A = B AND NOT LESS THAN C OR D
    ```

    is equivalent to

    ```
    ((A = B) AND NOT (A < C) OR (A < D))
    ```

- When both the subject and the relational operator are implied, NOT is considered to be part of the relational operator. For example,

    ```
    A > B AND NOT C
    ```

    is equivalent to

    ```
    A > B AND A NOT > C
    ```

In combined abbreviated relation conditions, VS COBOL II and OS/VS COBOL with LANGLVL (2) consider NOT to be as follows:

- Part of the relational operator in the forms NOT GREATER THAN, NOT >, NOT LESS THAN, NOT <, NOT EQUAL TO, and NOT = .

For example,

```
A = B AND NOT LESS THAN C OR D
```

is equivalent to

```
((A = B) AND (A NOT < C) OR (A NOT < D))
```

- NOT in any other position is considered to be a logical operator (and thus results in a negated relation condition).

For example

```
A > B AND NOT C
```

is equivalent to

```
A > B AND NOT A > C
```

To ensure that you get the execution results you want, expand all abbreviated combined conditions into their full unabbreviated forms.

Parenthesis evaluation. OS/VS COBOL accepts the use of parentheses within an abbreviated combined relational condition. (This is not a documented usage of OS/VS COBOL.) VS COBOL II supports most such parenthesis usage as IBM extensions. However, there are some incompatibilities/differences:

1. VS COBOL II accepts the logical NOT operator preceding a left parenthesis. OS/VS COBOL does not.
2. Within the scope of an abbreviated combined relation condition, VS COBOL II does not support relational operators inside parentheses.

For example,

```
A = B AND ( < C OR D)
```

is not accepted by VS COBOL II; it is accepted by OS/VS COBOL.

The optional word IS. OS/VS COBOL accepts the optional word IS immediately preceding objects within an abbreviated combined relation condition. For example,

A = B OR IS C AND IS D

VS COBOL II does not accept this usage of the optional word IS. Therefore, for VS COBOL II, delete the word IS when used in this way.

NOTE:
VS COBOL II does permit the use of the optional word IS as part of the relational operator in abbreviated combined relational conditions. For example,

```
A = B OR IS = C AND IS = D
```

ENTER statement. Obsolete. Should be removed.

EXIT PROGRAM/GOBACK statement changes. In OS/VS COBOL and in VS COBOL II with CMPR2, when an EXIT PROGRAM or GOBACK statement is executed, if the end of range of a PERFORM statement within it has not been reached, the PERFORM statement remains in an incomplete state. In VS COBOL II, when an EXIT PROGRAM or GOBACK statement is executed, the end of range of every PERFORM statement within it is considered to have been reached. If your OS/VS COBOL program depends upon PERFORM statements remaining incomplete between calls, use the CMPR2 option when compiling under VS COBOL II. This gives you the same execution results as you get under OS/VS COBOL. The element is affected by the VS COBOL II CMPR2/NOCMPR2 compiler option.

GREATER THEN (or > THEN) relational operator. THEN should be changed to THAN or left as >.

IF . . . OTHERWISE statement changes. OS/VS COBOL allows IF statements of the nonstandard format

```
IF condition THEN statement-1 OTHERWISE statement-2
```

VS COBOL II allows only IF statements having the standard format

```
IF condition THEN statement-1 ELSE statement-2
```

Therefore, OS/VS COBOL programs containing nonstandard IF . . . OTHERWISE statements must be changed to standard IF . . . ELSE statements.

LESS THEN (or < THEN) relational operator. THEN should be replaced by THAN or changed to <.

MOVE statements and comparisons—scaling changes. Using OS/VS COBOL with LANGLVL(1), the trailing zeros (0) are truncated if either the sending field in a MOVE statement or a field in a comparison is a scaled integer (that is, if the rightmost PICTURE symbols are the letter *P*) and the receiving field (or the field to be compared) is alphanumeric or numeric-edited. For example, after the following MOVE statement is executed

```
05  SEND-FIELD    PICTURE 999PPP VALUE 123000.
         05  RECEIVE-FIELD  PICTURE XXXXXX.
              .
              .
```

```
                    MOVE SEND-FIELD TO RECEIVE-FIELD.
```

RECEIVE-FIELD contains the value 123--- (left justified).

With VS COBOL II and OS/VS COBOL with the LANGLVL(2) option, a MOVE statement transfers the trailing zeros, and a comparison includes them. For example, after the following MOVE statement is executed

```
         05  SEND-FIELD      PICTURE 999PPP VALUE 123000.
         05  RECEIVE-FIELD   PICTURE XXXXXX.
             .
             .
             .
                    MOVE SEND-FIELD TO RECEIVE-FIELD.
```

RECEIVE-FIELD contains the value 123000.

ON statement. The ON statement is removed from support in VS COBOL II. This statement should be converted. The statement

```
    ON integer          imperative statement
```

may be converted to

```
    ADD 1 TO LCP-ONCTR-nn
    IF LCP-ONCTR-nn = integer       imperative statement
```

The statement

```
    ON integer-1 until integer 2        imperative statement
```

may be converted to

```
    ADD 1 TO LCP-ONCTR-nn   IF LCP-ONCTR-nn > (integer 1 - 1) & < integer-2
    imperative statement
```

A data item with the dataname LCP-ONCTR-nn (where nn is a sequence number) should be added into the WORKING STORAGE section with an initial value of zero.

ON SIZE ERROR option—changes in intermediate results. For OS/VS COBOL and VS COBOL II with CMPR2, the SIZE ERROR option for the DIVIDE and MULTIPLY statements applies to both intermediate and final results. For VS COBOL II with NOCMPR2, the SIZE ERROR option for the DIVIDE and MULTIPLY statements applies only to final results. Therefore, if your OS/VS COBOL depends upon SIZE ERROR detection for intermediate results, you must either change your program or compile it with the CMPR2 compiler option. The element is affected by the VS COBOL II CMPR2/NOCMPR2 compiler option.

For OS/VS COBOL and VS COBOL II with CMPR2, the SIZE ERROR option for the DIVIDE and MULTIPLY statements applies to both intermediate and final results. If your OS/VS COBOL relies upon SIZE ERROR detection for intermediate results, it must change or be compiled with the CMPR2 compiler option (see the subsection titled "Behaviors" in Section 1.6.1 for more on the CMPR2 compiler option). The statements

```
01      NUMERICS.
10      NUMBERIC-1 PICTURE  S9(16).
10         NUMERIC-2       PICTURE  S9(16).
10         NUMERIC-3       PICTURE  S9(16).
10         NUMERIC-4       PICTURE  S9(16).
10         TEMP      PICTURE  S9(30).
   MULTIPLY NUMERIC-1  BY NUMERIC-2 GIVING NUMERIC-3   NUMERIC-4.
```

should behave like the statements

```
MULTIPLY NUMERIC-1    BY NUMERIC-2  GIVING   TEMP          MOVE TEMPO-
RARY   TO NUMERIC-3       MOVE TEMPORARY  TO NUMERIC-4
```

TEMP is the intermediate result. An intermediate result will have at most thirty digits.

In the preceding example, if NUMERIC-1 , NUMERIC-2 , NUMERIC-3, and NUMERIC-4 are all defined as PIC S9(16), NUMERIC-1 will be multiplied by NUMERIC-2 , yielding a 32-digit result, which is moved to the 30-digit intermediate result, TEMP. TEMP is then moved to NUMERIC-3 and NUMERIC-4.

A size error may occur if the result exceeds the largest possible value of the result field, during a division by zero, or during an exponential expression.

PERFORM Statement—Changes in the VARYING/AFTER Options. In OS/VS COBOL and in VS COBOL II with CMPR2, if an inner condition tests as TRUE in a PERFORM statement with the VARYING/AFTER options, the following will occur:

1. The identifier/index associated with the inner condition is set to its current FROM value.

2. The identifier/index associated with the outer condition is augmented by its current BY value.

In VS COBOL II with NOCMPR2, when an inner condition tests as TRUE in such a PERFORM statement, the following actions take place in the following order:

1. The identifier/index associated with the outer condition is augmented by its current BY value.
2. The identifier/index associated with the inner condition is set to its current FROM value.

The following example illustrates the differences in execution:

```
            .
            .
            .
     PERFORM ABC VARYING X FROM 1 BY 1 UNTIL X > 3
                 AFTER Y FROM X BY 1 UNTIL Y > 3
            .
            .
            .
```

In OS/VS COBOL, ABC is executed eight times with the following values:

```
X:  1  1  1  2  2  2  3  3
Y:  1  2  3  1  2  3  2  3
```

In VS COBOL II, ABC is executed six times with the following values:

```
X:  1  1  1  2  2  3
Y:  1  2  3  2  3  3
```

By using nested PERFORM statements, you can achieve the same processing results in VS COBOL II as in OS/VS COBOL, as follows:

```
       MOVE 1 TO X, Y, Z
       PERFORM EX-1 VARYING X FROM 1 BY 1 UNTIL X > 3
       .
       .
   EX-1.
       PERFORM EX-2 VARYING Y FROM Z BY 1 UNTIL Y > 3.
       MOVE X TO Z.

   EX-2.
       PERFORM ABC.
   ABC.
       .
       .
```

The element is affected by the VS COBOL II CMPR2/NOCMPR2 compiler option.

READ and RETURN statement changes—INTO phrase. When the sending field is chosen for the move associated with a READ or RETURN . . . INTO identifier statement, OS/VS COBOL and VS COBOL II may select different records from under the FD or SD to use as the sending field.

RERUN clause changes. When the RERUN clause is specified, OS/VS COBOL takes a checkpoint on the first record. When the RERUN clause is specified, VS COBOL II does not take a checkpoint on the first record.

SEARCH statement changes. Under VS COBOL II, the WHEN phrase data name (the subject of the WHEN relation-condition) must be an ASCENDING/DESCENDING KEY data item in this table element, and identifier-2 (the object of the WHEN relation-condition) must not be an ASCENDING/DESCENDING key data item for this table element. Under OS/VS COBOL, these rules do not apply. The ASCENDING/DESCENDING KEY data item may be specified as either the subject or the object of the WHEN relation-condition. The following SEARCH example will execute under both VS COBOL II and OS/VS COBOL:

```
01  VAL  PIC X.
01  TABLE-01.
    05  TABLE-ENTRY
            OCCURS 100 TIMES
            ASCENDING KEY IS KEY-1
            INDEXED BY INDEX-NAME-1.
        10  FILLER PIC X.
        10  KEY-1 PIC X.
             .
             .
             .
    SEARCH ALL TABLE-ENTRY
        AT END DISPLAY "ERROR"
        WHEN KEY-1 ( INDEX-NAME-1 ) = VAL
            DISPLAY "TABLE RECORDS OK".
```

OS/VS COBOL accepts the following; VS COBOL II does not:

```
WHEN VAL = KEY-1 ( INDEX-NAME-1 )
    DISPLAY "TABLE RECORDS OK".
```

SORT Special Registers. The use of special registers in VS COBOL II is different than in OS/VS COBOL, as shown in Table 1.8.

> **NOTE:** See your sort manual for the meaning of keywords.

The SORT-CORE-SIZE, SORT-FILE-SIZE, SORT-MESSAGE, and SORT-MODE-SIZE special registers are supported under VS COBOL II, and they will be used in the SORT interface when they have non-default values. However, at run time, individual SORT special registers will be overridden by the corresponding parameters on control statements that are included in the SORT-CONTROL file, and a message will be issued. In addition, a compiler warning message (W-level) will be issued for each SORT special register that was set in the program.

START . . . USING KEY statement. The USING KEY clause of the START statement is not supported by the target language, VS COBOL

Table 1.8 Sorting in OS/VS COBOL and VS COBOL II

TO SPECIFY	IN OS/VS COBOL, USE	IN VS COBOL II, USE
Sort completion code	Special register: SORT-RETURN	Special register: SORT-RETURN
Name of file with sort control statements (by default IGZSRTCD)	SRTCDS (could contain only a sort/merge debug statement)	Special register: SORT-CONTROL
Modal length of records in a file with variable-length records	Special register: SORT-MODE-SIZE	SMS control statement: SMS=nnnnn or Special register: SORT-MODE-SIZE
Number of sort records	Special register: SORT-FILE-SIZE	OPTION control statement keyword: FILSZ (see note) or Special register: SORT-FILE-SIZE
Amount of main storage to be used	Special register: SORT-CORE-SIZE with value of +999999 or +99999999	OPTION control statement keyword: MAINSIZE=MAX (see note) or Special register: SORT-CORE-SIZE
Amount of main storage to be used	Special register: SORT-CORE-SIZE with a positive value	OPTION control statement keyword: MAINSIZE (see note) or Special register: SORT-CORE-SIZE
Amount of main storage to be reserved	Special register: SORT-CORE-SIZE with a negative value	OPTION control statement keyword: RESINV (see note) or Special register: SORT-CORE-SIZE
Name of sort message file (default SYSOUT)	Special register: SORT-MESSAGE	OPTION control statement keyword: MSGDDN (see note) or Special register: SORT-MESSAGE

II. START statements that specify this clause should be converted to START . . . KEY statements.

TO (as in = TO). TO should be removed in comparisons (IF A = TO B becomes IF A = B).

TRANSFORM statement. Change TRANSFORM to INSPECT.

UNSTRING Statements—Subscript Evaluation Changes. In OS/VS COBOL and in VS COBOL II with CMPR2, the UNSTRING statement for the following is evaluated immediately:

- DELIMITED BY, INTO, DELIMITER IN, and COUNT IN fields
- Any associated subscripting, indexing, or length calculation before the transfer of data into the receiving item

In VS COBOL II with NOCMPR2, the UNSTRING statement for these fields and any associated subscripting, indexing, or length calculation is evaluated once—immediately before the examination of the delimiter sending fields. If your UNSTRING statements under OS/VS COBOL have multiple receivers and contain items that are variably located, variable length, or subscripted, you should use the CMPR2 option to achieve identical processing results under VS COBOL II. For example,

```
01 ABC      PIC X(30).
   01 IND.
      02 IND-1 PIC 9.
   01 TAB.
      02 TAB-1 PIC X OCCURS 10 TIMES.
   01 ZZ      PIC X(30).

         UNSTRING ABC DELIMITED BY TAB-1 (IND-1) INTO IND ZZ.
```

Under OS/VS COBOL, subscript IND-1 is reevaluated before the second receiver IND is filled. Under VS COBOL II, the subscript IND-1 is evaluated only once at the beginning of the execution of the UNSTRING statement. Under OS/VS COBOL with LANGLVL(1), when the DELIMITED BY ALL option of UNSTRING is specified, two or more contiguous occurrences of any delimiter are treated as if they were only one occurrence. As much of the first occurrence as will fit is moved into the current delimiter receiving field (if specified), and each additional occurrence is moved only if the complete occurrence will fit. For more information on the behavior of this option in OS/VS COBOL, see the "IBM VS COBOL for OS/VS" manual. Under VS COBOL II, one or more contiguous occurrences of any delimiters are treated as if they were only one occurrence, and this one occurrence is moved to the delimiter receiving field (if specified). For example, assume ID-SEND contains 123**45678**90AB and consider the following statement:

```
UNSTRING ID-SEND DELIMITED BY ALL "*"
     INTO ID-R1 DELIMITER IN ID-D1 COUNT IN ID-C1
     INTO ID-R2 DELIMITER IN ID-D2 COUNT IN ID-C2
     INTO ID-R3 DELIMITER IN ID-D3 COUNT IN ID-C3
```

OS/VS COBOL (using LANGLVL(1)) will produce this result:

```
ID-R1   123     1D-D1   **      ID-C1   3
ID-R2   45678   1D-D2   **      ID-C2   5
ID-R3   90AB    1D-D3           ID-C3   4
```

and VS COBOL II will produce this result:

```
ID-R1   123     1D-D1   *       ID-C1   3
ID-R2   45678   1D-D2   *       ID-C2   5
ID-R3   90AB    1D-D3           ID-C3   4
```

WRITE AFTER POSITIONING Statement. OS/VS COBOL supports the WRITE statement with the AFTER POSITIONING option. VS COBOL II does not. Under VS COBOL II, delete the AFTER POSITIONING option of the WRITE statement, specify the NOADV compiler option, and specify RECFM=FBA in your JCL output DD statement.

OS/VS COBOL supports the WRITE statement with the AFTER POSITIONING phrase. COBOL for MVS & VM and COBOL/370 do not. In COBOL for MVS & VM and COBOL/370, you can use the WRITE . . . AFTER ADVANCING statement to receive behavior similar to WRITE . . . AFTER POSITIONING. The following two examples show OS/VS COBOL POSITIONING phrases and the equivalent COBOL for MVS & VM (or COBOL/370) phrases.

When using WRITE . . . AFTER ADVANCING with *literals*:

```
COBOL for MVS & VM
OS/VS COBOL                             COBOL/370

AFTER POSITIONING 0                     AFTER ADVANCING PAGE
AFTER POSITIONING 1                     AFTER ADVANCING 1 LINE
AFTER POSITIONING 2                     AFTER ADVANCING 2 LINES
AFTER POSITIONING 3                     AFTER ADVANCING 3 LINES
```

When using WRITE . . . AFTER ADVANCING with *nonliterals*:

```
WRITE OUTPUT-REC AFTER POSITIONING SKIP-CC.
```

```
COBOL for MVS & VM
OS/VS COBOL                                          COBOL/370
                          SKIP-CC

AFTER POSITIONING SKIP-CC    1       AFTER ADVANCING PAGE
AFTER POSITIONING SKIP-CC    ' '     AFTER ADVANCING 1 LINE
AFTER POSITIONING SKIP-CC    0       AFTER ADVANCING 2 LINES
AFTER POSITIONING SKIP-CC    -       AFTER ADVANCING 3 LINES
```

NOTE: With COBOL for MVS & VM and COBOL/370, channel skipping is only supported with references to SPECIAL-NAMES.

CCCA can automatically convert WRITE . . . AFTER POSITIONING statements. For example, given the following statement

```
WRITE OUTPUT-REC AFTER POSITIONING n.
```

if n is a literal, you should change this example to

```
WRITE . . . AFTER ADVANCING n LINES.
```

1.7 Migrating from OS/VS COBOL to VS COBOL II

The following three sections discuss some of the lessons we have learned during migrations from OS/VS COBOL to VS COBOL II. Data elements that did not behave the same in comparisons comprised a large portion of our issues (because of truncation issues or compiler options). Manage your source carefully. Regression tests will fail just as easily because the source code (preupgrade and postupgrade) differs as a result of production changes.

1.7.1 Testing for MVS COBOL

One of the first issues we encountered with our COBOL conversions was a result of how the different COBOL versions resolve file lengths at run time. OS/VS COBOL doesn't care if the file length specified in the FD statement matches the LRECL length specified in the JCL. With COBOL II, however, the file lengths must match exactly. We wrote a simple COBOL program that identifies the file length differences in the hope that we would catch and fix the anomalies before program testing. This anomaly is annoying, but it does not cause a functional change in the programs and can be fixed relatively quickly. Take care when resolving this issue; some file record lengths vary or have changed since the programs were originally written.

We also encountered a few programs (2 of 140) in which the COBOL conversion produced an unexpected, functional change in the program. The two programs were using a "LENGTH OF" statement that was actually coded incorrectly in OS/VS COBOL but seemed to be working. When the programs were converted to COBOL II, the statements caused a file to be severely truncated.

1.7.2 Commands: COBOL I versus COBOL II

There were some commands that worked in COBOL I but not in COBOL II. For example,

```
MOVE PFG-LABEL-REQUEST-RECORD TO PFG-LABEL-REQUEST-REC   (1:LENGTH OF
PFG-LABEL-REQUEST-REC)
```

The working storage areas being moved contained several OCCURS clauses. Both working storage areas were identical (5000 bytes). We believe the purpose of the length command was to ensure that the length of the two files would always be the same. In other words, if the first MOVE moved a file of 4000 bytes (not all of the OCCURS tables were filled) to the output and the second MOVE moved a 3500-byte record to the same output file, the output record would not have an extra 500 left over from the first MOVE. However, we don't believe this command ever worked because it is always specifying that the length of the output record be the length of the output record. It should have been referencing the length of the MOVE FROM file. This command worked in COBOL I but not COBOL II. The first file was being truncated to the length of the output file. Since the output file was initiated with a length of 24 the final result was a file that was severely truncated to 24 characters. The solution was to comment out the LENGTH OF statement.

1.7.3 High Values

We had a program ABENDing with a SOC7. High values were being moved to a group level item. An elementary item with a numeric definition was then being compared to another field. This comparison caused the ABEND.

COBOL/74 allows you to compare a numeric field that contains high values; COBOL II does not. Our resolution was to change the code to avoid the comparison when a numeric field contains high values.

1.8 Conclusion

Among the lessons you have hopefully learned in this chapter are the following:

- Train and educate programmers before you begin.
- Document and enforce standards:
    - Field names
    - How to change Report Writer code (more on that in Chapter 2)
    - How to change ISAM files (more on that in Chapter 2)
- Be prepared to develop a test strategy if you don't have one already:
    - Baseline test (what the code does today)
    - Unit tests
    - Integration tests within an application
    - Regression
- Organize. Organize. Organize. Plan milestones. Set schedules and stick to them.

CHAPTER 2

Report Writer, ISAM, BDAM, and Communications

This chapter will help you with the now obsolete OS/VS COBOL language elements Report Writer, ISAM file handling, BDAM file handling, and the communications feature.

2.1 Report Writer Conversion Options and Issues

The Report Writer language items no longer accepted by VS COBOL II or COBOL for MVS are as follows:

- GENERATE statement
- INITIATE statement
- LINE-COUNTER special register
- Nonnumeric literal IS mnemonic name
- PAGE-COUNTER special register
- PRINT-SWITCH special register
- REPORT clause of FD entry
- REPORT section
- TERMINATE statement
- USE BEFORE REPORTING declarative

To keep producing critical reports currently generated by OS/VS COBOL's Report Writer feature, and to upgrade your compilers, you will have to execute one of the following three options:

1. Keep your existing Report Writer code and use the Report Writer precompiler from IBM.

    When you recompile existing Report Writer applications (or newly written applications) with the Report Writer precompiler and use the output as input to the VS COBOL II or COBOL for MVS (or COBOL/370) compilers, your Report Writer applications can run above the 16M line. Through VS COBOL II or COBOL for MVS (or COBOL/370), you can also extend their processing capabilities.

    This method requires that you use both the Report Writer precompiler and the VS COBOL II COBOL for MVS (or COBOL/370) compiler. Installation takes a few days, but you get to keep your Report Writer code intact. At the time of this writing, the cost for the Precompiler was about $10,000 (this may vary depending on your CPU).

2. Convert existing Report Writer code using the Report Writer precompiler or other Report Writer conversion tool.

    If you permanently convert Report Writer code to non-Report Writer code, you can stop using the Report Writer precompiler and just use the VS COBOL II or COBOL for compilers. However, this may produce difficult-to-maintain COBOL code.

    When converting Report Writer code to non-Report Writer code using the IBM precompiler, the utility generates variable names and paragraph names. These names might not be familiar and so may be difficult to identify when you attempt to make changes to the program after the conversion. You can change the names to be meaningful, in line with your applications naming standards, but this might be difficult and time consuming.

    Another tool we have tested and used successfully is Prince Software's Translate R/W, which produced generally accurate code and appears to be easier to maintain.

3. Run existing OS/VS COBOL-compiled Report Writer programs under Language Environment.

You can run your existing OS/VS COBOL Report Writer applications using IBM's Language Environment (LE) without compiling with the VS COBOL II or COBOL for compilers. For details on running existing OS/VS COBOL programs using the Language Environment run-time library, see the IBM manual, *Compiler and Run-Time Migration Guide* (International Business Machines Corporation 1991, 1995), Chapter 5, Section 3.2, "Moving from the OS/VS COBOL Run Time."

NOTE:
To compile OS/VS COBOL applications with Report Writer statements, you must continue to use the OS/VS COBOL compiler. OS/VS COBOL Report Writer programs *will not run above the 16M line*.

2.1.1 About the COBOL Report Writer Precompiler

The Report Writer Precompiler has two functions. It can be used to precompile applications containing Report Writer statements so the code will be acceptable to the VS COBOL II, COBOL for MVS, and COBOL/370 compilers, or it can permanently convert Report Writer statements to valid VS COBOL II, COBOL for MVS, and COBOL/370 statements.

2.2 ISAM Conversion Options and Issues

IBM no longer supports ISAM. ISAM is dead. The VS COBOL II or COBOL for MVS compilers will not compile a program that has the NOMINAL KEY (for ISAM) clause coded. So if you have any programs using ISAM that you want to upgrade, you must change the ISAM files and programs. You will not be able to leave ISAM intact and only modify and compile them using the VS COBOL II or COBOL for MVS compilers.

Additionally, CICS/VS 1.7 and higher do not support ISAM files either. If you have been delaying the conversion process, do it now. VS COBOL II and COBOL for MVS & VM do not support the processing of ISAM files. Programs using any ISAM files should be converted to programs using Virtual Storage Access Method/Keyed Sequential Data Set (VSAM/KSDS) files. This can be done by using the VSAM utility program IDCAM.

The language elements that are affected and the conversion actions you can perform are documented in the following sections. There is a brief description of each item, followed by conversion suggestions.

ISAM File Handling Language Items Affected

The ISAM language items no longer accepted by VS COBOL II or COBOL for MVS & VM are as follows:

- ACTUAL KEY clause
- APPLY CORE-INDEX
- APPLY KEY
- APPLY RECORD-OVERFLOW clause
- APPLY REORG-CRITERIA
- File declarations for ISAM files
- NOMINAL KEY clause
- Organization parameter I
- TRACK-AREA clause
- TRACK-LIMIT clause
- FILE-LIMITS clause
- PROCESSING MODE
- SEEK statement
- TRACK-LIMIT clause
- USING KEY clause of START statement

ISAM Conversion Options and Issues

There are two options available to handle the ISAM conversion issues (assuming you want to upgrade your COBOL):

1. Convert the files to VSAM.
2. Extract the ISAM calls.

2.2.1 File Conversion Options

Two conversion tools can help you convert ISAM files to VSAM/KSDS files. You can use either IDCAMS REPRO or CCCA, Release 2.0, depending on the design of your application. The IDCAMS REPRO facility will perform the conversion unless the file has a hardware dependency.

Conversion involves two phases. Phase 1 consists of converting data sets from ISAM to VSAM, usually without modifying any COBOL programs. This phase involves using an IBM program product called IDCAMS.

2.2.2 Phase 1: File Conversion

File conversion requires the following two steps:

1. Convert the files from indexed sequential to KSDSs. This can be accomplished by allocating a KSDS using the DEFINE CLUSTER and REPRO commands to transfer all the records from the indexed sequential file into it. When allocating the KSDS, make sure that the record length, key length, and its offset are the same as those of the file being converted.

2. Convert the JCL job streams that are using the related files from indexed sequential to VSAM. While ISAM files require a long parameter list on the DD card, VSAM files need only the DSN and DISP parameters in most cases. When converting JCL job streams, the recovery and restart procedures must be reconsidered as they specifically apply to VSAM files. The programs and procedures that were used to reorganize ISAM files should also be modified. If the file was being deleted and defined using JCL statements, you will have to code the DELETE and DEFINE CLUSTER commands to perform the same function.

Once these two steps are finished, your file conversion is complete.

2.2.3 Phase 2: ISAM Program Conversion

ISAM program conversion involves changing the COBOL programs themselves to make use of VSAM verbs and statements. The COBOL conversion tool (CCCA, Release 2.0) can automatically convert the file definition and I/O statements from your ISAM COBOL language to VSAM/KSDS COBOL language, or you can perform these updates manually. The steps for manual updating are as follows:

- Change the assignment name.
- Remove NOMINAL KEY.

- Add "ORGANIZATION IS INDEXED."
- Generate a new data item, LCP-FILE-STATUS, in the Working Storage section to handle the return codes.
- The RECORD KEY field should be moved back to NOMINAL KEY after reading a record.
- The NOMINAL KEY field should be moved back to RECORD KEY to read a record.

2.3 ISAM Extraction

If the design of your application makes it impossible to convert to VSAM, you can restructure the application to separate the ISAM statements into an I/O program that can be compiled by the OS/VS COBOL compiler. You can then separate the rest of the application logic into programs that can be upgraded to VS COBOL II or COBOL for MVS. You can then run your application, which consists of both OS/VS COBOL programs and VS COBOL II or COBOL for MVS & VM programs, under Language Environment. See Figures 2.1 and 2.2 for a sample before and after conversion, respectively.

2.4 BDAM Conversion Issues

Converting BDAM files is much like converting ISAM files, and you have similar options. BDAM is no longer supported, so you can do either of the following:

1. Convert the BDAM files and the programs using them to VSAM.
2. Extract the BDAM calls to another program and maintain the BDAM files (see Section 2.3, "ISAM Extraction," for a similar method).

The following clauses specific to the BDAM access method are no longer accepted by VS COBOL II:

- ACTUAL KEY clause
- APPLY RECORD-OVERFLOW
- File declarations for BDAM files

```
SELECT INVENTORY-MASTER-FILE          ASSIGN TO DA-I-INVMASTR
        ACCESS IS RANDOM
        NOMINAL KEY IS WS-KEY
        RECORD KEY IS MAS-KEY.
I-O-CONTROL.
    APPLY CORE-INDEX ON INVENTORY-MASTER-FILE.

 DATA DIVISION.
 FILE SECTION.

 FD  INVENTORY-MASTER-FILE
     LABEL RECORDS ARE STANDARD
     BLOCK CONTAINS 120 RECORDS.
 01  INVENTORY-MASTER-RECORD.    COPY H6750B50.

WORKING STORAGE SECTION.
77  SUPERLIB                PIC 9(8) VALUE           0000
77  QOMDATEQ                PIC X(8) VALUE ZEROS.

01  HOUSEKEEPING-VARIABLES.
    05  WS-KEY.
        10  WS-ITEM         PIC 9(9) COMP-3 VALUE ZEROS.
        10  WS-INV          PIC 9(3) COMP-3 VALUE ZEROS.
01  WS-PROV-RECORD-IN.   COPY H6750B45.

 PROCEDURE DIVISION.
 *******************************************************************
 *******************************************************************
 *************    MAINLINE PROCEDURE    ****************************
 *******************************************************************
 *******************************************************************
  *******************************************************************
 *
 *   THIS PROCEDURE READS GISMO ISAM FILE #90.
 *
 *******************************************************************

 0200-GET-RECORD SECTION.
     MOVE 'YES'  TO VALID-KEY-FLAG.
     MOVE PROV-PRODUCT TO WS-ITEM.
     MOVE 90 TO WS-INV.
     READ INVENTORY-MASTER-FILE
        INVALID KEY PERFORM 0300-NOT-FOUND THRU 0300-END.
 0200-END. EXIT.

 *******************************************************************
```

Figure 2.1 Sample before conversion.

```
SELECT INVENTORY-MASTER-FILE        ASSIGN TO DA-V-INVMASTR
      FILE STATUS  IS LCP-FILE-STATUS-001
      ACCESS IS RANDOM
      RECORD KEY IS MAS-KEY
      ORGANIZATION IS INDEXED.

FD  INVENTORY-MASTER-FILE
    .
01  INVENTORY-MASTER-RECORD.
                                COPY H6750B50.
*                                                                      *
*01 INVENTORY-MASTER-RECORD.
    05  MAS-KEY.
        10  MAS-GENERIC-ITEM-NO     PIC 9(9)      COMP-3.
        10  MAS-INVENTORY-NO        PIC 9(3)      COMP-3.
*           (INVENTORY NUMBER IS 90)

WORKING STORAGE SECTION.
77  LCP-FILE-STATUS-001         PIC XX.
77  SUPERLIB                    PIC 9(8) VALUE
77  QOMDATEQ                    PIC X(8) VALUE ZEROS.
01  HOUSEKEEPING-VARIABLES.
    05  WS-KEY.
        10  WS-ITEM             PIC 9(9) COMP-3 VALUE ZEROS.
        10  WS-INV              PIC 9(3) COMP-3 VALUE ZEROS.
01  WS-PROV-RECORD-IN.
                         COPY H6750B45.
01  WS-PROVISIONS-REPORT-RECORD.
    05  PROV-RECORD-TYPE        PIC X.
        88  PROV-PROVISIONS-RECORD       VALUE 'P'.
    05  PROV-UPDATE-KEY         PIC X.
        1 = PRIOR INPUT FOR CURRENT AND PREVIOUS YEAR.
        2 = THIS WEEKS INPUT.
    05  PROV-PLANT              PIC 9(3)      COMP-3.
        PLANT TO RECEIVE THE SHIPMENT.
```

Figure 2.2 Sample after conversion.

- Organization parameters D, R, W
- SEEK statement
- TRACK-LIMIT clause

2.4.1 BDAM File-handling Migration Actions

You should convert any BDAM files to Virtual Storage Access Method/Relative Record Data Set (VSAM/RRDS) files. For such file

```
                    IF THE LOCATION THAT IS TO RECEIVE THE SHIPMENT IS
                    NOT A PLANT THEN THIS FIELD WILL BE THE PLANT
                    THAT PREPARED THE PURCHASE ORDER, NORMALLY 060.
        05   PROV-PRODUCT                PIC 9(9)      COMP-3.

    PROCEDURE DIVISION.
     DECLARATIVES.
     LCP-STATUS-001-SECTION SECTION.
         USE AFTER STANDARD ERROR PROCEDURE ON INVENTORY-MASTER-FILE.
     LCP-STATUS-001.
         DISPLAY 'INVENTORY-MASTER-FILE FILE STATUS IS '
                 LCP-FILE-STATUS-001
         CALL 'ILBOABN0'.
     END DECLARATIVES.
    *********************************************************************
    *********************************************************************
    *************       MAINLINE PROCEDURE     **************************
    *********************************************************************
    *********************************************************************
    *********************************************************************
    *
    *   THIS PROCEDURE READS GISMO ISAM FILE #90.
    *
    *********************************************************************

    0200-GET-RECORD SECTION.
         MOVE 'YES'  TO VALID-KEY-FLAG.
         MOVE PROV-PRODUCT TO WS-ITEM.
         MOVE 90 TO WS-INV.
         MOVE WS-KEY TO MAS-KEY
         READ INVENTORY-MASTER-FILE
                   INVALID KEY PERFORM 0300-NOT-FOUND THRU 0300-END.
    0200-END. EXIT.

    *********************************************************************
```

Figure 2.2 *(Continued)*

processing programs, convert BDAM files to VSAM/RRDS manually. The VSAM utility program, IDCAMS REPRO, will perform this conversion unless the file has a hardware dependency.

Convert your BDAM COBOL language to VSAM/RRDS COBOL language using the following steps:

1. The ASSIGN clause organization parameters.

    - sysnnn-class-device-organization-name

- class-device-organization name
- class-organization-name

should be *converted* to VS COBOL II format. Files that have a **D, W, U,** or **A** specified for the organization parameter in the assignment name (BDAM files) should be *converted* to VSAM/RRDS.

2. FILE STATUS clause should be added in the new VS COBOL II program because of VSAM.
3. ORGANIZATION IS RELATIVE clause should be there in the new VS COBOL II program.
4. ACCESS IS DYNAMIC or ACCESS IS RANDOM clause should be there in the new VS COBOL II program.
5. RELATIVE KEY clause should be there in the new VS COBOL II program.
6. The rest of the program logic in the Procedure Division should be manually converted.

2.5 Communications

COBOL's designers originally utilized the COMMUNICATION section of the Data Division as a computer terminal communications feature. The purpose of this section was to communicate direction with MVS. It was ultimately supplanted by CICS. This communications feature was rarely used and does not exist in VS COBOL II. In OS/VS COBOL it allowed the following statements:

- ACCEPT MESSAGE COUNT
- DISABLE, ENABLE
- RECEIVE
- SEND
- COMMUNICATION section

2.6 Conclusion

Seemingly unpopular, Report Writer, ISAM, BDAM, and Communications were dropped from support and now require that a serious effort be undertaken to replace their functionality. Although these features can all be converted manually, we found the automated conversion tools to be ideally suited to assisting in the conversion of these elements (except for the physical transition of the files themselves). In the next chapter, we will examine another upgrade that frequently accompanies older COBOL upgrades: CICS Release 2.X and up.

CHAPTER 3

Upgrading CICS Manually or by Using a Tool (CCCA)

VS COBOL II does not support CICS macro statements. If you need to convert CICS macro-level code to command-level code, then use the CICS Application Migration Guide (CAMG). If your operation is still in CICS Version 2, you may also want to consider upgrading to more recent versions (Version 4 or Version 5).

If the input COBOL source program includes CICS statements and uses the BLL mechanism for linking, you will need to convert these statements as well since they are no longer supported. The reason for using this compiler is to determine record lengths and the number of BLLs needed to address them.

3.1 Manually Converting CICS

VS COBOL II provides the CICS application programmer with additional programming functions. VS COBOL II also removes some CICS restrictions.

3.1.1 Elements to Consider When Converting CICS

The six CICS elements discussed in this section must be examined and/or changed in order to migrate to VS COBOL II or COBOL for MVS & VM.

Using the Static CALL Statement

With OS/VS COBOL, if multiple COBOL programs are separately compiled and then link-edited together, only the first program can contain CICS requests. With VS COBOL II, this restriction is removed. VS COBOL II fully supports static calls from VS COBOL II application programs running under CICS as well as calls to other VS COBOL II or assembler language programs that can contain CICS requests.

If your VS COBOL II program issues a static call, the calling program must pass the called VS COBOL II program the CICS EXEC interface block (DFHEIBLK) and the communication area (DFHCOMMAREA) as the first two parameters of the CALL statement. The CICS command language translator automatically inserts these parameters as the first two parameters on the corresponding PROCEDURE DIVISION USING statement in the called program.

Static calls between VS COBOL II programs and OS/VS COBOL programs running under CICS are not supported. (OS/VS COBOL subroutines should still be accessed by EXEC CICS LINK.)

Using the Dynamic CALL Statement

With VS COBOL II you can make dynamic calls to subprograms, and the dynamically called subprograms can contain CICS commands.

As with static calls, if your VS COBOL II program issues a dynamic call, the calling program must pass the called VS COBOL II program to the CICS EXEC interface block (DFHEIBLK) and the communication area (DFHCOMMAREA) as the first two parameters of the CALL statement. The CICS command language translator automatically inserts these parameters as the first two parameters on the corresponding PROCEDURE DIVISION USING statement in the called program.

Dynamic calls between VS COBOL II programs and OS/VS COBOL programs running under CICS are not supported. (OS/VS COBOL subroutines should still be accessed by EXEC CICS LINK.)

Using the LENGTH OF Special Register

With the LENGTH OF special register, you no longer need to pass explicit length arguments on many of the CICS commands where length is required. You can use the LENGTH OF special register in

COBOL statements as if it were an explicitly defined numeric data item. This lets you obtain information about the number of characters a data item occupies in the program.

Using Language Elements That Require GETMAIN Services

Certain statements cause OS/VS COBOL to dynamically request more storage during program execution using the OS GETMAIN macro. In a CICS environment, this imposes unpredictable virtual memory requirements. As a result, you cannot use STRING, UNSTRING, and INSPECT statements and the USE FOR DEBUGGING declarative in OS/VS COBOL CICS programs.

VS COBOL II uses CICS GETMAIN services for virtual memory management. This means that you can use STOP RUN, STRING, UNSTRING, and INSPECT statements and the USE FOR DEBUGGING declarative in VS COBOL II CICS programs.

SERVICE RELOAD Statement Changes

In OS/VS COBOL, in order for programs to be executed under CICS the SERVICE RELOAD statement is required to ensure addressability of items defined in the linkage section. In VS COBOL II, the SERVICE RELOAD statement is no longer required, and VS COBOL II treats it as a comment.

Base Addressability Considerations

Using OS/VS COBOL, the COBOL programmer must maintain addressability to storage areas not contained within the working storage section of the COBOL/CICS program. To satisfy program requests, an OS/VS COBOL program must keep track of storage area addresses allocated by CICS. This requires that the BLL cells within the application program be manipulated.

With VS COBOL II and the associated support within CICS, it is no longer necessary to maintain addressability. Therefore, when migrating from OS/VS COBOL to VS COBOL II, you must convert such programs.

NOTE:
If the COBOL/CICS program does not manipulate addressing BLL cells, conversion is **not necessary.**

3.1.2 CICS Conversion Summary

The following steps summarize the process for converting an OS/VS COBOL CICS program to a VS COBOL II CICS program:

1. Remove all SERVICE RELOAD statements. The VS COBOL II compiler treats these statements as comments. (Although desirable, removal is not absolutely necessary.)

2. Remove all operations dealing with addressing structures in the linkage section that are greater than 4K bytes in size. A typical statement is

   ```
   ADD +4096 D-PTR1 GIVING D-PTR2.
   ```

3. Remove all program code that assists in addressing COMMAREAs greater than 4K in size.

4. Remove redundant assignments and labels that OS/VS COBOL uses to ensure that CICS programs are correctly optimized. (This is good programming practice, but it is not essential.)

   Redundant assignments and labels include the following:
   - Artificial paragraph names that use BLL cells to address chained storage areas.
   - Artificial assignments from the object of an OCCURS . . . DEPENDING ON clause to itself.

5. Change every SET (P) option in the CICS commands to SET (ADDRESS OF L), where *L* is the linkage section structure that corresponds to the *P* BLL cell.

6. Specify REDEFINES clauses in the linkage section if multiple record formats are defined through the SET option.

7. Review programs that use Basic Mapping Support (BMS) data structures in their linkage section (i.e., check for maps that are not defined as STORAGE=AUTO). Move any such maps to the working storage section and remove any associated EXEC CICS GETMAIN commands.

3.1.3 DL/I Call Interface

After you have migrated to VS COBOL II, you might want to continue using CALL CBLTDLI. To do so, review your programs and make the following changes:

1. Remove BLL cells for addressing the User Interface Block (UIB) and Program Communication Blocks (PCBs).
2. In the linkage section, retain the DLIUIB declaration and at least one PCB declaration.
3. Change the PCB call to specify the UIB directly, as follows:
   ```
   CALL "CBLTDLI" USING PCB-CALL,
   PSB-NAME,
   ADDRESS OF DLIUI
   ```
4. Obtain the address of the required PCB from the address list in the UIB.

The following four examples give OS/VS COBOL and VS COBOL II examples of BLL cell manipulation.

Example 1: Receiving a Communications Area

In this example, a COBOL program defines a record area within the linkage section. This general technique is used in a number of COBOL/CICS programs that define structures outside of the working storage section.

During migration, do the following:

1. Remove the address list definition defining the BLL cells; under VS COBOL II, BLL cells are no longer explicitly defined in the linkage section.
2. In the SET option of the CICS command, use the ADDRESS OF special register when referring to the storage area instead of specifying the BLL cell name.

```
OS/VS COBOL


    LINKAGE SECTION.
       01 PARAMETER-LIST.
          05   PARM-FILLER              PIC S9(8) COMP.
          05   PARM-AREA1-POINTER       PIC S9(8) COMP.
          05   PARM-AREA2-POINTER       PIC S9(8) COMP.
       01  AREA1.
          05   AREA1-DATA               PIC X(100).
       01  AREA2.
```

continues

Example 1: *(Continued)*

```
           05  AREA2-DATA              PIC X(100).
                     .
                     .
                     .
       PROCEDURE DIVISION.

                     .
                     .
                     .
           EXEC CICS READ DATASET("INFILE")
               RIDFLD(INFILE-KEY)
               SET(PARM-AREA1-POINTER)
               LENGTH(RECORD-LEN)
           SERVICE RELOAD PARM-AREA1-POINTER.



VS COBOL II


   LINKAGE SECTION.
       01  AREA1.
           05  AREA1-DATA              PIC X(100).
       01  AREA2.
           05  AREA2-DATA              PIC X(100).

                     .
                     .
                     .
       PROCEDURE DIVISION.

                     .
                     .
                     .
           EXEC CICS READ DATASET("INFILE")
               RIDFLD(INFILE-KEY)
               SET(ADDRESS OF AREA1)
               LENGTH(RECORD-LEN).
```

Example 2: Processing Storage Areas Exceeding 4K

If a linkage section area is greater than 4096 bytes in length, you must add statements that provide addressability to the entire storage area.

The following example shows the coding for an OS/VS COBOL program, followed by the coding for a VS COBOL II program. During migration, do the following:

1. Remove the following statements used to maintain addressability:
   ```
   ADD +4096 TO RECORD-POINTER ....
   SERVICE RELOAD .....
   ```

2. Change the SET option of the CICS command from an intermediate BLL cell to the ADDRESS OF special register for the record.

```
OS/VS COBOL


       LINKAGE SECTION.
         01 PARMLIST.
               .
               .
               .
             05   RECORD-POINTERA            PIC S9(8) COMP.
             05   RECORD-POINTERB            PIC S9(8) COMP.
               .
               .
               .
         01 FILE-RECORD.
             05   REC-AREA1                  PIC X(2500).
             05   REC-AREA2                  PIC X(2500).
               .
               .
               .
       PROCEDURE DIVISION.
               .
               .
               .
             EXEC CICS READ DATASET("INFILE")
                 RIDFLD(INFILE-KEY)
```

continues

Example 2: (Continued)

```
                SET(RECORD-POINTERA)
                LENGTH(RECORD-LEN)
         END-EXEC
         SERVICE RELOAD RECORD-POINTERA
         ADD +4096 TO RECORD-POINTERA GIVING RECORD-POINTERB
         SERVICE RELOAD RECORD-POINTERB.



VS COBOL II
   LINKAGE SECTION.
      01 FILE-RECORD.
         05   REC-DATA1                    PIC X(2500).
         05   REC-DATA2                    PIC X(2500).

                    .
                    .
                    .
   PROCEDURE DIVISION.

                    .
                    .
                    .
         EXEC CICS READ DATASET("INFILE")
              RIDFLD(INFILE-KEY)
              SET(ADDRESS OF FILE-RECORD)
              LENGTH(RECORD-LEN)
         END-EXEC
```

Example 3: Accessing Chained Storage Areas

In an OS/VS COBOL CICS program, you can chain storage areas together by defining a storage area in the linkage section that contains a pointer to another storage area. To do this, you must copy the address of the next chained area from its location in one area to its associated BLL cell. In addition, you must code a paragraph name after any statement that changes the contents of the BLL cell used to address the chained areas.

During migration, do the following:

1. Change the code that moves the next address from within a storage area to the associated BLL cell. Perform the identical function in VS

COBOL II by using the ADDRESS OF special register associated with the current and next storage areas.
2. If you like, remove the dummy paragraph names that follow references that change the contents of BLL cells. (This is good programming practice, but it is not essential.)

```
OS/VS COBOL


      WORKING-STORAGE SECTION.
      01 WSDATA-HOLD PIC X(100).

             .
             .
             .

      LINKAGE SECTION.
      01 PARAMETER-LIST.

             .
             .
             .
           05   CHAINED-POINTER            PIC S9(8) COMP.

             .
             .
             .

      01 CHAINED-STORAGE.
           05   CHS-NEXT-AREA              PIC S9(8) COMP.
           05   CHS-DATA                   PIC X(100).

             .
             .
             .

      PROCEDURE DIVISION.

             .
             .
             .
           MOVE CHS-NEXT-AREA TO CHAINED-POINTER.
       ANY-PARAGRAPH-NAME.
           MOVE CHS-DATA TO WSDATA-HOLD.

             .
             .
             .
```

continues

Example 3: *(Continued)*

```
VS COBOL II

    WORKING-STORAGE SECTION.
    01 WSDATA-HOLD PIC X(100).
            .
            .
            .
    LINKAGE SECTION.
            .
            .
            .
    01 CHAINED-STORAGE.
        05   CHS-NEXT-AREA              USAGE IS POINTER.
        05   CHS-DATA                   PIC X(100).
            .
            .
            .
    PROCEDURE DIVISION.
            .
            .
            .
        SET ADDRESS OF CHAINED-STORAGE TO CHS-NEXT-AREA
        MOVE CHS-DATA TO WS-DATA-HOLD
```

Example 4: Using OCCURS DEPENDING ON

In OS/VS COBOL, if the object of an OCCURS DEPENDING ON clause is contained in the linkage section, you must ensure that the correct length of the group is used when the number of occurrences of the subject of the OCCURS clause changes. During migration, do the following:

1. In your VS COBOL II program, remove any code that resets the contents of the object of the OCCURS DEPENDING ON clause. (Such references are no longer necessary.)

```
OS/VS COBOL


    LINKAGE SECTION.
```

```
        01  PARMLIST.
            05   FILLER                         PIC S9(8).
            05   RECORD-POINTER                 PIC S9(8).

                   .
                   .
                   .
        01  VAR-RECORD.
            05   REC-OTHER-DATA                 PIC X(30).
            05   REC-AMT-CNT                    PIC 9(4).
            05   REC-AMT                        PIC 9(5)
                    OCCURS 1 TO 100 TIMES
                        DEPENDING ON REC-AMT-CNT.

                   .
                   .
                   .
        PROCEDURE DIVISION.

                   .
                   .
                   .
            EXEC CICS READ DATASET("INFILE")
                 RIDFLD(INFILE-KEY)
                 SET(RECORD-POINTER)
                    LENGTH(RECORD-LEN)
            END-EXEC.
            MOVE REC-AMT-CNT TO REC-AMT-CNT.
            MOVE REC-OTHER-DATA TO WS-DATA.
            MOVE VAR-RECORD TO WS-RECORD-HOLD.

                   .
                   .
                   .
```

VS COBOL II

```
        LINKAGE SECTION.
          01  VAR-RECORD.
              05   REC-OTHER-DATA               PIC X(30).
              05   REC-AMT-CNT                  PIC 9(4).
              05   REC-AMT                      PIC 9(5)
                      OCCURS 1 TO 100 TIMES
                          DEPENDING ON REC-AMT-CNT.
```

continues

Example 4: *(Continued)*

```
                .
                .
                .
        PROCEDURE DIVISION.

                .
                .
                .
        EXEC CICS READ DATASET("INFILE")
            RIDFLD(INFILE-KEY)
            SET(ADDRESS OF VAR-RECORD)
            LENGTH(RECORD-LEN)
        END-EXEC
        MOVE VAR-RECORD TO WS-RECORD-HOLD
```

3.1.4 Setting Compiler Options with CICS

CICS considerations for selected VS COBOL II recommended compiler options are as follows:

- RES
- RENT
- NODYNAM
- TRUNC(BIN)

3.1.5 Setting Run-time Options with CICS

Under CICS, you cannot use the PARM parameter to specify run-time options. Instead, you can use the VS COBOL II IGZEOPD or IGZEOPT modules:

- IGZEOPD—Global Default Run-time Module
- IGZEOPT—Application-Specific Run-time Module

3.2 Using CCCA to Convert CICS

Only the LINKAGE SECTION of the COBOL program is compiled, and if CICS option is chosen as Yes (Y) on CCCA's screen, then this will cause the

BLL to be deleted from the linkage section and reference to the BLLs to be flagged or changed, depending on the context of their occurrence.

Working Storage Section: CCCA, Release 2.0, generates the following code in the working storage section for use with the pointer facility:

```
77    LCP-WS-ADDR-COMP        PIC S9(8) COMP.
77    LCP-WS-ADDR-PNTR        REDEFINES
      LCP-WS-ADDR-COMP        USAGE     POINTER.
```

When you use CCCA, Release 2.0, and submit a batch conversion job with CICS programs, it is extremely important to choose the right option for CICS. When you choose the Batch Conversion (II) Panel, make sure that you do the following:

Choose "Y" for the CICS program with BLL cells.

Choose "O" for the CICS program with no BLL cells.

Choose "N" for the non-CICS program.

Choose "D" for DB/2 and the CICS program with BLL cells.

During the CCCA translation, the CCCA translator will try and resolve addresses within the BLL CELL definition. During this process, CCCA goes to each BLL CELL and attempts to match each BLL address to an '01' data item in the linkage section. If there is no one-to-one relationship, then the BLL errors will occur. During the CCCA translation, the CCCA translator removed all BLL CELL definitions in the linkage section. However, you will sometimes need to manually remove from PROCEDURE DIVISION any reference to these fields.

The programs are now being compiled with COBOL II versus COBOL. With the new release of the compiler, it appears that the new compiler is "flagging" coding techniques that did not get noticed with the old compiler. These types of "informational" messages are on a COBOL definition of a large area in working storage being "redefined" by a smaller area.

3.3 Converting CICS Statements

The following section discusses some lessons we have learned and issues we have encountered while converting CICS statements using the CCCA automated conversion utility.

We encountered the following errors with CCCA, Release 2.0.

Message IGYOS4007-U: Unexpected End-of-File

Problem:
Unexpected end-of-file was encountered on "SYSIN" from the VS COBOL II compiler.

Resolution:
Unexpected end-of-file was encountered because in the previous step the CCCA, Release 2.0, product did not produce any output. According to IBM, this problem occurs if you specify the wrong compiler for the "Compiler for CICS Conversions" Language Level Selection Panel (O.2) on the Options and Environment Setup Panel. *This should be set to the source compiler, not the target compiler.* Remember, when converting CICS programs with BLL cells, CCCA, Release 2.0, performs the process using the following sequence of operations:

1. Original Source
2. Extract Linkage Section
3. Compile with Old Compiler
4. Read/Analyze Linkage Map and Identify BLL Cells
5. Convert Original Source
6. Postconversion Compile Using Target Compiler

Ensure that the parameter setting on Panel 0.2 is correct and that the library names associated with the OLDLIB and OLDCOM parameters at the top of the ABJJ2 CLIST are associated with your old compiler.

SP Error Received in CICS Precompiler

Problem:
SP must be specified for application programs that contain special (SP) CICS commands or they will be rejected at translate time. These commands are ACQUIRE, COLLECT, DISABLE, DISCARD, ENABLE, EXTRACT, INQUIRE, PERFORM, RESYNC, and SET. These commands are generally used by system programmers.

Resolution:
You need to tailor the CICS translator so that "SP" is one of the default translation options.

806 Error Message When Converting CICS Program with BLL

Problem:
When you convert a CICS program with BLL structure, you will sometimes receive an 806 error (module not found).

> **Resolution:**
> According to IBM, this problem is caused by the fact that the wrong compiler has been specified on the STEPLIB override for the CMP step that is failing. Refer to the CCCA, Release 2.0's JCL listing as follows:
>
> ```
> //CMP.STEPLIB   DD   DSN=SYS1.COB2COMP,DISP=SHR
> ```
>
> You are trying to use the OS/VS COBOL compiler, yet the STEPLIB override appears to be pointing to a COBOL II library. Ensure that the parameter setting on Panel 0.2 is correct and that the library names associated with the OLDLIB and OLDCOM parameters at the top of the ABJJ2 CLIST are associated with your old compiler.
>
> **Question:**
> Can you do the conversion in the following steps?:
>   1. Convert the CICS portion of all of the programs.
>   2. Test the CICS portion.
>   3. Convert the COBOL portion.
>   4. Test the COBOL portion.
>
> **Answer:**
> No. According to IBM, CCCA can only convert CICS/COBOL in one pass.

3.4 Conclusion

Overall, CCCA performed well in upgrading CICS, and we had few unexpected issues. If you have a large conversion project, it is a good idea to capture your issues centrally (using an internal Web site, for example) so everyone involved has access to issues and resolutions.

CHAPTER 4

Upgrading VS COBOL II to COBOL/370 Manually

On March 25, 1997, IBM announced it was withdrawing support for VS COBOL II. For VS COBOL II, Version 1.3.X, marketing and service support was withdrawn on June 30, 1996. For VS COBOL II, Version 1.4.0, marketing support was withdrawn on June 30, 1997, and service support will be withdrawn March 31, 2001.

However, in terms of year 2000 compliance, IBM states that if your application has no date-related logic, then you can continue to run VS COBOL II programs indefinitely. Unfortunately, there are few commercial applications that don't have date-related logic. So continuing to run unchanged VS COBOL II programs is probably not an option for most IT managers.

4.1 Introduction

VS COBOL II is not year 2000 compliant. There is no four-digit-year date support. However, VS COBOL II shops can migrate to the LE run-time library and take advantage of its windowing logic, which enables two-digit-year dates to be correctly interpreted based on a one-hundred-year window. According to IBM, users can do a run-time migration now (Language Environment [LE] for MVS and VM) and then do a compiler migration later. This strategy guarantees IBM customers run-time support well into the twenty-first century, but no compile-time support.

The best year 2000 strategy is to migrate to a year 2000 compliant and supported compiler and a supported run-time library. However, if certain conditions exist that prohibit this (for example, lack of time), users should consider the LE option, keeping in mind that it will not work for applications that use data that does not fit into a one hundred-year window. In that case, an upgrade to COBOL for MVS (or COBOL/370) and VM (with expanded date fields) will be a better option.

Even though the conversion and compile is very clean to COBOL for MVS, the execution behavior may be different. Be careful and be prepared to test when you choose this migration path. From an upgrade standpoint, the only language difference between VS COBOL II, Release 4, and COBOL/370, Release 1, is the addition of two new reserved words: **FUNCTION** and **PROCEDURE-POINTER**. However, the COBOL UPGRADE to COBOL FOR MVS (COBOL/370) is much more complicated than just a compile.

You need to know about the following to make the migration successful:

- Language element behavior differences between VS COBOL II and COBOL for MVS (COBOL/370)
- Compile option differences
- Language Environment
- Run-time options
- Link-editing existing load modules

When you add a COBOL/370 program to an existing application, you are either recompiling an existing program with COBOL/370 or including a newly written COBOL/370 program. When you add COBOL/370 programs to your existing applications, you have the ability to do the following:

- Use a four-digit year in the date function for new applications and use IBM's strategic compiler
- Interpret two-digit-year data as four-digit years for existing applications
- Use Language Environment condition handling
- Upgrade your existing programs incrementally, as your shop's needs dictate

Once you begin adding COBOL/370 programs to your existing applications, you need to understand the implications of link-editing existing applications with Language Environment. First, you must use the **SCEELKED** link-edit library. When SCEELKED is used when you link-edit, *it impacts the remaining programs in the applications.* How it affects the existing application depends on whether the application is comprised of the following:

- Programs compiled RES
- Programs compiled NORES

When adding COBOL/370 programs to existing applications, you also need to be aware of AMODE and RMODE considerations. And, remember, COBOL for MVS & VM programs can run only under Language Environment, Release 5 or later.

Additionally, the same copy of Working Storage is used for each call for COBOL for MVS & VM programs that are compiled with the RENT option and dynamically called from VS COBOL II, COBOL/370, or COBOL for MVS & VM and then fetched and called by C or PL/I (or loaded and called by assembler) and run under Language Environment, Release 5 or later. In addition, the program is entered in its last-used state, unless there is an intervening CANCEL.

You must include the Language Environment Release 5 (or later) copy of ILBOSRV in the load module, in either of the following cases:

- If the existing load module contains and uses ILBOSTP0
- If the existing load module contains OS/VS COBOL NORES programs

4.1.1 Link-editing Existing Load Modules

If you create a COBOL for MVS & VM Release 2 program that makes static calls to a COBOL/370 Release 1 program or a VS COBOL II program, when you link-edit the load module with Language Environment Release 5, note the following:

- The link-edit job must contain a REPLACE statement to replace IGZEBST (the VS COBOL II bootstrap), if the VS COBOL II program was link-edited with the VS COBOL II Release 4 run time without APAR PN74000 applied.
- The link-edit job must contain a REPLACE statement to replace IGZEBST for VS COBOL II programs compiled with the RES com-

piler option that were link-edited with Language Environment/370, Release 2 or Release 3, without APAR PN74011 applied.

We encountered several problems that were related to a compile option that had been changed, which caused the program to act differently in the new environment (the **TRUNCATION option**). Another problem has been application assembler subroutines that needed to be changed to run "above the line."

Technically speaking, you may not need to recompile or relink all of your programs to the COBOL for MVS & VM compiler. However, unless you are confident that your code will have little need for future enhancements and are planning an organized test sequence (unit, integration, regression), recompiling and relinking is probably a good idea, and one step toward a clean room. And while you can run VS COBOL II and COBOL for MVS & VM programs in the same environment, there may be run-time conflicts. Refer to the IBM migration manual for more on run-time conflicts (which depend on your environment).

Other reasons (if you need more) to upgrade to COBOL for MVS & VM include the following:

1. To use COBOL programs as DB/2 stored procedures
2. To use COBOL for CICS, Version 4, Autoinstall Exit
3. To get COBOL programs, COBOL data, or I/O buffers above the 16 MB line
4. To use object-oriented COBOL syntax
5. To mix COBOL with C/C++ programs

4.2 COBOL Language Elements Converted to COBOL for MVS & VM

The following list of COBOL elements is similar to the one presented for converting from OS/VS to COBOL II in Section 1.6.1. However, the elements support is different in COBOL for MVS & VM.

4.2.1 Behaviors and Language Elements

In this section, we present the language elements that require changing and the code execution behavioral changes we have noted in our factory.

Behaviors

Will your code "behave" the same after you upgrade it? By this we mean to warn you that the processing flow that you had come to expect in your preupgraded code may not be identical to the processing flow in your postupgraded code. Why? Changes in commands and compiler options affect execution. You may have conditionals that tested true in COBOL II that no longer test true in COBOL for MVS & VM. This is why regression tests are so important in upgrade projects. The following paragraphs discuss the issues we detected in compiling and regression test failures.

EXIT PROGRAM. Under the ANSI 85 standard, statement control cannot flow beyond the last line of a called subprogram. The compiler generates an implicit EXIT program at the end of each program. The ANSI 68 and ANSI 74 standard behavior can be preserved under the ANSI 85 standard by adding, at the end of the program, a section with a call to the ABEND macro ILBOABN0. For example, CALL "ILBOABN0".

GOBACK statement. Under the ANSI 85 standard, control cannot flow beyond the last line of a called subprogram. The compiler generates an implicit EXIT PROGRAM at the end of each program. Under the ANSI 68 and ANSI 74 standard control can flow beyond the last line of a called program. When this happens the program ABENDs. The ANSI 68 and ANSI 74 standard behavior can be preserved under the ANSI 85 standard by adding, at the end of the program, a section with a call to an ABEND macro. For example, CALL "ILBOABN0".

PERFORM . . . VARYING . . . AFTER statement. Under the ANSI 85 standard the rules for augmenting variables have changed. If there are dependencies between variables of the statement, then the statement may behave differently. All PERFORM . . . VARYING . . . AFTER statements should be examined. You should check to see if there are any dependencies between the variables of the statement that will result in different behavior. If there are, you should modify the statement.

In OS/VS COBOL, when there is a PERFORM statement with the VARYING/AFTER phrase, two actions take place when an inner condition tests as TRUE:

1. The identifier/index associated with the inner condition is set to its current FROM value.

2. The identifier/index associated with the outer condition is augmented by its current BY value.

In COBOL/370 and COBOL for MVS & VM when there is a PERFORM statement with the VARYING/AFTER phrase, the following takes place when an inner condition tests as TRUE:

1. The identifier/index associated with the outer condition is augmented by its current BY value.
2. The identifier/index associated with the inner condition is set to its current FROM value.

The following example illustrates the differences in execution:

```
PERFORM ABC VARYING X FROM 1 BY 1 UNTIL X > 3
                AFTER Y FROM X BY 1 UNTIL Y > 3
```

In OS/VS COBOL, ABC is executed eight times with the following values:

```
X:  1  1  1  2  2  2  3  3
Y:  1  2  3  1  2  3  2  3
```

In COBOL/370 and COBOL for MVS & VM, ABC is executed six times with the following values:

```
X:  1  1  1  2  2  3
Y:  1  2  3  2  3  3
```

Performance Issues

You may find occasional degradation in performance when converting from VS COBOL II to COBOL for MVS. Large, CPU-intensive programs do not always perform as well, and some may suddenly exceed their previous batch windows (in our case, experiencing a 7.5 percent CPU increase). Be prepared to evaluate your new CPU usage.

STOP RUN Statement. Under the ANSI 85 standard, control cannot flow beyond the last line of a called subprogram. The compiler generates an implicit EXIT PROGRAM at the end of each program. Under the ANSI 68 and ANSI 74 standards control can flow beyond the last line of a called program. When this happens the program ABENDs. The ANSI 68 and ANSI 74 standard behavior can be preserved under the ANSI 85 standard by adding, at the end of the program, a section with a call to an ABEND macro. For example, CALL "ILBOABN0".

UNSTRING Statement. The statement requires examination if the PROGRAM COLLATING SEQUENCE established in the OBJECT COMPUTER paragraph identifies an alphabet that was defined with the ALSO clause. Under these circumstances, the statement will behave differently under the ANSI 85 standard.

Identification Division

The language upgrade changes to the Identification Division section, which briefly describes the program, are predominantly cosmetic, but they will cause compiler errors if they are not handled properly.

AUTHOR Paragraph. The AUTHOR paragraph in the Identification Division should be removed by commenting out the AUTHOR line.

DATE-COMPILED/ DATE-WRITTEN Paragraphs. These paragraphs in the Identification Division are obsolete and should be commented out.

INSTALLATION. The INSTALLATION paragraph in the Identification Division is obsolete and should be commented out.

MEMORY SIZE. The MEMORY SIZE clause of the OBJECT-COMPUTER paragraph is obsolete and should be removed.

SECURITY Paragraph. The SECURITY paragraph in the Identification Division is obsolete and should be commented out.

Environment Division

Most of the changes to the Environment Division, where COBOL defines outside elements, affect the obsolescence of items.

BLOCK CONTAINS Clause. You should remove the BLOCK CONTAINS clause from your VSAM file descriptions. The concept of blocking has no meaning for VSAM files.

DATA RECORDS. The DATA RECORDS clause is obsolete. It should be removed from the FD entry.

LABEL RECORDS. LABEL RECORDS is obsolete. The clause should be removed.

LABEL RECORDS . . . TOTALING/TOTALED AREA Option. LABEL RECORDS is obsolete and should be removed.

PROCESSING MODE clause. The PROCESSING MODE clause is obsolete and should be removed.

RECORD CONTAINS. The clause should be removed from the program, except for RECORD CONTAINS 0, which may be left in place.

RECORDING MODE clause. The COBOL for MVS compiler ignores this clause if it is specified for a VSAM file. If the clause is in a file description entry for a VSAM file or a file that is to be converted to VSAM, it may be removed.

Data Division

Upgrade changes to the Data Division, where data structures are defined, mostly involve the obsolescence of items.

ALPHABET clause. The keyword ALPHABET should be added in front of the alphabet name within the ALPHABET clause of the SPECIAL-NAMES paragraph.

CALL identifier statement. If the identifier has a PICTURE string consisting of characters only, a change is necessary.

The ANSI 74 standard classes the identifier fields as alphabetic, while the ANSI 85 standard classes them as alphanumeric-edited. You will have to make a change to the program because alphanumeric-edited identifiers are not permitted in the CALL statement.

IDMS. If your programs contain COPY IDMS statements, you should create a dummy copy member called IDMS. The copybook should just have a comment in it.

MULTIPLE FILE TAPE clause. The MULTIPLE FILE TAPE clause is obsolete and should be removed from the I-O-CONTROL paragraph.

VALUE OF clause. The VALUE OF clause is obsolete and should be removed from the FD entry.

Procedure Division

The Procedure Division, where COBOL places its executable commands, generally constitutes the majority of the code and, as such, also constitutes the majority of the upgrade changes. In this section, we'll present the commands that have been altered and what needs to change.

ALPHABETIC class. The ALPHABETIC clause should be changed to ALPHABETIC-UPPER.

CALL . . . ON OVERFLOW statement. Under the ANSI 85 standard the ON OVERFLOW phrase executes under more conditions than it does under the ANSI 68 and ANSI 74 standards. When an overflow condition occurs in a COBOL/370 program running under CICS, the ON OVERFLOW phrase will be invoked, if it is specified.

CALL . . . ON EXCEPTION statement. The ON EXCEPTION phrase in a VS COBOL II program is not invoked if the program is running under CICS. When an exception condition occurs in a COBOL for MVS program running under CICS, the ON EXCEPTION phrase will be invoked, if it is specified.

CANCEL statement. The statement needs modifications if there is an identifier in the statement with a PICTURE string that consists of characters only. The ANSI 74 standard classes these fields as alphabetic, while the ANSI 85 standard classes them as alphanumeric-edited. You will have to make a change to the program since alphanumeric-edited identifiers are not permitted in the CANCEL statement.

COPY . . . REPLACING statement. If there are lowercase alphabetic characters in operands of the REPLACING phrase that are not in nonnumeric literals, the statement may need modification. Under the ANSI 85 standard, lowercase characters are treated as their uppercase equivalent. You should check to see if this change will result in different text being copied into your program. If the operands of the REPLACING phrase contain a colon (:) character that is not in a nonnumeric literal, the statement is flagged. Under the ANSI 68 and ANSI 74 standards, the colon (:) is a non-COBOL character. Under the ANSI 85 standard, the colon character is treated as a separator. You should check to see if this change will result in different text being copied into your program. If the operands of the REPLACING phrase contain an ANSI 85 standard non-COBOL character that is not in a nonnumeric literal, the statement is flagged. Under the ANSI 68 and ANSI 74 standards, non-COBOL characters are permitted in the REPLACING option. Under the ANSI 85 standard, non-COBOL characters in the REPLACING phrase are diagnosed. You should remove all non-COBOL characters from the REPLACING phrase and from the copybook.

DIVIDE ... ON SIZE ERROR statement. DIVIDE ... ON SIZE ERROR statements with multiple receiving fields need modification because the ON SIZE ERROR phrase will not be executed for intermediate results under the ANSI 85 standard.

INSPECT statement. The statement needs changing if the PROGRAM COLLATING SEQUENCE established in the OBJECT COMPUTER paragraph identifies an alphabet that was defined with the ALSO clause to override the standard EBCDIC collating sequence. Under these circumstances, the statement will behave differently under the ANSI 85 standard. When coded, it affects the INSPECT, STRING, and UNSTRING statements.

The INSPECT statement also affects nonnumeric keys in a MERGE or SORT when the COLLATING SEQUENCE is not specified in the SORT or MERGE statement. The PROGRAM COLLATING SEQUENCE affects nonnumeric comparisons. In OS/VS COBOL it affects both explicitly coded conditions and implicitly performed conditions (those comparisons that the compiler deems necessary to perform) in INSPECT, STRING, and UNSTRING statements.

In VS COBOL II the PROGRAM COLLATING SEQUENCE only affects explicitly coded conditions in INSPECT statements.

MULTIPLY ... ON SIZE ERROR statement. MULTIPLY ... ON SIZE ERROR statements with multiple receiving fields require modification because the ON SIZE ERROR phrase will not be executed for intermediate results under the ANSI 85 standard. For OS/VS COBOL and VS COBOL II with CMPR2, the SIZE ERROR option for the DIVIDE and MULTIPLY statements applies to both intermediate and final results.

If your OS/VS COBOL relies upon SIZE ERROR detection for intermediate results, it must be changed or be compiled with the CMPR2 compiler option (see the subsection "Behaviors" earlier in this section for more on the CMPR2 compiler option). The statements

```
01      NUMERICS.
10      NUMBERIC-1 PICTURE  S9(16).
10         NUMERIC-2    PICTURE  S9(16).
10         NUMERIC-3    PICTURE  S9(16).
10         NUMERIC-4    PICTURE  S9(16).
10         TEMP              PICTURE  S9(30).

MULTIPLY NUMERIC-1  BY NUMERIC-2 GIVING NUMERIC-3    NUMERIC-4.
```

should behave like this:

```
MULTIPLY NUMERIC-1   BY NUMERIC-2  GIVING   TEMP
MOVE TEMPORARY   TO NUMERIC-3
MOVE TEMPORARY   TO NUMERIC-4
```

TEMP is the intermediate result. An intermediate result will have thirty digits at most.

In the example just given, if NUMERIC-1, NUMERIC-2, NUMERIC-3, and NUMERIC-4 are all defined as PIC S9(16), NUMERIC-1 will be multiplied by NUMERIC-2, yielding a 32-digit result, which is moved to the 30-digit intermediate result, TEMP. TEMP is then moved to NUMERIC-3 and NUMERIC-4.

A size error may occur if the result exceeds the largest possible value of the result field, during a division by zero, or during an exponential expression.

OCCURS DEPENDING ON clause (variable length receiver). COBOL statements that result in data transfer to a variable length receiver that contains its own OCCURS DEPENDING ON (ODO) object behave differently under the ANSI 85 standard. Under the ANSI 68 and ANSI 74 standards all ODO objects in sending and receiving fields must be set before the statement is executed. The actual lengths of the sender and receiver are calculated just before the execution of the data movement statement. Under the ANSI 85 standard, in some circumstances the maximum length of the variable length group is used when it is a receiver, whereas the ANSI 68 and ANSI 74 standards always use the actual length. You may preserve this behavior for the following statements:

- MOVE . . . TO identifier
- READ . . . INTO identifier
- RETURN . . . INTO identifier
- UNSTRING . . . INTO identifier
- DELIMITER IN identifier

If the identifier is a variable length data item that contains its own ODO object, then reference modification is added to it. For example,

```
MOVE...TO identifier
```

is changed to

```
MOVE...TO identifier (1:LENGTH OF identifier)
```

for the following statements:

```
RELEASE record-name FROM identifier
REWRITE record-name FROM identifier
WRITE record-name FROM identifier
```

If the identifier is a variable-length data item that contains its own ODO object, the FROM phrase should be removed from the statement and a MOVE statement with reference modification should be added before the statement. For example,

```
WRITE record-name FROM identifier
```

is changed to this:

```
MOVE identifier TO record-name (1:LENGTH OF record-name)
WRITE record-name
```

Note that in MOVE CORRESPONDING statements reference modification is not allowed when the CORRESPONDING phrase is specified.

PICTURE clause. If a scaled integer is compared with an alphanumeric or numeric edited field, you will have to convert this statement. If the scaled integer is compared with a nonnumeric field, you will have to convert the statement.

The trailing zeros (0) are truncated when using OS/VS COBOL with LANGLVL(1) if either the sending field in a MOVE statement or a field in a comparison is a scaled integer (i.e., if the rightmost PICTURE symbols are the letter *P*) and the receiving field (or the field to be compared) is alphanumeric or numeric-edited.

STRING statement. The statement is flagged if it has a receiving field with a PICTURE string that consists of letters only. The ANSI 74 standard classes these fields as alphabetic, while the ANSI 85 standard classes them as alphanumeric-edited.

You will have to make a change to the program because alphanumeric-edited receiving fields in the STRING statement are not permitted.

4.3 Migrating from COBOL II to COBOL for MVS

In this section, we will relate some lessons we learned while migrating COBOL II to COBOL for MVS. It cannot be stressed enough that this is not just a compile-only upgrade. There are genuine code changes that need to occur.

Reserved Word Issue

Problem:
This problem is related to a RESERVED WORD in the INSPECT or IF CONDITION statements. "CONVERTING" and "ALPHABETIC-UPPER" are reserved words for a feature supported by VS COBOL II and COBOL/370 compilers, and may occur if you performed a mass update and added a suffix to all user-defined words that are reserved words in the target language. Since "-74" was our default suffix for changing reserved word names, CONVERTING and ALPHABETIC-UPPER are changed to CONVERTING-74 and ALPHABETIC-UPPER-74.

For example, if you have the following condition

```
INSPECT FIELD-A CONVERTING SPACE TO ZERO.
```

the reserved word CONVERTING will be appended by a suffix "-74," hence, the converted code would look like this:

```
INSPECT FIELD-A CONVERTING-74 SPACE TO ZERO.
```

Also, once the program is compiled, you will get a compiler error message, as follows:

```
2106-S "CONVERTING-74" was found in the "INSPECT" statement.  It was not
allowed in this context.  The statement was discarded.
```

The following is an actual piece of code that serves as an example:

```
082400 2400-WRITE-GIS-ORDER.
082500*————————
*OLD**      INSPECT   WS-ORDERED-QUANTITY CONVERTING SPACE TO ZERO.
082600      INSPECT   WS-ORDERED-QUANTITY CONVERTING-74 SPACE TO ZERO.

00807    082300    ABJ6268 00  DATA NAME IS AN ANSI 85
00807    082300                RESERVED WORD.
                               SUFFIX HAS BEEN ADDED.
================================================================================
==========
COMPILER
082400 2400-WRITE-GIS-ORDER.
082500*————————
082600      INSPECT   WS-ORDERED-QUANTITY CONVERTING-74 SPACE TO ZERO.

2106-S "CONVERTING-74" was found in the "INSPECT" statement.  It was
not allowed in this context.  The statement was discarded.
```

Compiler Options (ZWB/NOZWB)

Problem:
With ZWB, the compiler removes the sign from a signed external decimal (DISPLAY) field when comparing this field to an alphanumeric elementary field during execution. If the external decimal item is a scaled item (contains the symbol *P* in its PICTURE character string), its use in comparisons is not affected by ZWB. Such items always have their sign removed before the comparison is made to the alphanumeric field.

Lesson learned:
ZWB affects how the program runs; the same COBOL source program can give different results, depending on the option setting. ZWB conforms to the COBOL/85 standard.

Resolution:
Use NOZWB if you want to test input numeric fields for SPACES.

4.4 Conclusion

There are important changes that need to occur when migrating from COBOL II to COBOL for MVS & VM. Integrating the Language Environment is just one of the environmental challenges you will face. In the next chapter, we will examine the same conversion topics, but this time using an automated tool to reduce much of the manual effort.

PART TWO

Upgrading COBOL Using a Tool

CHAPTER 5

Tool-Based COBOL Upgrades

The eliminated features of the old COBOL do not cause any real problems for the development and maintenance of new COBOL applications. However, they do pose considerable problems when you are converting old COBOL programs to new COBOL, depending on the level of the source code, the version of COBOL to which you are converting, and the needs of your specific environments. Although upgrade changes are not necessarily difficult to complete manually, they are very tedious and not the most exciting work for in-house COBOL programmers. For this reason, many organizations choose to use a conversion tool to automate the COBOL upgrade process. In addition, tools provide more consistent accuracy and greater speed. If you choose a tool, you should use it in all phases of the COBOL process to achieve consistent, higher-quality results in less time. A software tool can be the key to successful COBOL upgrades on a large scale.

If your organization has a sizable upgrade project, manual conversion may not be the best method for accomplishing your task. What is sizable? Consider the following:

- The cost of an upgrade tool (say, $30,000).
- Training time.
- Size of your programs (the average program we saw had fourteen hundred lines of code, excluding comments, but including lines brought in from copybooks).

- How far back is your compiler? If you're still on OS/VS COBOL and want to migrate to COBOL for MVS & VM, this is a more difficult job than migrating from VS COBOL II.
- Experience of your staff.
- Project schedule.

As a rule of thumb, if you have less than five hundred programs to upgrade, you are probably going to have equal success but higher cost if you use a tool than if you upgrade manually (see the introduction of this book for a comparison). If you upgrade between five hundred and one thousand programs, you will start breaking even. If you are faced with the prospect of upgrading over one thousand programs, a tool may be the best option.

5.1 Selecting a Tool

It is important to go through a careful tool selection process. Tools change and improve frequently. The following is a high-level summary of what you may want to look for in a tool:

- Availability
- Equipment configuration
- Technical environment
- Technical design features
- Flexibility
- Expandability
- Documentation
- Reporting capabilities
- User friendliness (learning curve)
- Vendor support
- Vendor reputation

We recommend that you follow these steps to select a tool:

- Identify tool vendors, for example:
    IBM's CCCA
    Prince Software's MHTRAN
    Computer Associates' CA-Migrate/COBOL

- Request thirty-day trials.
- Select various programs (we selected thirty in all) for trial, including the following:

    Large programs

    Programs with CICS

    Programs with CICS BLL

    Programs with ISAM (to see if they are flagged)

    Programs with Report Writer (to see if they are flagged)

    Programs with copybook issues (see Chapter 1)

    Programs with known reserved word issues (see Chapter 1)
- Run the tests with each tool.
- Compare the results of the test and the known, documented features (see Table 5.1).

Table 5.1 lists important findings for upgrade tools. We are listing only the results for IBM's utility, CCCA (5785-ABJ), Version 2.0. You will want to gather your own data. (See Appendix D for a comparison between CCCA, Version 2.0, and their newer release, CCCA, Version 2.1.) We have collected information on the other tools, but because new releases are issued frequently you should investigate all tools on your own.

Table 5.1 Selection Criteria

VENDOR PRODUCT SELECTION CRITERIA	IBM CCCA, RELEASE 2.0
Additional ISPF setup panels for usability?	Yes
CALL XREF—Print call/program report?	Yes
CALL XREF—Print program/call report?	Yes
Converts both source programs and copy modules?	Yes
Converts EXEC CICS commands?	Yes
Converts OS/VS COBOL to COBOL for MVS & VM?	Yes
Converts OS/VS COBOL to VS COBOL II ?	Yes
Converts VS COBOL II to COBOL for MVS & VM?	Yes
COPY XREF—Print copy/program report?	Yes
COPY XREF—Print program/copy report?	Yes
CURRENT-DATE handling?	Yes

continues

Table 5.1 (Continued)

VENDOR PRODUCT SELECTION CRITERIA	IBM CCCA, RELEASE 2.0
Eliminates conflicts between user-defined names and words reserved for VS COBOL II?	Yes
FILE XREF—Print file/program report?	Yes
Flexibility through an open converter design?	Yes
Is the Conversion Aid a menu-driven system?	Yes
Optional automatic compile of converted source code?	Yes
PROGRAM XREF—Print program/file report?	Yes
Removes and/or converts the Base Locator for Linkage (BLL) section mechanism and references?	Yes
Supports PANVALET/ENDEVOR/LIBRARIAN/SQL COPY?	Yes
Supports CA-PANVALET, CA-LIBRARIAN, CA-IDMS, IMS, DB/2, and more?	Yes
The option to specify the COBOL compiler of choice, for use by the tool?	Yes
Comparing packed decimal data against alphabetic data.	Manual translation is required.
WHEN-COMPILED.	Automatic conversion.
SECTION NAME.	No error message if name is too long.
CLOSE STATEMENT FOR FILE NAME.	No error message if there is no close statement.
The RECORD CONTAINS XX clause is removed from the program, except for RECORD CONTAINS 0, which is left in place.	Yes
The RECORDING MODE clause. The target language compilers ignore this clause if it is specified for a VSAM file. If the clause is in a file description entry for a VSAM file or a file that is to be converted to VSAM, it is removed.	Supposed to be removed automatically. Sometimes it does not remove.

REPORT WRITER (SECTION AND RD) These statements are not supported by the target languages:
   GENERATE
   INITIATE
   REPORT
   TERMINATE
   USE BEFORE REPORTING
	If you specify Y for the Report Writer Statement Flagging option on the Optional Processing Panel, they will be flagged.

VENDOR PRODUCT SELECTION CRITERIA	IBM CCCA, RELEASE 2.0
REMARKS paragraph is converted to comments by inserting an asterisk (*) in column 7 of the paragraph header and in all succeeding lines of the paragraph.	Converted for OS/VS COBOL; not for VS COBOL II.
Can we use COBOL Report Writer precompiler to perform two functions? 1. To permanently convert Report Writer statements to a valid COBOL statement that can be compiled in IBM COBOL for MVS & VM or IBM COBOL for VSE/ESA. 2. To precompile applications containing Report Writer statements so the code will be acceptable to the IBM COBOL for MVS & VM or IBM COBOL for VSE/ESA compiler.	Yes
First installed.	April 1986
Are ISPF setup panels services and education provided for this product?	Yes
Is this product mentioned in the 1991 DATAPRO report?	Yes
Hardware.	IBM System/370 architecture
Operating system.	MVS, MVS/SP, MVS/XA, MVS/ESA, and VM
Source languages.	COBOL, assembler, RPG
Source listings.	Not available

To summarize your evaluations, you should review the significant strengths and weaknesses identified for each tool package. The review should include documentation of any special concerns that will impact the development, implementation, and maintenance if the package is selected. The features we found important to our factory approach for upgrade projects included the following:

CCCA, Release 2.0, was able to convert VS COBOL II to COBOL for MVS & VM—a fundamental requirement (not limited to just OS/VS COBOL to VS COBOL II). If any conversion warning exists, CCCA, Release 2.0, does not force the job to ABEND in the postconversion compile step. This feature helped because it enabled us to do mass conversion and mass compilation.

CCCA, Release 2.0, was good at executing post conversion compile jobs. This is useful if you have a large upgrade inventory and want to mass compile immediately after upgrading.

In Chapter 6, we will tell you how to use IBM's conversion tool (CCCA, Release 2.0). Although there are different tools available, we have used CCCA to illustrate the conversion process and the issues that are related to it since they remain the same irrespective of the tool. CCCA, Release 2.0 (see Table 5.2), was not really a tool that IBM expected to be used regularly by customers. It was IBM's offering to customers to announce a new COBOL conversion tool and to obtain reactions from customers. The response was excellent from those who knew that in the near future their organization would be converting all of its old COBOL to newer COBOL releases.

5.2 The Conversion Process with CCCA

If you choose to do it yourself with a tool, then the process of converting old COBOL to new COBOL using CCCA, Release 2.0, may be divided into the following four phases (see Figure 5.1):

1. Preparing the inventory for the source programs.
2. Converting COBOL programs under MVS.
3. Compiling COBOL programs using the compile procedure of CCCA, Release 2.0.
4. Generating conversion and compile status reports and modifying control files.

In addition to following the tool conversion path, you need to make a human resources decision. Do you organize this effort by organization or application, or do you imitate a factory approach and have a few people convert the code? We recommend that you imitate the factory approach and dedicate resources to perform the upgrade but let the application teams focus on creating the test environments. It is also easier to enforce standards and centralize lessons learned (so there is no need to reinvent the wheel). Fewer people require training on the tool, and they can focus on the upgrades.

In either case, the process for upgrading your code is described in the remainder of Section 5.2.

5.2.1 Preparing the Inventory for the Source Programs

The purpose of the inventory phase is to identify the COBOL upgrade requirements. Once that has been done, an environment should be

Table 5.2 Specifications of CCCA, Release 2.0

CATEGORY	DESCRIPTION
Product Title	The COBOL and CICS/VS Command-Level Conversion Aid (CCCA, Release 2.0)
Product Number	5785-ABJ
Release/Version	Release 2.0
Function	By using CCCA, Release 2.0, it is possible for your organization to significantly reduce your COBOL upgrade effort.
Requirement	The CCCA, Release 2.0, requires that you have the COBOL for MVS & VM (or COBOL/370) and the OS/VS COBOL and/or VS COBOL II compilers available when converting CICS programs.
Benefit of using CCCA, Release 2.0	Most syntax differences between the following COBOL dialects can be converted: 1. OS/VS COBOL programs and COBOL/370 programs. 2. VS COBOL II programs and COBOL/370 programs. 3. OS/VS COBOL programs and COBOL for MVS & VM programs. 4. VS COBOL II programs and COBOL for MVS & VM programs. It's also possible to eliminate most conflicts between OS/VS COBOL and VS COBOL II user-defined names and COBOL for MVS & VM and COBOL/370 reserved words. The flagging of the old language elements that cannot be automatically converted is also possible. Diagnostic listing of source statement-by-statement can be produced. Cross-reference information such as where used reports for copybooks and files can be produced. Conversion of EXEC CICS commands is possible. Removal and/or conversion of the Base Locator Linkage (BLL) section mechanism and references.
Input to CCCA, Release 2.0	OS/VS COBOL source code or COBOL/74 Standard VS COBOL II (either VS COBOL II, Release 1 and 2, or VS or COBOL II, Release 3 and 4 [CMPR2]), source code
Output from CCCA, Release 2.0	COBOL 85 Standard VS COBOL II, Release 3 or 4 (NOCMPR2), source code. IBM COBOL for MVS & VM source code.

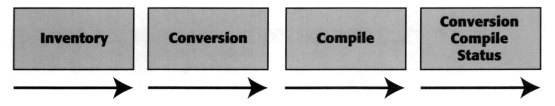

Figure 5.1 Conversion path for COBOL upgrades using a tool.

created for converting and compiling COBOL programs using the tool. Using the TSO/ISPF Search-for Utility (3.14), scan your entire company's source library, and identify the different types of sources included for the tool environment. This identification process facilitates the options and environment setup of an accurate set of programs for conversion and compile.

We organized different libraries to store our source based upon the different characteristics of the source modules. In this way, we could run CCCA against an entire PDS. We also noticed that we achieved optimum performance when running CCCA against no more than one hundred programs at a time. The first step in preparing a COBOL1 cluster for CCCA conversion is to separate the programs into the following categories:

- Batch program
- Online CICS program
- Program with ADABAS database
- Program with SQL database
- Program without a database
- Program with an ISAM file
- Program with Report Writer
- Program with or without BLL

This categorization should be done for each program so you select the correct CCCA options for conversion. This grouping will help you apply the same conversion solutions to a group of programs of the same type and will ensure a smoother conversion process. The following list gives the searching criteria for program type identification:

CICS program.

    Find string "CICS" in the program.

Table 5.3 Example of an Inventory

CATEGORY	DESCRIPTION
OS/VS COBOL or VS/COBOL II?	Due to requirements of the CCCA, Release 2.0, tool, we need to segregate the various versions of COBOL. OS/VS COBOL input source will require a different tool panel setting than COBOL II. One method used to make this determination is to scan for words such as END-IF or EVALUATE, which are unique to VS COBOL II or COBOL/ 370. Also check the content of LOAD LIBRARY for the IBM Product Number.
DB/2?	We also need to know if the input source is DB/2. This can be ascertained by scanning for words such as SQL, CURSOR, or SQLCODE. Again, the presence of DB/2 requires segregation into a separate file, and the appropriate panel selection needs to be chosen.
REPORT WRITER?	Report Writer, which appears in a number of OS/VS COBOL programs, is not supported for COBOL upgrade. We identify these programs by scanning for RD—or GENERATE. Any COBOL programs that use Report Writer are recorded in the Excel spreadsheet and reported to the company. You have the option of rewriting the report section or using another tool to do the upgrade.
CICS?	CICS programs using BLL (Base Locator Linkage) also need to be identified and placed into a separate file from other CICS programs. The appropriate panel options need to either be turned on or off.
100 PROGRAMS	Another constraint we need to deal with is cluster size. Any cluster of more than one hundred programs needs to be divided into separate files even though they may all be the same version and type, such as OS/VS COBOL batch and no CICS. If we run a file with more than one hundred programs, we do not get maximum throughput and can also experience tool issues.
COPYBOOK?	Copybook libraries also need to be controlled. The CCCA, Release 2.0, tool will read in any called-for copybooks and, if needed, update and write them out to a new file. Any copybooks not used are not written out.
	Once we have run all the various types of COBOL code and associated copybooks through the CCCA, Release 2.0, tool we are left with upgraded source and copybooks. One file contains the upgraded source and the other contains the upgraded copybooks. These files are generally copied to an output tape, or at times a file transfer is used if there is a small number of files.

Example: EXEC CICS

Note: "CICS" may be found in comments that will not guarantee a CICS program.

ADABAS program.

    Find string "ADABAS" in the program (not in the comments).

    Example: EXEC ADABAS

DB/2 program.

    Find string "SQL" in the program (not in the comments).

    Example: EXEC SQL

Program with **BLL**.

    Find string "BLL" in the Linkage Section of the program.

COBOL program with **Report Writer**.

    Find string "RD" in the File Section of the program.

    The CCCA tool does not convert COBOL programs with the Report Writer feature.

COBOL program with **Indexed Sequential File** (ISAM).

Find string "-I-" in the File Section of the program.

The CCCA tool does not convert COBOL programs with ISAM files. These files must be converted to a VSAM format, and programs should be modified to access converted files before attempting COBOL upgrades. For example, during the source preparation for one of our projects, the source data set was separated into the following smaller data sets based on the programs' type:

```
YJ.CCCA.CL#17.IN.OSVS.NAN.L1
YJ.CCCA.CL#17.IN.OSVS.NAN.L2
YJ.CCCA.CL#17.IN.OSVS.NSN.L1
YJ.CCCA.CL#17.IN.OSVS.NSN.L2
YJ.CCCA.CL#17.IN.OSVS.NNN.L1
YJ.CCCA.CL#17.IN.OSVS.NNN.L2
YJ.CCCA.CL#17.IN.OSVS.YAN.L1
YJ.CCCA.CL#17.IN.OSVS.YAN.L2
YJ.CCCA.CL#17.IN.OSVS.YAY.L1
YJ.CCCA.CL#17.IN.OSVS.YAY.L2
YJ.CCCA.CL#17.IN.OSVS.YAN.L1
YJ.CCCA.CL#17.IN.OSVS.YAY.L1
YJ.CCCA.CL#17.IN.OSVS.YSN.L1
YJ.CCCA.CL#17.IN.OSVS.YSY.L1
YJ.CCCA.CL#17.IN.OSVS.YNN.L1
YJ.CCCA.CL#17.IN.OSVS.YNY.L1
```

Each character of the data set name qualifier (in bold) represents the following program types:

- first character Y (CICS) or N (batch)
- second character A (ADABAS), S (DB/2), or N (nondatabase)
- third character N (no BLL) or Y (with BLL)

The last qualifier (L1 or L2) represents COBOL1 language level:

L1 or level 1 is ANSI COBOL 1968

L2 or level 2 is ANSI COBOL 1974

The following section offers some guidelines for language level identification.

Language-Level Identification

It is very important to correctly identify the COBOL1 language level before attempting upgrades from COBOL1 to COBOL2 using the CCCA tool. Some of the COBOL/68 (COBOL1 level 1) features were removed or modified with COBOL/74 (COBOL1 level 2). Selecting incorrect language-level parameters could cause errors during the conversion process.

The presence of one or more of the following keywords confirms that the language level of the COBOL1 program is level 1:

The **COPY statement** with the following format:

```
01  dataname  COPY  copybookname.
```

COBOL/74 requires a period before the COPY statement.

REMARKS

The REMARKS paragraph is used in COBOL/68 to put overall program documentation comments in the Identification Division of the program. COBOL/74 removed this feature. The asterisk is used instead to mark a statement as a comment.

EXHIBIT

This COBOL/68 statement was replaced by INSPECT for COBOL/74.

NOMINAL KEY

This clause was specified in the SELECT statement and was replaced by RECORD KEY for COBOL/74.

NOTE statement

The NOTE statement was provided for explanatory program documentation and was replaced by the asterisk in COBOL/74.

ACTUAL KEY

This statement was replaced by the RELATIVE clause in COBOL/74.

PROCESSING MODE IS SEQUENTIAL

This clause was used as the file control entry and was removed in COBOL/74.

INVALID KEY

This clause, used with READ/WRITE statements, was removed in COBOL/74.

5.2.2 Converting and Compiling COBOL Programs

The process of converting old COBOL to new COBOL using the CCCA, Release 2.0, tool and then compiling the converted programs is shown in Figure 5.2.

5.2.3 Generating Conversion and Compile Status Reports and Modifying the CONTROL File

The purpose of this section is to provide information on the Program/File Report, modifying the CONTROL File, and sample reports. The CONTROL File is a central file used by CCCA that collects all of the conversion options and program information. This file contains the conversion status, the files used, the copy members used, and the called subroutines that have been used.

Program/File Report

The report lists the programs converted after the last resetting of the CONTROL file. For each of these programs, it gives the following conversion information:

- The date and time that it was last converted
- The options that were specified for the conversion

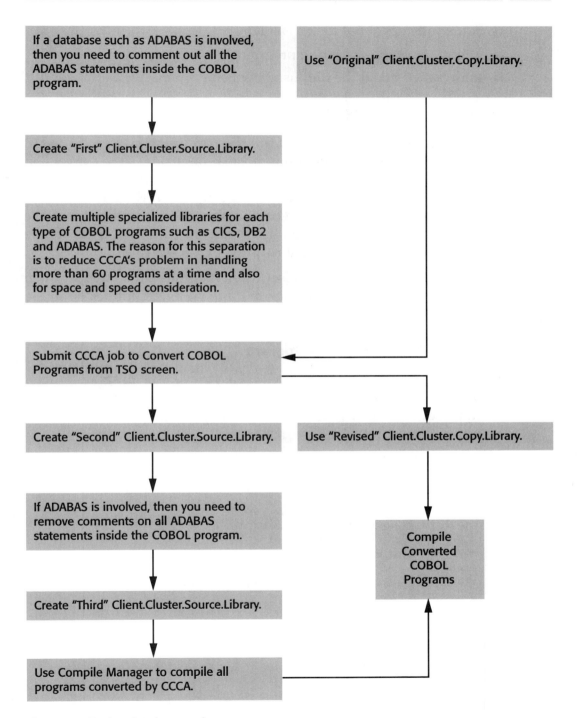

Figure 5.2 Tool-assisted conversion process.

- Some statistics about the conversion
- The status of the converted program
- Information about the files used by the program

Modifying the CONTROL File

All of the conversion options and program information are recorded in the CONTROL file. This program information includes the conversion status, the files used, the copy members used, and the called subroutines that have been referenced. Resetting the CONTROL file erases all the information that has been recorded about the programs you have converted. The only information that is not erased from the file are the default settings for the conversion options.

The CONTROL file should be reset when it becomes too large or when you have converted an application and are no longer interested in the program conversion information.

Easytrieve Plus Reporting Program

The authors developed the following Easytrieve Plus program to read the Program/File Report data set and to produce the following User-friendly Conversion and Compile Status Report:

```
//CO290EZR JOB (CO000P),'YOUNG CHAE',REGION=8M,
//         MSGCLASS=Z,NOTIFY=CO290,CLASS=A
//JOBLIB   DD DSN=SYS4.EZT62.CAILIB,DISP=SHR
//REPORT1  EXEC PGM=EZTPA00
//SYSOUT   DD  SYSOUT=*
//SORTWK01 DD SPACE=(CYL,(10,5)),AVGREC=K
//SORTWK02 DD SPACE=(CYL,(10,5)),AVGREC=K
//SORTWK03 DD SPACE=(CYL,(10,5)),AVGREC=K
//SORTWK04 DD SPACE=(CYL,(10,5)),AVGREC=K
//SORTWK05 DD SPACE=(CYL,(10,5)),AVGREC=K
//INFILE1  DD DSN=CO.CCCA.CO290.PROGREP.LIST,DISP=SHR
//SYSPRINT DD  SYSOUT=*
//SYSIN    DD *
FILE INFILE1 FB (133 9044)
   PFIRST   2   1   A
   PNAME    2   8   A
   PSTAT    65  9   A
   PCSTAT   65  9   A
   PCSTWRD  65  7   A
   PCSTCDE  76  2   A
   PMSTAT   62  17  A
```

```
            PDATE    63 10  A
            PDSLSH1  67  1  A
            PDSLSH2  70  1  A
            PCDATE   63 10  A
            PMDATE   63 10  A
            PCSLSH1  67  1  A
            PCSLSH2  70  1  A
            WFIRST   W   1  A
            WNAME    W   8  A
            WSTAT    W   9  A
            WCSTAT   W   9  A
            WCSTWRD  W   7  A
            WCSTCDE  W   2  A
            WMSTAT   W  17  A
            WDATE    W  10  A
            WCDATE   W  10  A
            WMDATE   W  10  A
            LNENBR   W   2  N VALUE 00
            GOODCTR  W   5  N VALUE 00000
            MNULCTR  W   5  N VALUE 00000
            WARNCTR  W   5  N VALUE 00000
            TOTLCTR  W   5  N VALUE 00000
            MNUALSW  W   1  A VALUE 'N'
            GOODCM   W   5  N VALUE 00000
            BADCOM   W   5  N VALUE 00000
   JOB INPUT NULL FINISH TERMINATE NAME CO2901
   READIP.
   GET INFILE1
      IF EOF INFILE1
         STOP
      END-IF
*
      IF (PFIRST NE ' ') AND (PFIRST NE '-')
         LNENBR = 1
         PRINT MMO-RPT
         WNAME = PNAME
         WSTAT    = '         '
         WCSTAT   = '         '
         WCSTWRD  = '       '
         WCSTCDE  = '  '
         WMSTAT   = '                 '
         WDATE    = '          '
         WCDATE   = '          '
         WMDATE   = '          '
         TOTLCTR = TOTLCTR + 1
         IF (PSTAT = 'NO CHANGE') OR (PSTAT = 'COMPLETE')
            GOODCTR = GOODCTR + 1
         ELSE
            IF PSTAT = 'WARNING '
               WARNCTR = WARNCTR + 1
```

```
                END-IF
            END-IF
            WSTAT = PSTAT
            LNENBR  = LNENBR + 1
        END-IF
   *
        IF (LNENBR = 2) AND (PDSLSH1 = '/') AND (PDSLSH2 = '/')
            WDATE = PDATE
            LNENBR  = LNENBR + 1
        END-IF
   *
        IF (LNENBR = 3) AND (PMSTAT = 'MANUAL COMPLETION')
            MNUALSW = 'Y'
            MNULCTR = MNULCTR + 1
            LNENBR  = LNENBR + 1
        END-IF
   *
        IF (LNENBR = 3) AND (PCSTWRD = 'COMPILE')
            WCSTCDE =  PCSTCDE
            LNENBR  = LNENBR + 1
            IF PCSTCDE < '08'
                GOODCM  = GOODCM + 1
            ELSE
                BADCOM  = BADCOM + 1
            END-IF
        END-IF
   *
        IF (LNENBR = 4) AND (PDSLSH1 = '/') AND (PDSLSH2 = '/')
            IF MNUALSW = 'Y'
                WMDATE = PMDATE
                MNUALSW = 'N'
                LNENBR  = LNENBR + 1
            ELSE
                WCDATE = PCDATE
                LNENBR  = LNENBR + 1
            END-IF
        END-IF
   *
        IF (LNENBR = 5) AND (PMSTAT = 'MANUAL COMPLETION')
            MNUALSW = 'Y'
            LNENBR  = LNENBR + 1
        END-IF
   *
        IF (LNENBR = 6) AND (PDSLSH1 = '/') AND (PDSLSH2 = '/')
            IF MNUALSW = 'Y'
                WMDATE = PMDATE
                MNUALSW = 'N'
                LNENBR  = LNENBR + 1
            END-IF
        END-IF
   *
```

```
      GOTO READIP.
*
TERMINATE. PROC
   PRINT MMO-RPT
   GOODCTR = TOTLCTR - (WARNCTR + MNULCTR)
   DISPLAY NEWPAGE                                        COL 30
   DISPLAY 'COBOL & CICS/VS COMMAND LEVEL CONVERSION'     COL 30
   DISPLAY 'SUMMARY REPORT'   ' '  SYSDATE                COL 30
   DISPLAY 'OS/VS COBOL AND VS COBOL II TO COBOL/370'     COL 30
   DISPLAY SKIP 5 '                                             '
   DISPLAY SKIP 2 'NUMBER OF TOTAL PROGRAMS           = ' TOTLCTR
   DISPLAY SKIP 2 'NUMBER OF PROGRAMS CONVERTED O.K. = ' GOODCTR
   DISPLAY SKIP 2 'NUMBER OF PROGRAMS W/WARNING      = ' WARNCTR
   DISPLAY SKIP 2 'NUMBER OF PROGRAMS MANUAL CONVRS  = ' MNULCTR
   DISPLAY SKIP 3 '                                             '
   DISPLAY SKIP 2 'NUMBER OF PROGRAMS COMPILED  O.K. = ' GOODCM
   DISPLAY SKIP 2 'NUMBER OF PROGRAMS COMPILED-ERROR = ' BADCOM
END-PROC
*
REPORT MMO-RPT LINESIZE   80
   SEQUENCE WNAME
   TITLE 01 'COBOL & CICS/VS COMMAND LEVEL CONVERSION DETAIL REPORT'
   HEADING WNAME ('PROGRAM' 'NAME')
   HEADING WSTAT ('CONVERSION' 'STATUS')
   HEADING WCSTCDE ('COMPILE' 'STATUS')
   HEADING WDATE ('CONVERSION' 'DATE   ')
   HEADING WCDATE ('COMPILE' 'DATE   ')
   HEADING WMDATE ('MANUAL ' 'COMPLETION')
   LINE 01 WNAME WSTAT WCSTCDE WDATE WCDATE WMDATE
*
END
//
```

User-friendly Conversion and Compile Status Report Sample

Metrics capturing was very important to us. It was how we measured progress and profitability. For a more detailed metrics report, see Appendix B. The following is a sample status report we developed to summarize our mass compiles after upgrading.

```
SUMMARY REPORT    7/29/97
OS/VS COBOL TO      VS COBOL II
-
-
-NUMBER OF TOTAL PROGRAMS           = 00281
-NUMBER OF PROGRAMS CONVERTED O.K.  = 00267
-NUMBER OF PROGRAMS W/WARNING       = 00001
-NUMBER OF PROGRAMS MANUAL CONVRS   = 00013
-
-NUMBER OF PROGRAMS COMPILED  O.K.  = 00253
```

```
-NUMBER OF PROGRAMS COMPILED-ERROR = 00015
1 7/29/97    COBOL & CICS/VS COMMAND LEVEL CONVERSION DETAIL REPORT PAGE  1
-
```

PROGRAM NAME	CONVERSION STATUS	COMPILE STATUS	CONVERSION DATE	COMPILE DATE	MANUAL COMPLETION
PRGJUL	COMPLETE	00	1997/07/25	1997/07/25	/ /
PRGNAME	COMPLETE	00	1997/07/25	1997/07/25	/ /
PRG5547	COMPLETE	00	1997/07/26	1997/07/26	/ /
PRGYDATE	COMPLETE	00	1997/07/25	1997/07/25	/ /
PRGCTL	COMPLETE	00	1997/07/25	1997/07/25	/ /
PRGDATE	COMPLETE	00	1997/07/25	1997/07/25	/ /
PRG0TBLO	COMPLETE	00	1997/07/25	1997/07/25	/ /
PRG0IRSO	COMPLETE	00	1997/07/25	1997/07/25	/ /
PRG0KWDO	COMPLETE	00	1997/07/25	1997/07/25	/ /
PR1001CA	COMPLETE	00	1997/07/25	1997/07/25	/ /
PR4550FP	COMPLETE	00	1997/07/25	1997/07/25	/ /
PR6750PB	COMPLETE	00	1997/07/25	1997/07/25	/ /
PR7110LJ	COMPLETE	00	1997/07/25	1997/07/25	/ /
PRG118CD	COMPLETE	04	1997/07/25	1997/07/25	/ /
PRG118CE	COMPLETE	04	1997/07/25	1997/07/25	/ /
PRG118CP	COMPLETE	04	1997/07/25	1997/07/25	/ /
PRG701CM	COMPLETE	00	1997/07/25	1997/07/25	/ /
PRG701CP	COMPLETE	00	1997/07/25	1997/07/25	/ /
PRG701DA	COMPLETE	00	1997/07/25	1997/07/25	/ /
PRG701DC	COMPLETE	00	1997/07/25	1997/07/25	/ /
PRG701LJ	COMPLETE	00	1997/07/25	1997/07/25	/ /
PRG701LP	COMPLETE	00	1997/07/25	1997/07/25	/ /
PRG701NP	COMPLETE	00	1997/07/25	1997/07/25	/ /
PRG701OP	COMPLETE	00	1997/07/25	1997/07/25	/ /
PRG701PL	COMPLETE	00	1997/07/25	1997/07/25	/ /
PRG701SB	COMPLETE	00	1997/07/25	1997/07/25	/ /
PRB0TCAB	COMPLETE	00	1997/07/25	1997/07/25	/ /

5.2.4 Postconversion Compile Jobs

One of the difficult tasks you will face in upgrading your COBOL will be to find the appropriate compile procedure for the different types of COBOL programs you have. Hence, it is quite important that you know the characteristics of the COBOL programs you need to convert and that you follow the naming conventions for the input as well as the output data sets. This will help you identify which compile procedure has to be used from the name of the output data set itself, which greatly reduces the duplication of effort. Moreover, with a utility like a compile manager—which does a mass compilation—you can convert and do postcompilation of the COBOL programs using a factory approach to deliver converted code that is consistently error free in as little time as possible.

One way to identify which compile procs are correct is to compile your programs in a separate environment and compare load modules. Your baseline test environment should feature these newly compiled programs rather than original load modules (otherwise, you may never know whether you have the right compilers and program versions).

Refer to Appendix C for sample compile procedures that we used specifically in postcompilation. These may not be exactly what your company needs, but they should provide you with information on how to handle the various COBOL programs using different compile procedures.

5.3 Running CCCA for Upgrading OS/VS COBOL to VS COBOL II

Rather than discuss the affected commands by division, we will present them in alphabetical order. When you manually upgrade programs, it's best to see upgrade elements in the order in which you will see them in the program. When using a tool (here, CCCA) you will need them in alphabetical order so you can find them more rapidly in your run outputs (giving you a better reference tool).

5.3.1 CCCA Recommendations

Here are some recommendations on using CCCA effectively:

- It is better to convert a program as COBOL/68 (LANGLVL1) than COBOL/74 (LANGLVL2). It gives you better results with fewer compiler errors.
- It is better to fix common errors, which the tool doesn't handle, in the input library rather than in the output library.
- Perform the conversion only once (if possible). After the conversion try to work only with output libraries, correct errors, and then recompile.
- If there are too many compiler errors, try to convert the program again.
- Resolve common problems before conversion.
- The CCCA tool uses DISP=OLD on output libraries. Therefore, do not edit, view, or browse output libraries while jobs are running.
- Do not run a whole cluster at once. First, process batch programs, then run CICS.

Before Conversion

Always use a blocking factor of 16,000 or less for COBOL copy library. CCCA uses the COBOL1 compiler to pre-recompile CICS programs before conversion. This is done to maintain addressability to storage and to keep track of the storage area addresses allocated by CICS. The COBOL1 compiler will not permit usage of a block size greater than 16K for a copy library.

CCCA inserts its own paragraphs/sections at the end of the upgraded program. If the program ends with a "COPY" statement, then all additional code inserted by the tool will be placed at the end of this copybook instead of at the end of the program. As a result, you will have an incorrect copybook. To resolve this problem, you should insert a dummy paragraph after the "COPY" statement. For example,

```
COPY   ABORTRTN.
       CCCA-DUMMY.                         <===   add this line at
column 8.
```

The tool does not handle SELECT statements that have copybooks with the SELECT statements. For example,

```
       SELECT INPUT-DATE-FILE      COPY    INDTCPY.
```

Copybook INDTCPY itself contains the following:

```
       SELECT INPUT-DATE-FILE    ASSIGN TO   INDTFLE.
```

To avoid compile errors (which will require a manual fix anyway), modify the source code in the input library instead of the output library:

```
***SELECT INPUT-DATE-FILE      COPY    INDTCPY.   <=== comment this
line
   COPY    INDTCPY.                <========  insert this line
```

The tool does not handle remarks such as MAINT-LOG, MAINTENANCE-LOG, DOC-LOG, and the like. It considers them to be reserved words that in return will cause compiler errors. To correct this, the input library should be edited to comment out these statements.

CCCA searches for literal delimiters and erroneously adds double quotation marks to a value in the "VALUE" clause whenever double quotation marks are used in comments at the beginning of a program. For example, VALUE "N" will become VALUE ""N"". To avoid this situation, change any double quotation marks to single quotation marks in program comments. Refer to the subsection "Behaviors" of the "Convert COBOL from OS/VS to VS COBOL II Manually" section in Chapter 3 to learn about compiler and run-time behavioral difference.

After Conversion

Examine the output to verify that the CNVx step was completed with either a 00, 01, 08, or 10 return code. If the CNVx step is not present then the program was only compiled and not converted. In most cases, choosing the wrong conversion option is the reason.

To resolve: Specify COBOL/74 for CCCA conversion options if COBOL/68 is used and run the conversion again.

Edit the output library and remove all CCCA-DUMMY lines. The CCCA tool comments out any copybooks following the REMARKS statement and before the ENVIRONMENT DIVISION.

To resolve: Examine the output library and remove comments from the commented "COPY" statements.

Recompile all programs outside of the CCCA by using your own JCL and fix all compiler errors. See Figure 5.3.

5.4 COBOL Language Elements Converted to VS COBOL II

CCCA, Release 2.0, analyzes valid OS/VS COBOL and DOS/VS COBOL and produces VS COBOL II source statements. In addition, CCCA indicates those old statements that either are not supported by VS COBOL II or are supported in a different manner. The input source program should be free of compilations and execution errors before you attempt to convert it. The following is an alphabetical list of COBOL language elements converted to VS COBOL II.

ACCEPT MESSAGE COUNT statement Communications feature. CCCA, Release 2.0, will *flag* this statement for the following input language levels: OS/VS COBOL LANGLVL(1) and OS/VS COBOL LANGLVL(2). This is a Communications statement. The Communications module is not supported by VS COBOL II, and there is nothing with which it can be replaced. CCCA, Release 2.0, will *flag* it.

```
CCCA OPTIONS
Lines per report page . . . . . .,===>,60,       01 to 99
Resequence source lines . . . .,===>,N,          Y/N
Sequence number increment . . .,===>,0010,       0001 to 9999
Reserved word suffix. . . . . .,===>,74,         Default value 74
Generate new program. . . . . .,===>,Y,          Y/N
Generate new copy members . . .,===>,Y,          Y/N
Replace like-named copy members,===>,Y,          Y/N
Print old source lines. . . . .,===>,Y,          Y/N
Print copy members. . . . . . .,===>,Y,          Y/N
Print diagnostics of level >= .,===>,00,         00 to 99
Report Heading. . . . . . . . .,===>,NISSAN CLUSTER 13       ,
Generate tokenization listing .,===>,N,          Y/N
    1. Check procedure names . . . . . .              ===>,Y,   Y/N
    2. Flag Report Writer statements . . . . . . . .  ===>,Y,   Y/N
    3. Remove obsolete elements. . . . . . . . . . .  ===>,Y,   Y/N
    4. Negate implicit EXIT PROGRAM. . . . . . . . .  ===>,N,   Y/N
    5. Generate END PROGRAM header . . . . . . . . .  ===>,N,   Y/N
    6. Compile after converting. . . . . . . . . . .  ===>,Y,   Y/N
    7. Flag manual changes in new source programs. .  ===>,N,   Y/N
    8. Add DATE FORMAT clause to date fields . . . .  ===>,N,   Y/N
    9. Remove VALUE clauses in File/Linkage sections  ===>,N,   Y/N
   10. Flag IF FILE-STATUS (NOT) = "00". . . . . . .  ===>,N,   Y/N
   11. Flag BLL cell arithmetic. . . . . . . . . . .  ===>,N,   Y/N
   12. BLL cell conversion method. . . . . . . . . .  ===>,A,   A/B
   13. Search source for literal delimiter . . . . .  ===>,Y,   Y/N
   14. Literal delimiter (QUOTE or APOST). . . . . .  ===>,A,   Q/A
   15. . . . . . . . . . . . . . . . . . . . . . . .  ===>,N,   Y/N
```

Figure 5.3 Listing of CCCA options.

ACTUAL KEY clause. CCCA, Release 2.0, will *convert* and *flag* this clause for the following input language levels: DOS/VS COBOL, OS/VS COBOL LANGLVL(1), and OS/VS COBOL LANGLVL(2).

The ACTUAL KEY clause should be for a BDAM file. ACTUAL KEY is replaced (*converted*) by RELATIVE KEY. Programs using BDAM files should be converted to programs using RRDS VSAM files. This can be done by using the VSAM utility program IDCAMS. The ACTUAL KEY is *flagged* if the new organization for the file is not RELATIVE. For additional information on this subject, you should refer to the ISAM section of Chapter 2 (Section 2.2, "ISAM Conversion Options and Issues").

ALPHABET clause. CCCA, Release 2.0, will *convert* this clause for the following input language levels: DOS/VS COBOL, OS/VS COBOL

LANGLVL(1), and OS/VS COBOL LANGLVL(2). CCCA, Release 2.0, will *convert* it as follows: The keyword ALPHABET is added in front of the alphabet name within the ALPHABET clause of the SPECIAL-NAMES paragraph.

ALPHABETIC class. CCCA Release 2.0 will *convert* this class for the following language levels: DOS/VS COBOL, OS/VS COBOL LANGLVL(1), and OS/VS COBOL LANGLVL(2).

CCCA Release 2.0 will *convert* ALPHABETIC to ALPHABETIC-UPPER.

APPLY CORE-INDEX clause. CCCA, Release 2.0, will *remove* this clause for the following input language levels: DOS/VS COBOL, OS/VS COBOL LANGLVL(1), and OS/VS COBOL LANGLVL(2).

CCCA, Release 2.0, will *remove* the clause from the I-O-CONTROL paragraph because this is an ISAM file-handling clause. For additional information on this subject, you should refer to the ISAM Section in Chapter 2 (Section 2.2).

APPLY CYL-INDEX clause. CCCA, Release 2.0, will *remove* this clause for the following input language level: DOS/VS COBOL.

CCCA, Release 2.0, will *remove* the clause from the I-O-CONTROL paragraph because this is an ISAM file-handling clause. For additional information on this subject, you should refer to the ISAM section in Chapter 2 (Section 2.2).

APPLY CYL-OVERFLOW clause. CCCA, Release 2.0, will *remove* this clause for the following input language level: DOS/VS COBOL. CCCA, Release 2.0, will *remove* the clause from the I-O-CONTROL paragraph because this is an ISAM file-handling clause. For additional information on this subject, you should refer to the ISAM section of Chapter 2 (Section 2.2).

APPLY EXTENDED-SEARCH clause. CCCA, Release 2.0, will *remove* this clause for the following language level: DOS/VS COBOL. CCCA, Release 2.0, will *remove* the clause from the I-O-CONTROL paragraph because this is an ISAM file-handling clause. For additional information on this subject, you should refer to the ISAM section of Chapter 2 (Section 2.2).

APPLY MASTER-INDEX clause. CCCA, Release 2.0, will *remove* this clause for the following input language level: DOS/VS COBOL. CCCA,

Release 2.0, will *remove* the clause from the I-O-CONTROL paragraph because this is an ISAM file-handling clause. For additional information on this subject, you should refer to the ISAM section of Chapter 2 (Section 2.2).

APPLY RECORD-OVERFLOW clause. CCCA, Release 2.0, will *remove* this clause for the following input language levels: OS/VS COBOL LANGLVL(1) and OS/VS COBOL LANGLVL(2).

CCCA, Release 2.0, will *remove* the APPLY RECORD-OVERFLOW clause from the I-O-CONTROL paragraph because this is an ISAM file-handling clause. For additional information on this subject, you should refer to the ISAM section of Chapter 2 (Section 2.2).

APPLY REORG-CRITERIA clause. CCCA, Release 2.0, will *remove* this clause for the following input language levels: OS/VS COBOL LANGLVL(1) and OS/VS COBOL LANGLVL(2).

CCCA, Release 2.0, will *remove* the APPLY RECORD-CRITERIA clause from the I-O-CONTROL paragraph because this is an ISAM file-handling clause. For additional information on this subject, you should refer to the ISAM section of Chapter 2 (Section 2.2).

APPLY WRITE-VERIFY clause. CCCA, Release 2.0, will *remove* this clause for the following input language level: DOS/VS COBOL. CCCA, Release 2.0, will *remove* the clause from the I-O-CONTROL paragraph because this is an ISAM file-handling clause. For additional information on this subject, you should refer to the ISAM section of Chapter 2 (Section 2.2).

ASSIGN clause organization parameter. CCCA, Release 2.0, will *convert* and *flag* this parameter for the following input language levels: DOS/VS COBOL, OS/VS COBOL LANGLVL(1), and OS/VS COBOL LANGLVL(2). Assignment names of the following formats are *converted* to VS COBOL II format:

- SYSnnn-class-device-organization-name
- class-device-organization name
- class-organization-name

Files that have a *D, W, U,* or *A* specified for the organization parameter in the assignment name (BDAM files) should be *converted* to RRDS

VSAM. For these files an ORGANIZATION IS RELATIVE clause is added to the File Control paragraph.

Files that have an *I* specified for the organization parameter in the assignment name (ISAM files) should be *converted* to VSAM/KSDS. For these files an ORGANIZATION IS INDEXED clause is added to the File Control paragraph. In DOS/VS COBOL, if the name is not coded for SYSnnn-devtype-device-organization-filename then SYSnnn is added as the external name. Programs using BDAM files should be converted to programs using RRDS VSAM files. This can be done by using the VSAM utility program IDCAMS. For additional information on this subject, you should refer to the ISAM section of Chapter 2 (Section 2.2).

ASSIGN integer system-name. CCCA, Release 2.0, will *remove* this integer for the following input language levels: DOS/VS COBOL, OS/VS COBOL LANGLVL(1), and OS/VS COBOL LANGLVL(2). CCCA, Release 2.0, will *remove* the integer from the clause.

ASSIGN . . . OR. CCCA, Release 2.0, will *remove* this statement for the following input language levels: DOS/VS COBOL, OS/VS COBOL LANGLVL(1), and OS/VS COBOL LANGLVL(2). CCCA, Release 2.0, will *remove* the OR from the clause.

AUTHOR paragraph. CCCA, Release 2.0, will *convert* this paragraph for the following input language levels: DOS/VS COBOL, OS/VS COBOL LANGLVL(1), and OS/VS COBOL LANGLVL(2). The AUTHOR paragraph in the Identification Division is *converted* by commenting out if the Obsolete Element Removal option on the Optional Processing Panel is specified as *Y* (yes).

Basic Direct Access Method (BDAM) files. CCCA, Release 2.0, will *convert* and *flag* these files for the following input language levels: DOS/VS COBOL, OS/VS COBOL LANGLVL(1), and OS/VS COBOL LANGLVL(2).

The VS COBOL II does not support the processing of BDAM files. Programs using BDAM files should be converted to programs using RRDS VSAM files. This can be done by using the VSAM utility program IDCAMS. CCCA, Release 2.0, converts the file definitions, but you must add the key algorithms manually. For additional information on this subject, you should refer to the ISAM section of Chapter 2 (Section 2.2).

BLANK WHEN ZERO clause. CCCA, Release 2.0, will *remove* this clause for the following input language levels: DOS/VS COBOL, OS/VS COBOL LANGLVL(1), and OS/VS COBOL LANGLVL(2). CCCA, Release 2.0, will *remove* the BLANK WHEN ZERO clause if the data description entry has a BLANK WHEN ZERO clause and a PICTURE string with a * (zero suppression) symbol in it.

BLOCK CONTAINS clause. CCCA, Release 2.0, will *remove* this clause for the following input language levels: DOS/VS COBOL, OS/VS COBOL LANGLVL(1), and OS/VS COBOL LANGLVL(2). CCCA, Release 2.0, will *remove* the clause from VSAM file descriptions if you specify Y for the Obsolete Element Removal option on the Optional Processing Panel. The concept of blocking has no meaning for VSAM files.

CALL identifier statement. CCCA, Release 2.0, will *flag* this statement for the following input language levels: OS/VS COBOL LANGLVL(1) and OS/VS COBOL LANGLVL(2).

CCCA, Release 2.0, will *flag* the statement if the identifier has a PICTURE string consisting of characters only. The ANSI 74 standard classes these fields as alphabetic, while the ANSI 85 standard classes them as alphanumeric-edited. You will have to make a change to the program because alphanumeric-edited identifiers are not permitted in the CALL statement.

CALL . . . ON OVERFLOW statement. CCCA, Release 2.0, will *flag* this statement for the following input language levels: DOS/VS COBOL, OS/VS COBOL LANGLVL(1), and OS/VS COBOL LANGLVL(2). Under the ANSI 85 standard, the ON OVERFLOW phrase executes under more conditions than it does under the ANSI 68 and ANSI 74 standards. The ON OVERFLOW phrase in a DOS/VS COBOL, OS/VS COBOL, or VS COBOL II program is not invoked if the program is running under CICS.

CALL statement. CCCA, Release 2.0, will *convert* this statement for the following input language level: DOS/VS COBOL. If there are no literal delimiters around the name of the called program, it is put in quotation marks if the literal delimiter for the program is quotation marks or in apostrophes if the literal delimiter is apostrophes.

CALL . . . USING statement. CCCA, Release 2.0, will *flag* this statement for the following input language levels: DOS/VS COBOL, OS/VS COBOL LANGLVL(1), and OS/VS COBOL LANGLVL(2). If identifiers following USING are VSAM file names, then the statement is flagged. If identifiers following USING are procedure names and the Procedure Name Checking option on the Optional Processing Panel is set to Y, then the statement is flagged.

CANCEL statement. CCCA, Release 2.0, will *flag* this statement for the following language levels: DOS/VS COBOL, OS/VS COBOL LANGLVL(1), and OS/VS COBOL LANGLVL(2).

The statement is *flagged* if there is an identifier in the statement with a PICTURE string that consists of characters only. The ANSI 74 standard classes these fields as alphabetic, while the ANSI 85 standard classes them as alphanumeric-edited. You will have to make a change to the program because alphanumeric-edited identifiers are not permitted in the CANCEL statement.

CLOSE . . . REEL/UNIT FOR REMOVAL statement. CCCA, Release 2.0, will *flag* this statement for the following input language levels: OS/VS COBOL LANGLVL(1) and OS/VS COBOL LANGLVL(2). CLOSE . . . REEL/UNIT FOR REMOVAL statements are flagged because in VS COBOL II the FOR REMOVAL option is treated as a comment.

CLOSE WITH DISP /CLOSE . . . WITH POSITIONING statements. CCCA, Release 2.0, will *remove* these statements for the following input language levels: OS/VS COBOL LANGLVL(1) and OS/VS COBOL LANGLVL(2). The WITH DISP option and the WITH POSITIONING option are removed.

COMMUNICATIONS SECTION. CCCA, Release 2.0, will *flag* a COMMUNICATIONS SECTION for the following input language levels: OS/VS COBOL LANGLVL(1) and OS/VS COBOL LANGLVL(2). The Communications module is not supported by VS COBOL II, and there is nothing with which it can be replaced.

COM-REG special register. CCCA, Release 2.0, will *flag* this special register for the following input language level: DOS/VS COBOL. The COM-REG special register is not supported by VS COBOL II. You should remove all references to it from the program.

CONFIGURATION SECTION header. CCCA, Release 2.0, will *convert* and *flag* a CONFIGURATION SECTION header for the following language levels: DOS/VS COBOL, OS/VS COBOL LANGLVL(1), and OS/VS COBOL LANGLVL(2).

The CONFIGURATION SECTION header is added, if it is missing and a SOURCE-COMPUTER, an OBJECT-COMPUTER, or a SPECIAL-NAMES paragraph is present. If the CONFIGURATION SECTION header is coded out of sequence, then you must attempt to put it in its

Copybook Issue 1

Problem:
The description of the *problem* for this case is as follows:
OS/VS COBOL allows COPY statements with associated names; VS COBOL II does not. For example, consider the following copy member (PROGC01L):

```
01  PROGC01L.
    05  RECORD-TYPE         PIC X.
    05  CTL-LOC             PIC X(4).
    05  SUB-LOC             PIC X(4).
    05  JOB-NO              PIC X(4).
    05  PLT-NO              PIC X(4).
```

The *problem* is that the following coding technique is valid in OS/VS COBOL but not valid in VS COBOL II:

```
01  1-SAVE-AREA   COPY   PROGC01L.
```

In this case, the 01 level element in the Copybook member (PROGC01L) is PROGC01L and is *not the same* as 1-SAVE-AREA, which is the 01 level field in the COPY statement.

EXAMPLE: The original OS/VS COBOL coding is

```
01 1-SAVE-AREA COPY PROGC01L.
```

PROBLEM: After conversion by CCCA, this COPY statement was converted as

```
01 1-SAVE-AREA.
   COPY PROGC01L.
```

After compiling the program under VS COBOL II, the following two errors were generated:

```
000506        050600 01 1-SAVE-AREA

000506==> IGYDS1159-E A "PICTURE" clause was not found for elementary
item "1-SAVE-AREA"
              "PICTURE X(1)" was assumed.
```

correct place. If this cannot be done, then the CONFIGURATION SECTION header is flagged.

COPY . . . REPLACING statement. CCCA, Release 2.0, will *flag* this statement for the following input language levels: DOS/VS COBOL,

```
000507                                                      COPY PROGC01L.
000508C           000100 01   PROGC01L.

000508==> IGYDS1082-E A period was required.  A period was assumed
before "01"
000509C           000200 05   RECORD-TYPE          PIC X.
```

When the PROCEDURE DIVISION uses a 05 level field like RECORD-TYPE, it will associate RECORD-TYPE with PROGC01L instead of 1-SAVE-AREA.

Resolution:
The description of the resolution for this problem is as follows. The program was manually revised for VS COBOL II compiler as follows:

```
COPY  PROGC01L   REPLACING   PROGC01L
   BY    1-SAVE-AREA.
```

The majority of problems we experienced during this conversion were these types of COPY statements:

```
000507        050700      COPY PROGC01L REPLACING PROGC01L BY 1-
                          SAVE-AREA.
000508C       000100 01   1-SAVE-AREA.
000509C       000200   05 RECORD-TYPE          PIC X.
000510C       000300   05 CTL-LOC              PIC X(4).
000511C       000400   05 SUB-LOC              PIC X(4).
000512C       000500   05 JOB-NO               PIC X(4).
000513C       000600   05 PLT-NO               PIC X(4).
000514C       000700   05 FILLER               PIC X(10).
000515C       000800   05 CTL-DESC             PIC X(30).
000516C       000900   05 JOB-DESC             PIC X(30).
000517C       001000   05 PLT-DESC             PIC X(30).
000518C       001100   05 JOB-BUDGET           PIC S9(9)V9(2)
                                               COMP-3.
000519C       001200   05 PRT-DETAIL           PIC X.
000520C       001300      88 PRT-DET                    VALUE 'Y'.
000521C       001400   05 JOB-BALANCE          PIC S9(9)V9(2)
                                               COMP-3.
000522C       001500   05 JB-DATE              PIC X(4).
000523C       001600   05 PR-OPT               PIC X.
```

Copybook Issue 2

Problem:
The description of the *problem* for this case is as follows: OS/VS COBOL allows COPY statements with associated names; VS COBOL II does not. For example, consider the following copy member (PROGM16L):

```
01  PROGM16L.
      05   FILLER                  PIC X(12) VALUE 'CHART-MAP***'.
```

The *problem* is that the following coding technique is valid in OS/VS COBOL but not valid in VS COBOL II:

```
01  PROGM16L    COPY  PROGM16L.
```

In this case, the 01 level element in the copybook member (PROGM16L) is PROGM16L and is the *same* as PROGM16L, which is the 01 level field in the COPY statement.

EXAMPLE: The original OS/VS coding is

```
01  PROGM16L    COPY PROGM16L.
```

PROBLEM: This copy statement was converted by CCCA as

```
01  PROGM16L.
    COPY PROGM16L.
```

After compiling the program under VS COBOL II, the following two errors were generated:

```
016200 01   PROGM16L

==> IGYDS1159-E A "PICTURE" clause was not found for elementary item
"PROGM16L".
             "PICTURE X(1)" was assumed.

                                                    COPY PROGM16L.
    C       000100 01   PROGM16L.

==> IGYDS1082-E A period was required.  A period was assumed before
"01".

    C       000700     05   FILLER              PIC X(12) VALUE 'CHART-
MAP***'.
```

OS/VS COBOL LANGLVL(1), and OS/VS COBOL LANGLVL(2). See Copybook issues 1 and 2 for samples of problems we encountered.

If there are lowercase alphabetic characters in operands of the REPLACING phrase that are not in nonnumeric literals, the state-

```
              016300
              016400  01   PROGM17L
```

Resolution:
The description of the resolution for this problem is as follows. The program was manually revised for VS COBOL II compiler as follows:

```
COPY PROGM16L.
```

Some of the problems we experienced during this conversion were of this type of COPY statement:

```
    016800*01  PROGM16L.                COPY PROGM16L.
    016900                               COPY PROGM16L.
    000100 01  PROGM16L.

000200********************************************************
000300********************************************************
    000400**
    000500**     SSA'S AND I/O AREAS, CHART MASTER DATA BASE
    000600*****
    000700     05  FILLER              PIC X(12) VALUE 'CHART-
MAP***'.
    017000
COPY PROBLEM
000071          007100 01  HEADER-HISTORY-RECORD
000071==> IGYDS1159-E A "PICTURE" clause was not found for elementary item
                "HEADER-HISTORY-RECORD".  "PICTURE X(1)" was assumed.
000072                                    COPY DEMDHIST.
000073C         000100 01  HISTORY-RECORD.
000073==> IGYDS1082-E A period was required.  A period was assumed before "01"
000074C         000200   05  PARTS-HISTORY-KEY.
000075C         000300     10  PART-NUMBER     PIC X(12).
000076C         000400   05  DEMAND-TABLE.
000077C         000500     10  DEPOT-DEMAND    OCCURS 15 TIMES
```

ment is flagged. Under the ANSI 68 and ANSI 74 standards, the REPLACING phrase is case sensitive. Under the ANSI 85 standard, lowercase characters are treated as their uppercase equivalent. You should check to see if this change will result in different text being copied into your program. If the operands of the REPLACING phrase contain a colon (":") character that is not in a nonnumeric literal, the statement is flagged. Under the ANSI 68 and ANSI 74 standards, the colon (":") is a non-COBOL character. Under the ANSI 85 standard, the colon character is treated as a separator. You should check to see if this change will result in different text being copied into your program.

If the operands of the REPLACING phrase contain an ANSI 85 standard non-COBOL character that is not in a nonnumeric literal, the statement is flagged. Under the ANSI 68 and ANSI 74 standards, non-COBOL characters are permitted in the REPLACING option. Under the ANSI 85 standard, non-COBOL characters in the REPLACING phrase are diagnosed. You should remove all non-COBOL characters from the REPLACING phrase and from the copybook.

COPY statement. CCCA, Release 2.0, will convert this statement for the following input language levels: DOS/VS COBOL and OS/VS COBOL LANGLVL(1). COPY statements with associated names are not supported by VS COBOL II. The following example illustrates how all such statements are converted. The COPY statement for the member (MBR-A) before conversion looks like this:

```
01 RECORD1 COPY MBR-A.
01 RECORD-A.
   05 FIELD-A...
   05 FIELD-B...
```

The statement after conversion is as follows:

```
01 RECORD1         COPY MBR-A REPLACING    ==01 RECORD-A.== BY ==      ==.
```

CURRENCY SIGN. CCCA, Release 2.0, will *flag* a CURRENCY SIGN for the following input language levels: DOS/VS COBOL and OS/VS COBOL LANGLVL(1). VS COBOL II does not accept the / (slash) character or the = (equal) character in the CURRENCY SIGN clause.

CURRENT-DATE special register. CCCA, Release 2.0, will *convert* this special register for the following language levels: DOS/VS COBOL, OS/VS COBOL LANGLVL(1), and OS/VS COBOL LANGLVL(2). The CURRENT-DATE register is not supported by the target languages. Whenever CURRENT-DATE is referenced in the program, it is replaced by code that contains the date from the system and puts it in the format of the CURRENT-DATE register. The fields required for the reformatting are generated in the WORKING-STORAGE section.

For CICS programs, the date is retrieved from the system using an EXEC CICS ASKTIME statement. CICS Release 1.7 or later is required. For non-CICS programs, the ACCEPT . . . FROM DATE statement is used to obtain the date. For DOS/VS COBOL, there are two different formats for the CURRENT-DATE register. You must specify the date format that is used at your installation in the DATE FORMAT field on the Conversion Parameters Panel. If you specify the wrong one, CCCA, Release 2.0, will not convert this language element correctly.

DATA RECORDS clause. CCCA, Release 2.0, will *remove* this clause for the following language levels: DOS/VS COBOL, OS/VS COBOL LANGLVL(1), and OS/VS COBOL LANGLVL(2). If you specify Y for the Obsolete Element Removal option on the Optional Processing Panel, the DATA RECORDS clause is removed from the FD entry. The word RECORDS is added if it is missing when the clause is not removed.

DATE-COMPILED/DATE-WRITTEN headers. CCCA, Release 2.0, will *convert* these headers for the following language levels: DOS/VS COBOL, OS/VS COBOL LANGLVL(1), and OS/VS COBOL LANGLVL(2). If the hyphen after the DATE is missing, it is added.

DATE-COMPILED/DATE-WRITTEN paragraphs. CCCA, Release 2.0, will *convert* these paragraphs for the following language levels: DOS/VS COBOL, OS/VS COBOL LANGLVL(1), and OS/VS COBOL LANGLVL(2). If you specify Y for the Obsolete Element Removal option on the Optional Processing Panel, these paragraphs in the Identification Division are commented out.

DATE-COMPILED header. CCCA, Release 2.0, will *convert* this header for the following language levels: DOS/VS COBOL, OS/VS COBOL LANGLVL(1), and OS/VS COBOL LANGLVL(2). If you specify N for the Obsolete Element Removal option on the Optional Processing Panel and there is no period after the header, a period is added.

DEBUG card and packet. CCCA, Release 2.0, will *remove* a DEBUG card and packet for the following language levels: DOS/VS COBOL, OS/VS COBOL LANGLVL(1), and OS/VS COBOL LANGLVL(2). These are commented out.

DISABLE statement Communications feature. CCCA, Release 2.0, will *flag* this statement for the following language levels: DOS/VS COBOL, OS/VS COBOL LANGLVL(1), and OS/VS COBOL LANGLVL(2). This is a Communications statement. The Communications module is not supported by the target languages, and there is nothing with which it can be replaced. CCCA, Release 2.0, will *flag* it.

DIVIDE ... ON SIZE ERROR statement. CCCA, Release 2.0, will *flag* this statement for the following input language levels: DOS/VS COBOL, OS/VS COBOL LANGLVL(1), and OS/VS COBOL LANGLVL(2). DIVIDE ... ON SIZE ERROR statements with multiple receiving fields are flagged because the ON SIZE ERROR phrase will not be executed for intermediate results under the ANSI 85 standard.

ENABLE statement Communications feature. CCCA, Release 2.0, will *flag* this statement for the following input language levels: DOS/VS COBOL, OS/VS COBOL LANGLVL(1), and OS/VS COBOL LANGLVL(2). This is a Communications statement. The Communications module is not supported by the target languages, and there is nothing with which it can be replaced. CCCA, Release 2.0, will *flag* it.

ENTER statement. CCCA, Release 2.0, will *remove* this statement for the following language levels: DOS/VS COBOL, OS/VS COBOL LANGLVL(1), and OS/VS COBOL LANGLVL(2). If you specify Y for the Obsolete Element Removal option on the Optional Processing Panel, the ENTER statement is removed.

ERROR declaratives. CCCA, Release 2.0, will *convert* an ERROR declarative for the following language levels: DOS/VS COBOL, OS/VS COBOL LANGLVL(1), and OS/VS COBOL LANGLVL(2). An ERROR declarative SECTION is generated for each file that is to be converted to VSAM. The code in the SECTION includes a DISPLAY of the returned file status and a GOBACK.

ERROR declaratives GIVING option. CCCA, Release 2.0, will *remove* this option and provide you with information for the following language levels: DOS/VS COBOL, OS/VS COBOL LANGLVL(1), and OS/VS COBOL LANGLVL(2). The GIVING option is removed from the program.

EXAMINE. CCCA, Release 2.0, will *convert* this statement for the following language levels: DOS/VS COBOL, OS/VS COBOL LANGLVL(1), and OS/VS COBOL LANGLVL(2). The EXAMINE statement is changed to an INSPECT statement, and the statement MOVE ZERO TO TALLY is put in front of it.

EXHIBIT statement. CCCA, Release 2.0, will *convert* this statement for the following language levels: DOS/VS COBOL, OS/VS COBOL LAN-

GLVL(1), and OS/VS COBOL LANGLVL(2). The EXHIBIT statement is changed to a DISPLAY statement.

EXIT PROGRAM. CCCA, Release 2.0, will *convert* this program for the following language levels: DOS/VS COBOL, OS/VS COBOL LANGLVL(1), and OS/VS COBOL LANGLVL(2). Under the ANSI 85 standard, statement control cannot flow beyond the last line of a called subprogram. The compiler generates an implicit EXIT PROGRAM at the end of each program.

Under the ANSI 68 and ANSI 74 standard, control can flow beyond the last line of a called program. When this happens, the program ABENDs. The ANSI 68 and ANSI 74 standard behavior can be preserved under the ANSI 85 standard by adding, at the end of the program, a section with a call to an ABEND macro. If you specify Y for the Call "ILBOABN0" Statement Generation option on the Optional Processing Panel and if EXIT PROGRAM, STOP RUN, or GOBACK is not the last physical statement in the program, a section that includes a CALL to the ABEND macro ILBOABN0 will be inserted at the end of the program.

FILE-LIMIT/FILE-LIMITS clauses. CCCA, Release 2.0, will *remove* these clauses for the following language levels: DOS/VS COBOL, OS/VS COBOL LANGLVL(1), and OS/VS COBOL LANGLVL(2). The clause is removed from the FILE-CONTROL paragraph.

FILE STATUS clause. CCCA, Release 2.0, will *convert* this clause for the following language levels: DOS/VS COBOL, OS/VS COBOL LANGLVL(1), and OS/VS COBOL LANGLVL(2). A FILE STATUS clause,

```
FILE-STATUS IS LCP-FILE STATUS-nn
```

is added to the FILE-CONTROL paragraph for each file that is to be converted to VSAM. The status key data item LCP-FILE-STATUS-nn referred to in the clause is added to the WORKING-STORAGE section (nn is a sequence number).

FILE STATUS codes. CCCA, Release 2.0, will *flag* these codes for the following language levels: DOS/VS COBOL, OS/VS COBOL LANGLVL(1), and OS/VS COBOL LANGLVL(2). The file status codes returned under ANSI 85 standard COBOL are different from those returned under ANSI 68 and ANSI 74 standard COBOL. You should check all references to the file status key in the program and update the values of the file status codes where it is required.

FOR MULTIPLE REEL/UNIT clause. CCCA, Release 2.0, will *remove* this clause for the following language levels: DOS/VS COBOL, OS/VS COBOL LANGLVL(1), and OS/VS COBOL LANGLVL(2). The clause is removed from the program.

GOBACK statement. CCCA, Release 2.0, will *convert* this statement for the following input language levels: DOS/VS COBOL, OS/VS COBOL LANGLVL(1), and OS/VS COBOL LANGLVL(2). Under the ANSI 85 standard, control cannot flow beyond the last line of a called subprogram. The compiler generates an implicit EXIT PROGRAM at the end of each program. Under the ANSI 68 and ANSI 74 standard, control can flow beyond the last line of a called program. When this happens the program ABENDs. The ANSI 68 and ANSI 74 standard behavior can be preserved under the ANSI 85 standard by adding, at the end of the program, a section with a call to an ABEND macro. If you specify Y for the Call "ILBOABN0" Statement Generation option on the Optional Processing Panel and if EXIT PROGRAM, STOP RUN, or GOBACK is not the last physical statement in the program, a section that includes a CALL to the ABEND macro ILBOABN0 will be inserted at the end of the program.

GREATER THEN relational operator. CCCA, Release 2.0, will *convert* this relational operator for the following language levels: DOS/VS COBOL, OS/VS COBOL LANGLVL(1), and OS/VS COBOL LANGLVL(2). THEN is changed to THAN.

IDMS. CCCA, Release 2.0, will *flag* this statement for the following input language levels: DOS/VS COBOL, OS/VS COBOL LANGLVL(1), and OS/VS COBOL LANGLVL(2). If your programs contain COPY IDMS statements, you should create a dummy copy member called IDMS. The copybook should just have a comment in it.

IF statement. CCCA, Release 2.0, will *convert* and *flag* this statement for the following language levels: DOS/VS COBOL, OS/VS COBOL LANGLVL(1), and OS/VS COBOL LANGLVL(2). Brackets immediately prior to relational operators are removed, but you should inspect the conversion. For example,

```
if A (= B)
```

is converted to

```
IF A = B
```

The target languages do not accept the following statements:

```
IF dataname ZEROS...
IF dataname ZEROES...
```

They are converted to

```
IF dataname zero...
```

Indexes (qualified). CCCA, Release 2.0, will *flag* qualified indexes for the following language levels: OS/VS COBOL LANGLVL(1) and OS/VS COBOL LANGLVL(2). CCCA, Release 2.0, will flag any reference to a qualified index because qualified indexes are no longer permitted in VS/COBOL II.

INSPECT statement. CCCA, Release 2.0, will *flag* this statement for the following language levels: OS/VS COBOL LANGLVL(1) and OS/VS COBOL LANGLVL(2). The statement is flagged if the PROGRAM COLLATING SEQUENCE established in the OBJECT COMPUTER paragraph identifies an alphabet that was defined with the ALSO clause to override the standard EBCDIC collating sequence. In these circumstances, the statement will behave differently under the ANSI 85 standard.

When coded, it affects the INSPECT, STRING, and UNSTRING statements. (It also affects nonnumeric keys in a MERGE or SORT when the COLLATING SEQUENCE is not specified in the SORT or MERGE statement.) The PROGRAM COLLATING SEQUENCE affects nonnumeric comparisons. In OS/VS COBOL, it affects both explicitly coded conditions and implicitly performed conditions (those comparisons that the compiler deems necessary to perform) in INSPECT, STRING, and UNSTRING statements.

In VS COBOL II, the PROGRAM COLLATING SEQUENCE only affects explicitly coded conditions in these statements.

INSTALLATION paragraph. CCCA, Release 2.0, will *convert* this paragraph for the following language levels: DOS/VS COBOL, OS/VS COBOL LANGLVL(1), and OS/VS COBOL LANGLVL(2). If you specify Y for the Obsolete Element Removal option on the Optional Processing Panel, the INSTALLATION paragraph in the Identification Division is commented out.

ISAM files. CCCA, Release 2.0, will *convert* these files for the following language levels: DOS/VS COBOL, OS/VS COBOL LANGLVL(1), and OS/VS COBOL LANGLVL(2).

Programs using ISAM files should be converted to programs using Key Sequenced Data Set (KSDS) Virtual Storage Access Method (VSAM) files. This can be done by using the VSAM utility program IDCAMS. CCCA, Release 2.0, will convert the file definition and I/O statements for ISAM files. VS COBOL II does not support the processing of ISAM files.

JUSTIFIED RIGHT clause. CCCA, Release 2.0, will *convert* and *flag* this clause for the following input language levels: DOS/VS COBOL, OS/VS COBOL LANGLVL(1), and OS/VS COBOL LANGLVL(2).

Under the ANSI 68 standard, if a JUSTIFIED clause is specified together with a VALUE clause for a data description entry, the initial data is right justified. Under the ANSI 85 standard, the initial data is not right justified. To preserve the ANSI 68 standard behavior of this language element, CCCA, Release 2.0, makes the following conversion. If the length of the nonnumeric literal in the VALUE clause is less than the length of the field as specified in the PICTURE clause, spaces are added to the front of the literal string until their lengths are equal. The clause will be flagged, instead of converted, if the literal has more than twenty-eight characters.

LABEL RECORDS clause. CCCA, Release 2.0, will *remove* this clause for the following language levels: DOS/VS COBOL, OS/VS COBOL LANGLVL(1), and OS/VS COBOL LANGLVL(2). If you specify Y for the Obsolete Element Removal option on the Optional Processing Panel, this clause is removed. The word RECORDS is added, if missing, when the clause is not removed.

LABEL RECORDS . . . TOTALING/TOTALED AREA option. CCCA, Release 2.0, will *remove* this option and provide you with information for the following language levels: DOS/VS COBOL, OS/VS COBOL LANGLVL(1), and OS/VS COBOL LANGLVL(2). This option is removed from the program. The data name associated with this option is listed at the end of the diagnostic listing.

LESS THEN relational operator. CCCA, Release 2.0, will *convert* this relational operator for the following language levels: DOS/VS COBOL, OS/VS COBOL LANGLVL(1), and OS/VS COBOL LANGLVL(2). THEN is changed to THAN.

Literals—Nonnumeric. CCCA, Release 2.0, will *convert* and *flag* nonnumeric literals for the following input language levels: DOS/VS COBOL, OS/VS COBOL LANGLVL(1), and OS/VS COBOL LANGLVL(2). If the continuation of a nonnumeric literal begins in Area A, it is shifted to the right until its whole length lies within Area B. If the continuation is too long to fit in Area B, it is flagged.

MEMORY SIZE clause. CCCA, Release 2.0, will *remove* this clause for the following language levels: DOS/VS COBOL, OS/VS COBOL LANGLVL(1), and OS/VS COBOL LANGLVL(2). If you specify Y for the Obsolete Element Removal option on the Optional Processing Panel, the MEMORYSIZE clause of the OBJECT-COMPUTER paragraph is removed.

MOVE ALL literal. CCCA, Release 2.0, will *flag* this literal for the following language levels: DOS/VS COBOL, OS/VS COBOL LANGLVL(1), and OS/VS COBOL LANGLVL(2). MOVE ALL literal TO numeric will be *flagged* with a warning.

MOVE CORR/CORRESPONDING statement. CCCA, Release 2.0, will *convert* this statement for the following language levels: DOS/VS COBOL, OS/VS COBOL LANGLVL(1), and OS/VS COBOL LANGLVL(2). The target languages do not allow multiple receiving fields in the MOVE CORRESPONDING statement. If the statement has multiple receiving fields, it is replaced by separate MOVE CORRESPONDING statements for each of the receiving fields.

MULTIPLE FILE TAPE clause. CCCA, Release 2.0, will *remove* this clause for the following language levels: DOS/VS COBOL, OS/VS COBOL LANGLVL(1), and OS/VS COBOL LANGLVL(2). If you specify Y for the Obsolete Element Removal option on the Optional Processing Panel, this clause is removed from the I-O-CONTROL paragraph.

MULTIPLY . . . ON SIZE ERROR statement. CCCA, Release 2.0, will *flag* this statement for the following language levels: DOS/VS COBOL, OS/VS COBOL LANGLVL(1), and OS/VS COBOL LANGLVL(2).

MULTIPLY . . . ON SIZE ERROR statements with multiple receiving fields are flagged because the ON SIZE ERROR phrase will not be executed for intermediate results under the ANSI 85 standard. For OS/VS COBOL and VS COBOL II with CMPR2, the SIZE ERROR option for the DIVIDE and MULTIPLY statements applies to both intermediate and final results.

If your OS/VS COBOL relies upon SIZE ERROR detection for intermediate results, it must change or be compiled with the CMPR2 compiler option (see Chapter 4, Section 4.21 on behaviors for more on that). The statements

```
01    NUMERICS.
10    NUMBERIC-1 PICTURE  S9(16).
10        NUMERIC-2    PICTURE  S9(16).
10        NUMERIC-3    PICTURE  S9(16).
10        NUMERIC-4    PICTURE  S9(16).
10        TEMP         PICTURE  S9(30).

      MULTIPLY NUMERIC-1  BY NUMERIC-2 GIVING NUMERIC-3   NUMERIC-4.
```

should behave like this:

```
                MULTIPLY NUMERIC-1    BY NUMERIC-2   GIVING   TEMP
                MOVE TEMPORARY    TO NUMERIC-3
                MOVE TEMPORARY    TO NUMERIC-4
```

TEMP is the intermediate result. An intermediate result will have at most thirty digits. In the preceding example, if NUMERIC-1, NUMERIC-2 , NUMERIC-3 , and NUMERIC-4 are all defined as PIC S9(16), NUMERIC-1 will be multiplied by NUMERIC-2 , yielding a thirty-two-digit result, which is moved to the thirty-digit intermediate result, TEMP. TEMP is then moved to NUMERIC-3 and NUMERIC-4.

A size error may occur if the result exceeds the largest possible value of the result field, during a division by zero, or during an exponential expression.

MOVE statement. CCCA, Release 2.0, will *remove* this statement for the following input language levels: DOS/VS COBOL, OS/VS COBOL LANGLVL(1), and OS/VS COBOL LANGLVL(2). Superfluous TOs are removed.

NOMINAL KEY clause. CCCA, Release 2.0, will *convert* or *remove* this clause for the following input language levels: DOS/VS COBOL, OS/VS COBOL LANGLVL(1), and OS/VS COBOL LANGLVL(2). You should convert this file to a Virtual Storage Access Method (VSAM) file. If the new organization for the file is INDEXED, the NOMINAL KEY clause is removed. Before every I/O statement for these files, the following statement is added prior to the I/O statement:

```
MOVE nominal-key-name TO record-key-name
```

After the I/O statement, the statement,

```
MOVE record-key-name TO nominal-key-name
```

is replaced by RELATIVE KEY if the new organization for the file is RELATIVE NOMINAL KEY.

NOT. CCCA, Release 2.0, will *convert* and *flag* this expression for the following language levels: DOS/VS COBOL and OS/VS COBOL LANGLVL(1). NOT in an abbreviated combined relation will be *changed* into an unabbreviated relation condition. If more than one NOT is involved, the expression is *flagged*. You will have to update the expression manually.

NOTE statement. CCCA, Release 2.0, will *convert* this statement for the following language levels: DOS/VS COBOL, OS/VS COBOL LANGLVL(1), and OS/VS COBOL LANGLVL(2).

It is removed from VS COBOL II. CCCA, Release 2.0, fully converts this statement by commenting it out. The NOTE statement is used to write comments in the source program. It is not supported by the target languages. CCCA, Release 2.0, fully converts this statement by commenting it out. If the NOTE sentence is the first sentence of a paragraph, an asterisk ("*") is placed in column 7 of each line in the paragraph. If the NOTE sentence is not the first sentence of the paragraph, an asterisk is placed in column 7 of all lines up to the first period. If other language elements not part of the NOTE statement are on the first or last line of the NOTE statement, the line is split in order to isolate the NOTE.

NSTD-REELS special register. CCCA, Release 2.0, will *flag* this special register for the following input language level(s): DOS/VS COBOL. The NSTD-REELS special register is not supported in the target languages. You should remove all references to it from the program.

OCCURS clause. CCCA, Release 2.0, will *flag* this clause for the following language levels: DOS/VS COBOL, OS/VS COBOL LANGLVL(1), and OS/VS COBOL LANGLVL(2).

OS/VS COBOL and DOS/VS COBOL allow a nonstandard order for phrases in the OCCURS clause. They allow the DEPENDING ON phrase to be inserted after or among the ASCENDING/DESCENDING phrases. They also allow the DEPENDING ON phrase after the INDEXED BY phrase. VS COBOL II and COBOL/370 only allow phrases in the standard order. OCCURS clauses with phrases in nonstandard order are flagged.

OCCURS DEPENDING ON clause (variable-length record). CCCA, Release 2.0, will *convert* this clause for the following language levels:

DOS/VS COBOL, OS/VS COBOL LANGLVL(1), and OS/VS COBOL LANGLVL(2).

COBOL statements that result in data transfer to a variable-length receiver that contains its own OCCURS DEPENDING ON (ODO) object behave differently under the ANSI 85 standard. Under the ANSI 68 and ANSI 74 standards, all ODO objects in sending and receiving fields must be set before the statement is executed. The actual lengths of the sender and receiver are calculated just before the execution of the data movement statement. Under the ANSI 85 standard, in some circumstances the maximum length of the variable-length group is used when it is a receiver, whereas the ANSI 68 and ANSI 74 standard always use the actual length. CCCA, Release 2.0, preserves the ANSI 68 and ANSI 74 behavior in the following way. For the following statements,

```
MOVE...TO identifier
READ...INTO identifier
RETURN...INTO identifier
UNSTRING...INTO identifier DELIMITER IN identifier
```

If the identifier is a variable-length data item that contains its own ODO object, then reference modification is added to it. For example,

```
MOVE...TO identifier
```

is changed to

```
MOVE...TO identifier (1:LENGTH OF identifier)
```

For the following statements,

```
RELEASE record-name FROM identifier
REWRITE record-name FROM identifier
WRITE record-name FROM identifier
```

if the identifier is a variable-length data item that contains its own ODO object, the FROM phrase is removed from the statement and a MOVE statement with reference modification is added before the statement. For example,

```
WRITE record-name FROM identifier
```

is changed to

```
MOVE identifier TO record-name (1:LENGTH OF record-name)
WRITE record-name
```

MOVE CORRESPONDING statements are flagged because reference modification is not allowed when the CORRESPONDING phrase is specified.

ON statement. CCCA, Release 2.0, will *convert* and *flag* this statement for the following language levels: DOS/VS COBOL, OS/VS COBOL LANGLVL(1), and OS/VS COBOL LANGLVL(2). It is removed from VS COBOL II. This statement will be converted. More complex ON statements are flagged. The ON statement is not supported by the target languages. The statement,

```
ON integer
```

imperative statement is converted to

```
ADD 1 TO LCP-ONCTR-nn
IF LCP-ONCTR-nn = integer
```

imperative statement. The statement,

```
ON integer-1 until integer 2
```

imperative statement is converted to

```
ADD 1 TO LCP-ONCTR-nn
  IF LCP-ONCTR-nn > (integer 1 - 1) & < integer-2
```

imperative statement.

A data item with the data name LCP-ONCTR-nn (where nn is a sequence number) is added into the WORKING-STORAGE section with an initial value of zero. More complex ON statements are flagged.

OPEN . . . DISP/ OPEN . . . LEAVE / OPEN . . . REREAD statements. CCCA, Release 2.0, will *convert* these statements for the following language levels: OS/VS COBOL LANGLVL(1) and OS/VS COBOL LANGLVL(2). CCCA, Release 2.0, will remove the DISP option, LEAVE option, and REREAD option.

OPEN . . . REVERSED statement. CCCA, Release 2.0, will *flag* this statement for the following input language levels: OS/VS COBOL LANGLVL(1) and OS/VS COBOL LANGLVL(2). You should check whether the file in the OPEN statement has multiple reels. If it does, you will have to make a change to the program because for the target languages this option is only valid for single-reel files. OS/VS COBOL handles single-reel files and, in an undocumented extension, multireel files.

ORGANIZATION clause. CCCA, Release 2.0, will *convert* this clause for the following language levels: DOS/VS COBOL, OS/VS COBOL LANGLVL(1), and OS/VS COBOL LANGLVL(2). For VSAM files, this clause is removed.

OTHERWISE. CCCA, Release 2.0, will *convert* OTHERWISE for the following input language levels: DOS/VS COBOL, OS/VS COBOL LANGLVL(1), and OS/VS COBOL LANGLVL(2). OTHERWISE is replaced by ELSE.

PERFORM/ALTER. CCCA, Release 2.0, will *flag* PERFORM/ALTER for the following language levels: DOS/VS COBOL, OS/VS COBOL LANGLVL(1), and OS/VS COBOL LANGLVL(2). The section is checked for a priority number less than 49 and for the presence of ALTER. If this is not the case, manual changes may be required if this independent section is performed from outside the section.

PERFORM . . . VARYING . . . AFTER statement. CCCA, Release 2.0, will *flag* this statement for the following language levels: DOS/VS COBOL, OS/VS COBOL LANGLVL(1), and OS/VS COBOL LANGLVL(2). Under the ANSI 85 standard, the rules for augmenting variables have changed. If there are dependencies between variables of the statement, then the statement may behave differently.

All PERFORM . . . VARYING . . . AFTER statements are flagged. You should check to see if there are any dependencies between the variables of the statement that will result in different behavior. If there are, you should modify the statement. In OS/VS COBOL, in a PERFORM statement with the VARYING . . . AFTER phrase, two actions take place when an inner condition tests as TRUE:

- The identifier/index associated with the inner condition is set to its current FROM value.
- The identifier/index associated with the outer condition is augmented by its current BY value.
- With such a PERFORM statement in COBOL/370 and COBOL for MVS & VM, the following takes place when an inner condition tests as TRUE:
- The identifier/index associated with the outer condition is augmented by its current BY value.
- The identifier/index associated with the inner condition is set to its current FROM value.

The following example illustrates the differences in execution:

```
PERFORM ABC VARYING X FROM 1 BY 1 UNTIL X > 3
            AFTER Y FROM X BY 1 UNTIL Y > 3
```

In OS/VS COBOL, ABC is executed eight times with the following values:

```
X:  1  1  1  2  2  2  3  3
Y:  1  2  3  1  2  3  2  3
```

In COBOL/370 and COBOL for MVS & VM, ABC is executed six times with the following values:

```
X:  1  1  1  2  2  3
Y:  1  2  3  2  3  3
```

Periods. CCCA, Release 2.0, will *convert* periods for the following language levels: DOS/VS COBOL, OS/VS COBOL LANGLVL(1), and OS/VS COBOL LANGLVL(2). If there is no period immediately before or immediately after paragraph names or section headers in the PROCEDURE DIVISION, one is inserted.

PICTURE clause scaled integers. CCCA, Release 2.0, will *flag* these scaled integers and provide you with information for the following language levels: DOS/VS COBOL and OS/VS COBOL LANGLVL(1). Scaled integers (i.e., data items that have a *P* as the rightmost symbol in their PICTURE strings) are flagged. If the scaled integer is the sending field in a MOVE statement and the receiving field is alphanumeric- or numeric-edited, you will have to convert this. If the scaled integer is compared with an alphanumeric- or numeric-edited field, you will have to convert this statement. Scaled integers are flagged.

PICTURE P in RELATIVE KEY. CCCA, Release 2.0, will *flag* PICTURE P in RELATIVE KEY for the following language levels: DOS/VS COBOL, OS/VS COBOL LANGLVL(1), and OS/VS COBOL LANGLVL(2). This is flagged.

PROCESSING MODE clause. CCCA, Release 2.0, will *remove* this clause for the following language levels: DOS/VS COBOL, OS/VS COBOL LANGLVL(1), and OS/VS COBOL LANGLVL(2). The PROCESSING MODE clause is removed.

PROGRAM-ID header. CCCA, Release 2.0, will *convert* the header for the following language levels: DOS/VS COBOL, OS/VS COBOL LANGLVL(1), and OS/VS COBOL LANGLVL(2). If the PROGRAM-ID header begins in Area B, it is moved to the left so that it begins in Area A.

Program name. CCCA, Release 2.0, will *convert* the program name for the following language levels: DOS/VS COBOL, OS/VS COBOL LAN-

GLVL(1), and OS/VS COBOL LANGLVL(2). VS COBOL II does not allow a data item to have a data name that is the same as the program name.

If there is one in the program, the data name will be suffixed, in the same manner as data names that are reserved words. In the called subprogram, the name of the program and the argument name in the procedure statement cannot be the same.

READ statement ISAM files. CCCA, Release 2.0, will *convert* these files for the following language levels: DOS/VS COBOL, OS/VS COBOL LANGLVL(1), and OS/VS COBOL LANGLVL(2). For randomly accessed indexed (ISAM) files, the following statement is added prior to the READ statement:

```
MOVE nominal-key-name TO record-key-name.
```

After the READ statement, the statement,

```
MOVE record-key-name TO nominal-key-name
```

is added. You should convert the file to VSAM.

READY TRACE statement. CCCA, Release 2.0, will *remove* this statement for the following language levels: DOS/VS COBOL, OS/VS COBOL LANGLVL(1), and OS/VS COBOL LANGLVL(2).

RECEIVE statement. CCCA, Release 2.0, will *flag* this statement for the following language levels: OS/VS COBOL LANGLVL(1) and OS/VS COBOL LANGLVL(2). This is a Communications statement. The Communications module is not supported by the target languages, and there is nothing with which it can be replaced. CCCA, Release 2.0, will flag it.

RECORD CONTAINS. CCCA, Release 2.0, will *remove* this clause for the following language levels: DOS/VS COBOL, OS/VS COBOL LANGLVL(1), and OS/VS COBOL LANGLVL(2). The clause is removed from the program, except for RECORD CONTAINS 0, which is left in place.

RECORDING MODE clause. CCCA, Release 2.0, will *remove* this clause for the following language levels: DOS/VS COBOL, OS/VS COBOL LANGLVL(1), and OS/VS COBOL LANGLVL(2). VS COBOL II compiler ignores this clause if it is specified for a VSAM file. If the clause is in a file description entry for a VSAM file or a file that is to be converted to VSAM, it is removed.

REDEFINES clause in FD or SD entry. CCCA, Release 2.0, will *convert* this clause for the following language levels: DOS/VS COBOL, OS/VS COBOL LANGLVL(1), and OS/VS COBOL LANGLVL(2). VS COBOL II does not permit REDEFINES clauses in FD or SD entries. Because they are superfluous, they are removed.

REMARKS paragraph. CCCA, Release 2.0, will *convert* a REMARKS paragraph for the following language levels: DOS/VS COBOL, OS/VS COBOL LANGLVL(1), and OS/VS COBOL LANGLVL(2). It is removed from VS COBOL II. CCCA, Release 2.0, fully converts this statement by commenting it out with an asterisk ("*") inserted in column 7 of the paragraph header and all succeeding lines of the paragraph.

REPORT WRITER statements. CCCA, Release 2.0, will *flag* these statements for the following language levels: DOS/VS COBOL, OS/VS COBOL LANGLVL(1), and OS/VS COBOL LANGLVL(2). The following statements are not supported by VS COBOL II:

- GENERATE
- INITIATE
- REPORT
- TERMINATE
- USE BEFORE REPORTING

If you specify Y for the Report Writer Statement *Flagging* option on the Optional Processing Panel, they will be flagged.

RESERVE ALTERNATE AREAS. CCCA, Release 2.0, will *convert* RESERVE ALTERNATE AREAS for the following language levels: DOS/VS COBOL, OS/VS COBOL LANGLVL(1), and OS/VS COBOL LANGLVL(2). The following changes are performed: from RESERVE NO/n ALTERNATE AREA/AREAS to RESERVE 1/n + 1 AREA/AREAS

RESERVE AREAS. CCCA, Release 2.0, will *convert* RESERVE AREAS for the following language levels: DOS/VS COBOL, OS/VS COBOL LANGLVL(1), and OS/VS COBOL LANGLVL(2). The following changes are performed:

- from ANS68 RESERVE n AREA
- to ANS74 RESERVE n+1 AREA /AREAS

Reserved words. CCCA, Release 2.0, will *convert* reserved words for the following language levels: DOS/VS COBOL, OS/VS COBOL LANGLVL(1), and OS/VS COBOL LANGLVL(2). A suffix is appended to all user-defined words that are reserved words in the target language. You specify the suffix that you want appended in the RESERVED word suffix field of the Conversion Parameters Panel. The number 74 is the default suffix.

RESET TRACE statement. CCCA, Release 2.0, will *remove* this statement for the following language levels: DOS/VS COBOL, OS/VS COBOL LANGLVL(1), and OS/VS COBOL LANGLVL(2).

REWRITE statement ISAM files. CCCA, Release 2.0, will *convert* these files for the following language levels: DOS/VS COBOL, OS/VS COBOL LANGLVL(1), and OS/VS COBOL LANGLVL(2). For randomly accessed indexed (ISAM) files, the following statement is added prior to the REWRITE statement:

```
MOVE nominal-key-name TO record-key-name
```

After the REWRITE statement, the statement

```
MOVE record-key-name TO nominal-key-name
```

is added. You should convert the file to VSAM.

SAME AREA clause. CCCA, Release 2.0, will *convert* this clause for the following language levels: DOS/VS COBOL, OS/VS COBOL LANGLVL(1), and OS/VS COBOL LANGLVL(2). SAME AREA is changed to SAME RECORD AREA.

SEARCH ALL. CCCA, Release 2.0, will *flag* this statement for the following input language levels: DOS/VS COBOL and OS/VS COBOL LANGLVL(1).

SEARCH . . . WHEN. CCCA, Release 2.0, will *convert* this statement for the following language levels: DOS/VS COBOL, OS/VS COBOL LANGLVL(1), and OS/VS COBOL LANGLVL(2).

In DOS/VS COBOL and OS/VS COBOL, the ASCENDING/DESCENDING KEY data item may be specified as either the subject or the object of the WHEN relation condition. In the target languages, it must be specified as the subject. If the key is not the subject, the condition is reversed, so that the subject becomes the object. NEXT SENTENCE is added if no statement is found.

SECURITY paragraph. CCCA, Release 2.0, will *convert* this paragraph for the following language levels: DOS/VS COBOL, OS/VS COBOL LANGLVL(1), and OS/VS COBOL LANGLVL(2). If you specify Y for the Obsolete Element Removal option on the Optional Processing Panel, the SECURITY paragraph in the Identification Division is commented out.

SEEK. CCCA, Release 2.0, will *remove* this statement for the following language levels: DOS/VS COBOL, OS/VS COBOL LANGLVL(1), and OS/VS COBOL LANGLVL(2). CCCA, Release 2.0, removes this statement from the program because this is a BDAM file-handling statement. Programs using BDAM files should be converted to programs using RRDS VSAM files. This can be done by using the VSAM utility program IDCAMS.

SELECT OPTIONAL. CCCA, Release 2.0, will remove this phrase for the following language levels: DOS/VS COBOL, OS/VS COBOL LANGLVL(1), and OS/VS COBOL LANGLVL(2). The OPTIONAL phrase is removed from the program.

SEND statement. CCCA, Release 2.0, will *flag* this statement for the following input language levels: OS/VS COBOL LANGLVL(1) and OS/VS COBOL LANGLVL(2). CCCA, Release 2.0, will flag it because this is a Communications statement. The Communications module is not supported by the target languages, and there is nothing with which it can be replaced.

Signed VALUE. CCCA, Release 2.0, will *convert* this sign for the following language levels: DOS/VS COBOL, OS/VS COBOL LANGLVL(1), and OS/VS COBOL LANGLVL(2). The sign is removed from the value if PIC is unsigned.

SORT-OPTION clause. CCCA, Release 2.0, will *remove* this clause for the following language level(s): DOS/VS COBOL. The clause is removed from the SD entry.

START . . . USING KEY statement. CCCA, Release 2.0, will *convert* this statement for the following language levels: DOS/VS COBOL, OS/VS COBOL LANGLVL(1), and OS/VS COBOL LANGLVL(2). The USING KEY clause of the START statement is not supported by the target languages. START statements that specify this clause are converted to START . . . KEY statements.

STOP RUN statement. CCCA, Release 2.0, will *convert* this statement for the following language levels: DOS/VS COBOL, OS/VS COBOL LANGLVL(1), and OS/VS COBOL LANGLVL(2).

Under the ANSI 85 standard, control cannot flow beyond the last line of a called subprogram. The compiler generates an implicit EXIT PROGRAM at the end of each program. Under the ANSI 68 and ANSI 74 standards, control can flow beyond the last line of a called program. When this happens, the program ABENDs. The ANSI 68 and ANSI 74 standard behavior can be preserved under the ANSI 85 standard by adding, at the end of the program, a section with a call to an ABEND macro. If you specify Y for the Call "ILBOABN0" Statement Generation option on the Optional Processing Panel and EXIT PROGRAM, STOP RUN, or GOBACK is not the last physical statement in the program, a section that includes a CALL to the ABEND macro ILBOABN0 will be inserted at the end of the program.

STRING statement. CCCA, Release 2.0, will *flag* this statement for the following language levels: OS/VS COBOL LANGLVL(1) and OS/VS COBOL LANGLVL(2). The statement is flagged if it has a receiving field with a PICTURE string that consists of As and Bs only. The ANSI 74 standard classes these fields as alphabetic, while the ANSI 85 standard classes them as alphanumeric-edited. You will have to make a change to the program because alphanumeric-edited receiving fields in the STRING statement are not permitted.

The statement is flagged if the PROGRAM COLLATING SEQUENCE established in the OBJECT COMPUTER paragraph identifies an alphabet that was defined with the ALSO clause. Under these circumstances, the statement will behave differently under the ANSI 85 standard.

The following string statements,

```
STRING identifier-1 DELIMITED BY identifier-2
INTO identifier-3 WITH POINTER identifier-4 . . .
```

are flagged where identifier-1 or identifier-2 is the same as identifier-3 or identifier-4 or where identifier-3 is the same as identifier-4.

> THAN relational operator. CCCA, Release 2.0, will *convert* this relational operator for the following language levels: DOS/VS COBOL, OS/VS COBOL LANGLVL(1), and OS/VS COBOL LANGLVL(2). THAN is removed.

< THAN relational operator. CCCA, Release 2.0, will *convert* this relational operator for the following language levels: DOS/VS COBOL, OS/VS COBOL LANGLVL(1), and OS/VS COBOL LANGLVL(2). THAN is removed.

> THEN relational operator. CCCA, Release 2.0, will *convert* this relational operator for the following language levels: DOS/VS COBOL, OS/VS COBOL LANGLVL(1), and OS/VS COBOL LANGLVL(2). THEN is removed.

< THEN relational operator. CCCA, Release 2.0, will *convert* this relational operator for the following language levels: DOS/VS COBOL, OS/VS COBOL LANGLVL(1), and OS/VS COBOL LANGLVL(2). The THEN relational operator is removed.

THEN. CCCA, Release 2.0, will *remove* this statement for the following language levels: DOS/VS COBOL, OS/VS COBOL LANGLVL(1), and OS/VS COBOL LANGLVL(2). THEN used between statements is removed.

TIME-OF-DAY special register. CCCA, Release 2.0, will *convert* this special register for the following language levels: DOS/VS COBOL, OS/VS COBOL LANGLVL(1), and OS/VS COBOL LANGLVL(2). Whenever TIME-OF-DAY is referenced in the program, it is replaced by code that contains the date from the system and puts it in the format of the TIME-OF-DAY register.

The TIME-OF-DAY register is not supported by the target languages. The fields required for the reformatting are generated in the WORKING-STORAGE section. For CICS programs, the time is retrieved from the system using an EXEC CICS ASKTIME statement. CICS Release 1.7 or later is required. For non-CICS programs, the ACCEPT . . . FROM TIME statement is used to obtain the time.

=TO relational operator. CCCA, Release 2.0, will *convert* this relational operator for the following language levels: DOS/VS COBOL, OS/VS COBOL LANGLVL(1), and OS/VS COBOL LANGLVL(2). TO is removed.

TOTALING/TOTALED AREA. CCCA, Release 2.0, will *remove* this option and provide information for the following language levels: OS/VS COBOL LANGLVL(1) and OS/VS COBOL LANGLVL(2). This option is removed from the program. The data name associated with this option is listed at the end of the diagnostic listing.

TRACK-AREA. CCCA, Release 2.0, will *remove* this clause for the following language levels: DOS/VS COBOL, OS/VS COBOL LANGLVL(1), and OS/VS COBOL LANGLVL(2). The clause is removed from the program by CCCA Release 2.0.

TRACK-LIMIT clause. CCCA, Release 2.0, will *remove* this clause for the following input language levels: OS/VS COBOL LANGLVL(1) and OS/VS COBOL LANGLVL(2). The clause is removed from the program by CCCA Release 2.0.

TRANSFORM statement. CCCA, Release 2.0, will *convert* this statement for the following language levels: DOS/VS COBOL, OS/VS COBOL LANGLVL(1), and OS/VS COBOL LANGLVL(2). CCCA, Release 2.0,. changes TRANSFORM to INSPECT.

UNSTRING statement. CCCA, Release 2.0, will *flag* this statement for the following language level(s): OS/VS COBOL LANGLVL(1). The UNSTRING statement is flagged if an ALL is specified in the DELIMITED BY phrase. CCCA, Release 2.0, will *convert* this statement for the following input language level(s): OS/VS COBOL LANGLVL(2).

Insert the word OR between identifiers in the DELIMITED BY PHRASE if it is missing. CCCA, Release 2.0, will *convert* this statement for the following input language level(s): OS/VS COBOL LANGLVL(2). Remove the word IS if it appears in the POINTER phrase. CCCA, Release 2.0, will *flag* this statement for the following input language levels: OS/VS COBOL LANGLVL(1) and OS/VS COBOL LANGLVL(2).

The statement is flagged if the PROGRAM COLLATING SEQUENCE established in the OBJECT COMPUTER paragraph identifies an alphabet that was defined with the ALSO clause. Under these circumstances, the statement will behave differently under the ANSI 85 standard.

UPSI name. CCCA, Release 2.0, will *convert* and *flag* this name for the following language levels: DOS/VS COBOL, OS/VS COBOL LANGLVL(1), and OS/VS COBOL LANGLVL(2). Condition names are added. UPSI-n is replaced by condition name, for example,

```
LCP-ON-UPSI-n
```

and

```
LCP-OFF-UPSI-n
```

where n is a number from 0 to 7.

USE AFTER STANDARD . . . ON . . . GIVING. CCCA, Release 2.0, will *remove* this option and provide information for the following language levels: DOS/VS COBOL, OS/VS COBOL LANGLVL(1), and OS/VS COBOL LANGLVL(2). The GIVING option is removed from the program. A list of GIVING affected data names is printed in the conversion listing.

USE BEFORE STANDARD. CCCA, Release 2.0, will *remove* USE BEFORE STANDARD for the following language levels: DOS/VS COBOL, OS/VS COBOL LANGLVL(1), and OS/VS COBOL LANGLVL(2). USE BEFORE STANDARD is removed from the program.

USE FOR DEBUGGING. CCCA, Release 2.0, will *flag* this statement for the following input language levels: DOS/VS COBOL, OS/VS COBOL LANGLVL(1), and OS/VS COBOL LANGLVL(2). If an identifier following DEBUGGING is a file name, then the statement is flagged. If an identifier following DEBUGGING is not a procedure name and the Procedure Name Checking option on the Optional Processing Panel is set to Y, then the statement is flagged.

VALUE in 88 level. CCCA, Release 2.0, will *convert* a VALUE in 88 level for the following language levels: DOS/VS COBOL, OS/VS COBOL LANGLVL(1), and OS/VS COBOL LANGLVL(2). If the value of a level 88 refers to a variable defined with a PICTURE X and the value is not enclosed between quotation marks or apostrophes, quotation marks or apostrophes will be added.

VALUE OF clause. CCCA, Release 2.0, will *remove* this clause for the following language levels: DOS/VS COBOL, OS/VS COBOL LANGLVL(1), and OS/VS COBOL LANGLVL(2). If you specify Y for the Obsolete Element Removal option on the Optional Processing Panel, the VALUE OF clause is removed from the FD entry.

VALUES. CCCA, Release 2.0, will *convert* VALUES for the following language levels: DOS/VS COBOL, OS/VS COBOL LANGLVL(1), and OS/VS COBOL LANGLVL(2). If not used in 88 level, VALUES is changed to VALUE.

WHEN-COMPILED. CCCA, Release 2.0, will *convert* this special register for the following language levels: DOS/VS COBOL, OS/VS COBOL LANGLVL(1), and OS/VS COBOL LANGLVL(2). Both VS COBOL II and OS/VS COBOL support the use of the WHEN-COMPILED special

Table 5.4 When Compiled Date/Time Formats

IN OS/VS COBOL, THE FORMAT IS:	IN VS COBOL II, THE FORMAT IS:
hh.mm.ssMMM DD, YYYY	MM/DD/YYhh.mm.ss
(hour.minute.secondMONTH DAY, YEAR)	(MONTH/DAY/YEARhour.minute.second

register. The rules for using the special register are the same for both compilers. However, the format of the data differs, as shown in Table 5.4.

Wherever WHEN-COMPILED is referenced in the program, code is inserted that changes the data from the register to the old format. The fields required for the reformatting are generated in the WORKING-STORAGE section.

WRITE statement ISAM files. CCCA, Release 2.0, will *convert* these files for the following language levels: DOS/VS COBOL, OS/VS COBOL LANGLVL(1), and OS/VS COBOL LANGLVL(2). For randomly accessed indexed (ISAM) files, the following statement is added prior to the WRITE statement:

```
MOVE nominal-key-name TO record-key-name
```

After the WRITE statement, the statement "MOVE record-key-name TO nominal-key-name" is added. You should convert the file to VSAM.

WRITE . . . AFTER POSITIONING n. CCCA, Release 2.0, will *convert* WRITE . . . AFTER POSITIONING n for the following language levels: DOS/VS COBOL, OS/VS COBOL LANGLVL(1), and OS/VS COBOL LANGLVL(2).

If n is a literal, this is changed to WRITE . . . AFTER lines ADVANCING n LINES. If n is an identifier, SPECIAL-NAMES are generated and a section is added at the end of the program. Note: When compiling the converted program with the VS COBOL II Compiler, use the NOADV option. If POSITIONING and ADVANCING are used in the old program, you should review the ADV option.

WRITE . . . BEFORE/AFTER ADVANCING mnemonic-name LINE/LINES. CCCA, Release 2.0, will *convert* LINE or LINES for the following language levels: DOS/VS COBOL, OS/VS COBOL LANGLVL(1), and OS/VS COBOL LANGLVL(2). VS COBOL II does not accept LINE or LINES in this statement. They are removed.

5.5 VSAM Problem with CCCA

If the file name contains an "-I-", the conversion tool flags the file as ISAM when it is actually VSAM. The programs containing this error on conversion can be complied manually. (The tool will not automatically compile programs receiving errors during the conversion.)

5.6 Conclusion

Because of the volume of upgrades of OS/VS COBOL to COBOL II we had to perform, CCCA shortened our turnaround time and improved our consistency. We have migrated to CCCA, Release 2.1, now, which has improved our automated percentage (versus manual fixes) by more than 50 percent over CCCA, Release 2.0. In the next chapter, we'll look at how to use CCCA to upgrade COBOL II to COBOL/370, which is just one step away from the current COBOL for MVS & VM.

CHAPTER 6

Upgrading OS/VS COBOL to VS COBOL/370 Using CCCA

If your upgrade project is tool based, your environment is OS/VS, and you'd like to skip migrating to COBOL II and proceed directly to COBOL for MVS & VM, this chapter will help you get there. There are similarities between migrating to COBOL II and migrating to COBOL for MVS & VM, but there are differences as well. You may do well to read the migration to COBOL II first, because many of the steps are the same, but going to COBOL for MVS & VM directly has its own challenges.

6.1 Ideal Migration Path

Because of the long-term support issues and the powerful intrinsic date functions of COBOL for MVS & VM (or COBOL/370), the ideal situation would be to have users with OS/VS COBOL migrate directly to IBM COBOL for MVS & VM (or COBOL/370) and the IBM Language Environment for MVS & VM (run-time library) if the IBM Language Environment for MVS & VM prerequisites are met.

There is no reason to go to VS COBOL II. Instead, go directly to COBOL for MVS & VM (or COBOL/370). Some people prefer to do an assessment and modification/recompile (if necessary), and "flash-cut" by putting LE in LINKLST, while most prefer to slowly STEPLIB into the new environment.

6.2 COBOL Language Elements Converted to COBOL/370

Rather than organize the affected commands by division in this section, we will present them in alphabetic order. When you manually upgrade programs, it's best to see upgrade elements in the order in which you will see them in the program. When using a tool (here, CCCA) you will need them in alphabetic order so you can find them more rapidly in your run outputs (offering you a better reference).

ACCEPT MESSAGE COUNT statement Communications feature. CCCA, Release 2.0, will *flag* this statement for the following input language levels: OS/VS COBOL LANGLVL(1) and OS/VS COBOL LANGLVL(2).

This is a Communications statement. The Communication module is not supported by COBOL for MVS & VM (or COBOL/370), and there is nothing with which it can be replaced. CCCA, Release 2.0, will *flag* it.

ACTUAL KEY clause. CCCA, Release 2.0, will *convert* and *flag* this statement for the following language levels: DOS/VS COBOL and OS/VS COBOL LANGLVL(1).

In OS/VS COBOL LANGLVL(2), the ACTUAL KEY clause should be for a BDAM file. ACTUAL KEY is replaced (*converted*) by RELATIVE KEY. Programs using BDAM files should be *converted* to programs using RRDS VSAM files. This can be done by using the VSAM utility program IDCAMS. The ACTUAL KEY is *flagged* if the new organization for the file is not RELATIVE. For additional information on this subject, you should refer to the ISAM section of Chapter 2 (Section 2.2, "ISAM Conversion Options and Issues").

ALPHABET clause. CCCA, Release 2.0, will *convert* this statement for the following input language levels: DOS/VS COBOL, OS/VS COBOL LANGLVL(1), and OS/VS COBOL LANGLVL(2).

CCCA, Release 2.0, will *convert* it as follows: The keyword ALPHABET is added in front of the alphabet name within the ALPHABET clause of the SPECIAL-NAMES paragraph.

ALPHABETIC class. CCCA, Release 2.0, will *convert* this statement for the following input language levels: DOS/VS COBOL and OS/VS COBOL LANGLVL(1).

OS/VS COBOL LANGLVL(2), CCCA, Release 2.0, will *convert* ALPHABETIC to ALPHABETIC-UPPER. In OS/VS COBOL, only uppercase letters and the space character are considered to be ALPHABETIC. In COBOL for MVS & VM and COBOL/370, uppercase letters, lowercase letters, and the space character are considered to be ALPHABETIC.

APPLY CORE-INDEX clause. CCCA, Release 2.0, will *remove* this statement for the following input language levels: DOS/VS COBOL and OS/VS COBOL LANGLVL(1).

OS/VS COBOL LANGLVL(2), CCCA, Release 2.0, will *remove* the clause from the I-O-CONTROL paragraph because this is an ISAM file-handling clause. For additional information on this subject, you should refer to the ISAM section of Chapter 2 (Section 2.2).

APPLY CYL-INDEX clause. CCCA, Release 2.0, will *remove* this statement for the following input language level: DOS/VS COBOL.

CCCA, Release 2.0, will *remove* the clause from the I-O-CONTROL paragraph because this is an ISAM file-handling clause. For additional information on this subject, you should refer to the ISAM section of Chapter 2 (Section 2.2).

APPLY CYL-OVERFLOW clause. CCCA, Release 2.0, will *remove* this statement for the following input language level: DOS/VS COBOL. CCCA, Release 2.0, will *remove* the clause from the I-O-CONTROL paragraph because this is an ISAM file-handling clause. For additional information on this subject, you should refer to the ISAM section of Chapter 2 (Section 2.2).

APPLY EXTENDED-SEARCH clause. CCCA, Release 2.0, will *remove* this statement for the following input language level: DOS/VS COBOL. CCCA, Release 2.0, will *remove* the clause from the I-O-CONTROL paragraph because this is an ISAM file-handling clause. For additional information on this subject, you should refer to the ISAM section of Chapter 2 (Section 2.2).

APPLY MASTER-INDEX clause. CCCA, Release 2.0, will *remove* this statement for the following input language level: DOS/VS COBOL. CCCA, Release 2.0, will *remove* the clause from the I-O-CONTROL paragraph because this is an ISAM file-handling clause. For additional information on this subject, you should refer to the ISAM section of Chapter 2 (Section 2.2).

APPLY RECORD-OVERFLOW clause. CCCA, Release 2.0, will *remove* this statement for the following input language levels: OS/VS COBOL LANGLVL(1) and OS/VS COBOL LANGLVL(2).

CCCA, Release 2.0, will *remove* the APPLY RECORD-OVERFLOW clause from the I-O-CONTROL paragraph because this is an ISAM file-handling clause. For additional information on this subject, you should refer to the ISAM section of Chapter 2 (Section 2.2).

APPLY REORG-CRITERIA clause. CCCA, Release 2.0, will *remove* this statement for the following input language levels: OS/VS COBOL LANGLVL(1) and OS/VS COBOL LANGLVL(2).

CCCA, Release 2.0, will *remove* the APPLY RECORD-CRITERIA clause from the I-O-CONTROL paragraph because this is an ISAM file-handling clause. For additional information on this subject, you should refer to the ISAM section of Chapter 2 (Section 2.2).

APPLY WRITE-VERIFY clause. CCCA, Release 2.0, will *remove* this statement for the following input language level: DOS/VS COBOL. CCCA, Release 2.0, will *remove* the clause from the I-O-CONTROL paragraph because this is an ISAM file-handling clause. For additional information on this subject, you should refer to the ISAM section of Chapter 2 (Section 2.2).

ASSIGN clause organization parameter. CCCA, Release 2.0, will *convert* and *flag* this statement for the following language levels: OS/VS COBOL LANGLVL(1) and OS/VS COBOL LANGLVL(2).

Assignment names of the following formats are *converted* to COBOL/370 format:

- sysnnn-class-device-organization-name
- class-device-organization name
- class-organization-name

Files that have a *D*, *W*, *U*, or *A* specified for the organization parameter in the assignment name (BDAM files) should be *converted* to RRDS VSAM. For these files an ORGANIZATION IS RELATIVE clause is added to the FILE-CONTROL paragraph.

Files that have an *I* specified for the organization parameter in the assignment name (ISAM files) should be *converted* to VSAM/KSDS. For these files an ORGANIZATION IS INDEXED clause is added to the

FILE-CONTROL paragraph. In DOS/VS COBOL, if the name is not coded for SYSnnn-devtype-device-organization-filename then SYSnnn is added as the external name.

Programs using BDAM files should be converted to programs using RRDS VSAM files. This can be done by using the VSAM utility program IDCAMS. For additional information on this subject, you should refer to the ISAM section of Chapter 2 (Section 2.2). COBOL for MVS & VM and COBOL/370 support only the following format of the ASSIGN clause:

```
ASSIGN TO assignment-name
```

where assignment-name can have the following forms:

```
QSAM Files [comments-][S-]name
VSAM Sequential Files [comments-][AS-]name
VSAM Indexed or Relative Files [comments-]name
```

If your OS/VS COBOL program uses other formats of the ASSIGN clause or other forms of the assignment-name, you must change it to conform to the format supported by COBOL for MVS & VM and COBOL/370.

ASSIGN integer system-name. CCCA, Release 2.0, will *remove* this statement for the following input language levels: DOS/VS COBOL, OS/VS COBOL LANGLVL(1), and OS/VS COBOL LANGLVL(2). CCCA, Release 2.0, will *remove* the integer from the clause.

ASSIGN . . . OR. CCCA, Release 2.0, will *remove* this statement for the following input language levels: DOS/VS COBOL, OS/VS COBOL LANGLVL(1), and OS/VS COBOL LANGLVL(2). CCCA, Release 2.0, will *remove* the OR from the clause.

AUTHOR paragraph. CCCA, Release 2.0, will *convert* this statement for the following input language levels: DOS/VS COBOL, OS/VS COBOL LANGLVL(1), and OS/VS COBOL LANGLVL(2).

The AUTHOR paragraph in the Identification Division is *converted* by commenting out if the Obsolete Element Removal option on the Optional Processing Panel is specified as *Y* (yes).

Basic Direct Access Method (BDAM) files. CCCA, Release 2.0, will *convert* and *flag* this statement for the following language levels: DOS/VS COBOL, OS/VS COBOL LANGLVL(1), and OS/VS COBOL LANGLVL(2).

The COBOL/370 does not support the processing of BDAM files. Programs using BDAM files should be *converted* to programs using RRDS VSAM files. This can be done by using the VSAM utility program IDCAMS. CCCA, Release 2.0, *converts* the file definitions, but you must add the key algorithms manually. For additional information on this subject, you should refer to the ISAM section of Chapter 2 (Section 2.2).

BLANK WHEN ZERO clause. CCCA, Release 2.0, will *remove* this statement for the following input language levels: DOS/VS COBOL, OS/VS COBOL LANGLVL(1), and OS/VS COBOL LANGLVL(2). CCCA, Release 2.0, will *remove* the BLANK WHEN ZERO clause if the data description entry has a BLANK WHEN ZERO clause and a PICTURE string with a * (zero suppression) symbol in it.

BLOCK CONTAINS clause. CCCA, Release 2.0, will *remove* this statement for the following input language levels: DOS/VS COBOL, OS/VS COBOL LANGLVL(1), and OS/VS COBOL LANGLVL(2). CCCA, Release 2.0, will *remove* the clause from VSAM file descriptions if you specify Y for the Obsolete Element Removal option on the Optional Processing Panel. The concept of blocking has no meaning for VSAM files.

CALL identifier statement. CCCA, Release 2.0, will *flag* this statement for the following input language levels: OS/VS COBOL LANGLVL(1) and OS/VS COBOL LANGLVL(2). CCCA, Release 2.0, will *flag* the statement if the identifier has a PICTURE string consisting of As and Bs only. The ANSI 74 standard classes these fields as alphabetic, while the ANSI 85 standard classes them as alphanumeric-edited. You will have to make a change to the program because alphanumeric-edited identifiers are not permitted in the CALL statement.

CALL . . . ON EXCEPTION statement. CCCA, Release 2.0, will *flag* this statement for the following input language level: VS COBOL II. The ON EXCEPTION phrase in a COBOL/370 program is not invoked if the program is running under CICS. When an exception condition occurs in a COBOL/370 program running under CICS, the ON EXCEPTION phrase will be invoked, if it is specified. The statement is *flagged* if the target language is COBOL/370.

CALL . . . ON OVERFLOW statement. CCCA, Release 2.0, will *flag* this statement for the following input language levels: DOS/VS COBOL, OS/VS COBOL LANGLVL(1), and OS/VS COBOL LANGLVL(2).

Under the ANSI 85 standard, the ON OVERFLOW phrase executes under more conditions than it does under the ANSI 68 and ANSI 74 standards. The ON OVERFLOW phrase in a DOS/VS COBOL, OS/VS COBOL, or COBOL/370 program is not invoked if the program is running under CICS.

CALL statement. CCCA, Release 2.0, will *convert* this statement for the following input language level: DOS/VS COBOL. If there are no literal delimiters around the name of the called program, it is put in quotation marks if the literal delimiter for the program is quotation marks or in apostrophes if the literal delimiter is apostrophes. OS/VS COBOL accepts paragraph names, section names, and file names in the USING phrase of the CALL statement. COBOL for MVS & VM and COBOL/370 CALL statements do not accept procedure names and only accept QSAM file names in the USING phrase. Therefore, you must *remove* the procedure names and make sure that file names used in the USING phrase of the CALL statement name QSAM physical sequential files.

CALL . . . USING statement. CCCA, Release 2.0, will *flag* this statement for the following input language levels: DOS/VS COBOL, OS/VS COBOL LANGLVL(1), and OS/VS COBOL LANGLVL(2).

If identifiers following USING are VSAM file names, then the statement is *flagged*. If identifiers following USING are procedure names and the Procedure Name Checking option on the Optional Processing Panel is set to Y, then the statement is *flagged*.

CANCEL statement. CCCA, Release 2.0, will *flag* this statement for the following input language levels: DOS/VS COBOL, OS/VS COBOL LANGLVL(1), and OS/VS COBOL LANGLVL(2).

The statement is *flagged* if there is an identifier in the statement with a PICTURE string consisting of As and Bs only. The ANSI 74 standard classes these fields as alphabetic, while the ANSI 85 standard classes them as alphanumeric-edited. You will have to make a change to the program because alphanumeric-edited identifiers are not permitted in the CANCEL statement.

CLOSE . . . REEL/UNIT FOR REMOVAL statement. CCCA, Release 2.0, will *flag* this statement for the following input language levels: OS/VS COBOL LANGLVL(1), and OS/VS COBOL LANGLVL(2). CLOSE . . . REEL/UNIT FOR REMOVAL statements are *flagged* because in COBOL for MVS & VM (or COBOL/370) the FOR REMOVAL option is treated as a comment.

CLOSE WITH DISP /CLOSE . . .WITH POSITIONING statements. CCCA, Release 2.0, will *remove* these statements for the following input language levels: OS/VS COBOL LANGLVL(1), and OS/VS COBOL LANGLVL(2). The WITH DISP option and the WITH POSITIONING option are *removed*.

COMMUNICATIONS SECTION. CCCA, Release 2.0, will *flag* COMMUNICATIONS SECTION for the following input language levels: OS/VS COBOL LANGLVL(1) and OS/VS COBOL LANGLVL(2). The Communications module is not supported by COBOL for MVS & VM (or COBOL/370), and there is nothing with which it can be replaced.

COM-REG special register. CCCA, Release 2.0, will *flag* COM-REG for the following input language level: DOS/VS COBOL. The COM-REG special register is not supported by COBOL for MVS & VM (or COBOL/370). You should *remove* all references to it from the program.

CONFIGURATION SECTION header. CCCA, Release 2.0, will *convert* and *flag* this header for the following input language levels: DOS/VS COBOL, OS/VS COBOL LANGLVL(1), and OS/VS COBOL LANGLVL(2).

The CONFIGURATION SECTION header is added, if it is missing and a SOURCE-COMPUTER, an OBJECT-COMPUTER, or a SPECIAL-NAMES paragraph is present. If the CONFIGURATION SECTION header is coded out of sequence, then you must attempt to put it in its correct place. If this cannot be done, then the CONFIGURATION SECTION header is *flagged*.

COPY . . . REPLACING statement. CCCA, Release 2.0, will *flag* this statement for the following input language levels: DOS/VS COBOL, OS/VS COBOL LANGLVL(1), and OS/VS COBOL LANGLVL(2).

If there are lowercase alphabetic characters in operands of the REPLACING phrase that are not in nonnumeric literals, the statement is *flagged*. Under the ANSI 68 and ANSI 74 standards, the REPLACING phrase is case sensitive. Under the ANSI 85 standard, lowercase characters are treated as their uppercase equivalent. You should check to see if this change will result in different text being copied into your program. If the operands of the REPLACING phrase contain a colon (":") character that is not in a nonnumeric literal, the statement is *flagged*. Under the ANSI 68 and ANSI 74 standards, the colon (":") is a non-COBOL character. Under the ANSI 85 standard, the colon character is treated as a separator. You should check to see if this change will result in different text being copied into your program.

If the operands of the REPLACING phrase contain an ANSI 85 standard non-COBOL character that is not in a nonnumeric literal, the statement is *flagged*. Under the ANSI 68 and ANSI 74 standards, non-COBOL characters are permitted in the REPLACING option. Under the ANSI 85 standard, non-COBOL characters in the REPLACING phrase are diagnosed. You should *remove* all non-COBOL characters from the REPLACING phrase and from the copybook.

COPY statement. CCCA, Release 2.0, will *convert* this statement for the following input language levels: DOS/VS COBOL and OS/VS COBOL LANGLVL(1). COPY statements with associated names are not supported by COBOL/370. The following example illustrates how all such statements are *converted*. The COPY member (MBR-A) before conversion looks like this:

```
01 RECORD1 COPY MBR-A.
01 RECORD-A.
    05 FIELD-A...
    05 FIELD-B...
```

The statement after conversion is as follows:

```
01 RECORD1        COPY MBR-A REPLACING    ==01 RECORD-A.== BY ==    ==.
```

CURRENCY SIGN. CCCA, Release 2.0, will *flag* this statement for the following input language levels: DOS/VS COBOL and OS/VS COBOL LANGLVL(1). COBOL/370 does not accept the / (slash) character or the = (equal) character in the CURRENCY SIGN clause.

CURRENT-DATE special register. CCCA, Release 2.0, will *convert* this statement for the following input language levels: DOS/VS COBOL and OS/VS COBOL LANGLVL(1). In OS/VS COBOL LANGLVL(2), the CURRENT-DATE register is not supported by the target languages.

Whenever CURRENT-DATE is referenced in the program, it is replaced by code that contains the date from the system and puts it in the format of the CURRENT-DATE register. The fields required for the reformatting are generated in the WORKING-STORAGE section. For CICS programs, the date is retrieved from the system using an EXEC CICS

ASKTIME statement. CICS, Release 1.7 or later, is required. For non-CICS programs, the ACCEPT . . . FROM DATE statement is used to obtain the date.

For DOS/VS COBOL, there are two different formats for the CURRENT-DATE register. You must specify the date format that is used at your installation in DATE FORMAT field on the Conversion Parameters Panel. If you specify the wrong one, CCCA, Release 2.0, will not *convert* this language element correctly.

DATA RECORDS clause. CCCA, Release 2.0, will *remove* this statement for the following input language levels: DOS/VS COBOL and OS/VS COBOL LANGLVL(1).

In OS/VS COBOL LANGLVL(2), if you specify Y for the Obsolete Element Removal option on the Optional Processing Panel, the DATA RECORDS clause is *removed* from the FD entry. The word RECORDS is added if missing when the clause is not *removed*.

DATE-COMPILED/DATE-WRITTEN headers. CCCA, Release 2.0, will *convert* this statement for the following input language levels: DOS/VS COBOL, OS/VS COBOL LANGLVL(1), and OS/VS COBOL LANGLVL(2). If the hyphen after DATE is missing, it is added.

DATE-COMPILED/DATE-WRITTEN paragraphs. CCCA, Release 2.0, will *convert* this statement for the following input language levels: DOS/VS COBOL, OS/VS COBOL LANGLVL(1), and OS/VS COBOL LANGLVL(2). If you specify Y for the Obsolete Element Removal option on the Optional Processing Panel, these paragraphs in the Identification Division are commented out.

DATE-COMPILED header. CCCA, Release 2.0, will *convert* this statement for the following input language levels: DOS/VS COBOL, OS/VS COBOL LANGLVL(1), and OS/VS COBOL LANGLVL(2). If you specify N for the Obsolete Element Removal option on the Optional Processing Panel and there is no period after the header, a period is added.

DEBUG card and packet. CCCA, Release 2.0, will *remove* this statement for the following input language levels: DOS/VS COBOL, OS/VS COBOL LANGLVL(1), and OS/VS COBOL LANGLVL(2). These are commented out.

DISABLE statement Communications feature. CCCA, Release 2.0, will *flag* this statement for the following input language levels: OS/VS

COBOL LANGLVL(1) and OS/VS COBOL LANGLVL(2). This is a Communications statement. The Communications module is not supported by the target languages, and there is nothing with which it can be replaced. CCCA, Release 2.0, will *flag* it.

DIVIDE . . . ON SIZE ERROR statement. CCCA, Release 2.0, will *flag* this statement for the following input language levels: DOS/VS COBOL, OS/VS COBOL LANGLVL(1), and OS/VS COBOL LANGLVL(2). DIVIDE . . . ON SIZE ERROR statements with multiple receiving fields are *flagged* because the ON SIZE ERROR phrase will not be executed for intermediate results under the ANSI 85 standard.

ENABLE statement Communications feature. CCCA, Release 2.0, will *flag* this statement for the following input language levels: OS/VS COBOL LANGLVL(1) and OS/VS COBOL LANGLVL(2). This is a Communications statement. The Communications module is not supported by the target languages, and there is nothing with which it can be replaced. CCCA, Release 2.0, will *flag* it.

ENTER statement. CCCA, Release 2.0, will *remove* this statement for the following input language levels: DOS/VS COBOL, OS/VS COBOL LANGLVL(1), and OS/VS COBOL LANGLVL(2). If you specify Y for the Obsolete Element Removal option on the Optional Processing Panel, the ENTER statement is *removed*.

ERROR declaratives. CCCA, Release 2.0, will *convert* ERROR declaratives for the following input language levels: DOS/VS COBOL, OS/VS COBOL LANGLVL(1), and OS/VS COBOL LANGLVL(2). An ERROR declarative SECTION is generated for each file that is to be *converted* to VSAM. The code in the SECTION includes a DISPLAY of the returned file status and a GOBACK.

ERROR declaratives GIVING option. CCCA, Release 2.0, will *remove* this option and provide you with information for the following input language levels: DOS/VS COBOL, OS/VS COBOL LANGLVL(1), and OS/VS COBOL LANGLVL(2). The GIVING option is *removed* from the program.

EXAMINE. CCCA, Release 2.0, will *convert* this statement for the following input language levels: DOS/VS COBOL, OS/VS COBOL LANGLVL(1), and OS/VS COBOL LANGLVL(2). The EXAMINE statement is changed to an INSPECT statement, and the statement MOVE ZERO TO TALLY is put in front of it.

EXHIBIT statement. CCCA, Release 2.0, will *convert* this statement for the following input language levels: DOS/VS COBOL, OS/VS COBOL LANGLVL(1), and OS/VS COBOL LANGLVL(2). The EXHIBIT statement is changed to a DISPLAY statement.

EXIT PROGRAM. CCCA, Release 2.0, will *convert* this statement for the following input language levels: DOS/VS COBOL, OS/VS COBOL LANGLVL(1), and OS/VS COBOL LANGLVL(2). Under the ANSI 85 standard, statement control cannot flow beyond the last line of a called subprogram. The compiler generates an implicit EXIT PROGRAM at the end of each program. Under the ANSI 68 and ANSI 74 standard control can flow beyond the last line of a called program. When this happens the program ABENDS.

The ANSI 68 and ANSI 74 standard behavior can be preserved under the ANSI 85 standard by adding, at the end of the program, a section with a call to an ABEND macro. If you specify *Y* for the Call "ILBOABN0" Statement Generation option on the Optional Processing Panel and if EXIT PROGRAM, STOP RUN, or GOBACK is not the last physical statement in the program, a section that includes a CALL to the ABEND macro ILBOABN0 will be inserted at the end of the program.

FILE-LIMIT/FILE-LIMITS clauses. CCCA, Release 2.0, will *remove* these clauses for the following input language levels: DOS/VS COBOL, OS/VS COBOL LANGLVL(1), and OS/VS COBOL LANGLVL(2). The clause is *removed* from the FILE-CONTROL paragraph.

FILE STATUS clause. CCCA, Release 2.0, will *convert* this clause for the following input language levels: DOS/VS COBOL, OS/VS COBOL LANGLVL(1), and OS/VS COBOL LANGLVL(2). A FILE STATUS clause,

```
FILE-STATUS IS LCP-FILE STATUS-nn
```

is added to the FILE-CONTROL paragraph for each file that is to be *converted* to VSAM. The status key data item LCP-FILE-STATUS-nn referred to in the clause is added to the WORKING-STORAGE section. nn is a sequence number.

FILE STATUS codes. CCCA, Release 2.0, will *flag* FILE STATUS codes for the following input language levels: DOS/VS COBOL, OS/VS COBOL LANGLVL(1), and OS/VS COBOL LANGLVL(2).

The file status codes returned under ANSI 85 standard COBOL are different from those returned under ANSI 68 and ANSI 74 standard COBOL. You should check all references to the file status key in the program and update the values of the file status codes where it is required.

FOR MULTIPLE REEL/UNIT clause. CCCA, Release 2.0, will *remove* this clause for the following input language levels: DOS/VS COBOL, OS/VS COBOL LANGLVL(1), and OS/VS COBOL LANGLVL(2). The clause is *removed* from the program.

GOBACK statement. CCCA, Release 2.0, will *convert* this statement for the following input language levels: DOS/VS COBOL, OS/VS COBOL LANGLVL(1), and OS/VS COBOL LANGLVL(2).

Under the ANSI 85 standard, control cannot flow beyond the last line of a called subprogram. The compiler generates an implicit EXIT PROGRAM at the end of each program. Under the ANSI 68 and ANSI 74 standard, control can flow beyond the last line of a called program. When this happens the program ABENDS. The ANSI 68 and ANSI 74 standard behavior can be preserved under the ANSI 85 standard by adding, at the end of the program, a section with a call to an ABEND macro. If you specify Y for the Call "ILBOABN0" Statement Generation option on the Optional Processing Panel and if EXIT PROGRAM, STOP RUN, or GOBACK is not the last physical statement in the program, a section that includes a CALL to the ABEND macro ILBOABN0 will be inserted at the end of the program.

GREATER THEN relational operator. CCCA, Release 2.0, will *convert* this statement for the following input language levels: DOS/VS COBOL, OS/VS COBOL LANGLVL(1), and OS/VS COBOL LANGLVL(2). THEN is changed to THAN.

IDMS. CCCA, Release 2.0, will *flag* this statement for the following input language levels: DOS/VS COBOL, OS/VS COBOL LANGLVL(1), and OS/VS COBOL LANGLVL(2). If your programs contain COPY IDMS statements, you should create a dummy copy member called IDMS. The copybook should just have a comment in it.

IF statement. CCCA, Release 2.0, will *convert* and *flag* this statement for the following language levels: DOS/VS COBOL, OS/VS COBOL LANGLVL(1), and OS/VS COBOL LANGLVL(2). Brackets immediately prior to relational operators are *removed*, but you should inspect the conversion. For example,

```
IF A (= B)
```

is *converted* to:

```
IF A = B
```

The target languages do not accept the following statements:

```
IF dataname ZEROS...
IF dataname ZEROES...
```

They are *converted* to:

```
IF dataname zero...
```

Indexes (qualified). CCCA, Release 2.0, will *flag* qualified indexes for the following input language levels: OS/VS COBOL LANGLVL(1) and OS/VS COBOL LANGLVL(2). CCCA, Release 2.0, will *flag* any reference to a qualified index because qualified indexes are no longer permitted in VS/COBOL for MVS & VM (or COBOL/370).

INSPECT statement. CCCA, Release 2.0, will *flag* this statement for the following input language levels: OS/VS COBOL LANGLVL(1) and OS/VS COBOL LANGLVL(2).

The statement is *flagged* if the PROGRAM COLLATING SEQUENCE established in the OBJECT COMPUTER paragraph identifies an alphabet that was defined with the ALSO clause to override the standard EBCDIC collating sequence. Under these circumstances, the statement will behave differently under the ANSI 85 standard. When coded, it affects the INSPECT, STRING, and UNSTRING statements. (It also affects nonnumeric keys in a MERGE or SORT when the COLLATING SEQUENCE is not specified in the SORT or MERGE statement.) The PROGRAM COLLATING SEQUENCE affects nonnumeric comparisons. In OS/VS COBOL, it affects both explicitly coded conditions and implicitly performed conditions (those comparisons that the compiler deems necessary to perform) in INSPECT, STRING, and UNSTRING statements. In VS COBOL II, the PROGRAM COLLATING SEQUENCE only affects explicitly coded conditions in these statements.

INSTALLATION paragraph. CCCA, Release 2.0, will *convert* the INSTALLATION paragraph for the following input language levels: DOS/VS COBOL, OS/VS COBOL LANGLVL(1), and OS/VS COBOL LANGLVL(2). If you specify Y for the Obsolete Element Removal option on the Optional Processing Panel, the INSTALLATION paragraph in the Identification Division is commented out.

ISAM files. CCCA, Release 2.0, will *convert* ISAM files for the following input language levels: DOS/VS COBOL, OS/VS COBOL LANGLVL(1), and OS/VS COBOL LANGLVL(2).

Programs using ISAM files should be *converted* to programs using Key Sequenced Data Set (KSDS) Virtual Storage Access Method (VSAM) files. This can be done by using the VSAM utility program IDCAMS. CCCA, Release 2.0, will *convert* the file definition and I/O statements for ISAM files. The COBOL for MVS & VM (or COBOL/370) does not support the processing of ISAM files.

JUSTIFIED RIGHT clause. CCCA, Release 2.0, will *convert* and *flag* a JUSTIFIED clause for the following language levels: DOS/VS COBOL, OS/VS COBOL LANGLVL(1), and OS/VS COBOL LANGLVL(2).

Under the ANSI 68 standard, if a JUSTIFIED clause is specified together with a VALUE clause for a data description entry, the initial data is right justified. Under the ANSI 85 standard, the initial data is not right justified. To preserve the ANSI 68 standard behavior of this language element, CCCA, Release 2.0, makes the following conversion. If the length of the nonnumeric literal in the VALUE clause is less than the length of the field as specified in the PICTURE clause, spaces are added to the front of the literal string until their lengths are equal. The clause will be *flagged*, instead of *converted*, if the literal has more than twenty-eight characters.

LABEL RECORDS clause. CCCA, Release 2.0, will *remove* a LABEL RECORDS clause for the following input language levels: DOS/VS COBOL, OS/VS COBOL LANGLVL(1), and OS/VS COBOL LANGLVL(2).

If you specify Y for the Obsolete Element Removal option on the Optional Processing Panel, this clause is *removed*. The word RECORDS is added, if missing, when the clause is not *removed*.

LABEL RECORDS ... TOTALING/TOTALED AREA option. CCCA, Release 2.0, will *remove* this option and provide you with information for the following input language levels: DOS/VS COBOL, OS/VS COBOL LANGLVL(1), and OS/VS COBOL LANGLVL(2). This option is *removed* from the program. The data name associated with this option is listed at the end of the diagnostic listing.

LESS THEN relational operator. CCCA, Release 2.0, will *convert* LESS THEN relational operators for the following input language levels: DOS/VS COBOL, OS/VS COBOL LANGLVL(1), and OS/VS COBOL LANGLVL(2). THEN is changed to THAN.

Literals—Nonnumeric. CCCA, Release 2.0, will *convert* or *flag* a nonnumeric literal for the following input language levels: DOS/VS COBOL, OS/VS COBOL LANGLVL(1), and OS/VS COBOL LANGLVL(2). If the continuation of a nonnumeric literal begins in Area A, it is shifted to the right until its whole length lies within Area B. If the continuation is too long to fit in Area B, it is *flagged*.

MEMORY SIZE clause. CCCA, Release 2.0, will *remove* a MEMORY SIZE clause for the following input language levels: DOS/VS COBOL, OS/VS COBOL LANGLVL(1), and OS/VS COBOL LANGLVL(2). If you specify Y for the Obsolete Element Removal option on the Optional Processing Panel, the MEMORY SIZE clause of the OBJECT-COMPUTER paragraph is *removed*.

MOVE ALL literal. CCCA, Release 2.0, will *flag* MOVE ALL literal TO numeric for the following input language levels: DOS/VS COBOL, OS/VS COBOL LANGLVL(1), and OS/VS COBOL LANGLVL(2). MOVE ALL literal TO numeric will be *flagged* with a warning.

MOVE CORR/CORRESPONDING statement. CCCA, Release 2.0, will *convert* this statement for the following input language levels: DOS/VS COBOL, OS/VS COBOL LANGLVL(1), and OS/VS COBOL LANGLVL(2). The target languages do not allow multiple receiving fields in the MOVE CORRESPONDING statement. If the statement has multiple receiving fields, it is replaced by separate MOVE CORRESPONDING statements for each of the receiving fields.

MOVE statement. CCCA, Release 2.0, will *remove* this statement for the following input language levels: DOS/VS COBOL, OS/VS COBOL LANGLVL(1), and OS/VS COBOL LANGLVL(2). Superfluous TOs are *removed*.

MULTIPLE FILE TAPE clause. CCCA, Release 2.0, will *remove* this clause for the following input language levels: DOS/VS COBOL, OS/VS COBOL LANGLVL(1), and OS/VS COBOL LANGLVL(2). If you specify Y for the Obsolete Element Removal option on the Optional Processing Panel, this clause is *removed* from the I-O-CONTROL paragraph.

MULTIPLY . . . ON SIZE ERROR statement. CCCA, Release 2.0, will *flag* this statement for the following input language levels: DOS/VS COBOL, OS/VS COBOL LANGLVL(1), and OS/VS COBOL LANGLVL(2).

MULTIPLY . . . ON SIZE ERROR statements with multiple receiving fields are *flagged* because the ON SIZE ERROR phrase will not be executed for intermediate results under the ANSI 85 standard. For OS/VS COBOL and VS COBOL II with CMPR2, the SIZE ERROR option for the DIVIDE and MULTIPLY statements applies to both intermediate and final results. If your OS/VS COBOL relies upon SIZE ERROR detection for intermediate results, it must change or be compiled with the CMPR2 compiler option (see Chapter 4, Section 4.2.1on behaviors for additional information on the compiler option). The statements

```
01     NUMERICS.
10     NUMERIC-1 PICTURE S9(16).
10 NUMERIC-2          PICTURE S9(16).
10 NUMERIC-3          PICTURE S9(16).
10 NUMERIC-4          PICTURE S9(16).
10 TEMP PICTURE S9(30).

   MULTIPLY NUMERIC-1 BY NUMERIC-2 GIVING NUMERIC-3 NUMERIC-4.
```

should behave like this:

```
   MULTIPLY NUMERIC-1 BY NUMERIC-2 GIVING TEMP
   MOVE TEMPORARY TO NUMERIC-3
   MOVE TEMPORARY TO NUMERIC-4
```

TEMP is the intermediate result. An intermediate result will have at most thirty digits.

In the preceding example, if NUMERIC-1 , NUMERIC-2 , NUMERIC-3, and NUMERIC-4 are all defined as PIC S9(16), NUMERIC-1 will be multiplied by NUMERIC-2 , yielding a thirty-two-digit result, which is moved to the thirty-digit intermediate result, TEMP. TEMP is then moved to NUMERIC-3 and NUMERIC-4. A size error may occur if the result exceeds the largest possible value of the result field, during a division by zero, or during an exponential expression.

NOMINAL KEY clause. CCCA, Release 2.0, will *convert* or *remove* this clause for the following input language levels: DOS/VS COBOL, OS/VS COBOL LANGLVL(1), and OS/VS COBOL LANGLVL(2). You should *convert* this file to Virtual Storage Access Method (VSAM) file.

If the new organization for the file is INDEXED, the NOMINAL KEY clause is *removed*. Before every I/O statement for these files, the following statement is added prior to the I/O statement:

```
MOVE nominal-key-name TO record-key-name
```

After the I/O statement, the statement

```
MOVE record-key-name TO nominal-key-name
```

is replaced by RELATIVE KEY if the new organization for the file is RELATIVE NOMINAL KEY.

NOT. CCCA, Release 2.0, will *convert* and *flag* this expression for the following input language levels: DOS/VS COBOL and OS/VS COBOL LANGLVL(1). NOT in an abbreviated combined relation will be changed into an unabbreviated relation condition. If more than one NOT is involved, the expression is *flagged*. You will have to update the expression manually.

NOTE statement. CCCA, Release 2.0, will *convert* this statement for the following input language levels: DOS/VS COBOL, OS/VS COBOL LANGLVL(1), and OS/VS COBOL LANGLVL(2).

It is *removed* from COBOL for MVS & VM (or COBOL/370). CCCA, Release 2.0, fully *converts* this statement by commenting it out. The NOTE statement is used to write comments in the source program. It is not supported by the target languages. CCCA, Release 2.0, fully *converts* this statement by commenting it out. If the NOTE sentence is the first sentence of a paragraph, an asterisk ("*") is placed in column 7 of each line in the paragraph. If the NOTE sentence is not the first sentence of the paragraph, an asterisk is placed in column 7 of all lines up to the first period. If other language elements not part of the NOTE statement are on the first or last line of the NOTE statement, the line is split in order to isolate the NOTE.

NSTD-REELS special register. CCCA, Release 2.0, will *flag* NSTD-REELS special register for the following input language level: DOS/VS COBOL. The NSTD-REELS special register is not supported in the target languages. You should *remove* all references to it from the program.

OCCURS clause. CCCA, Release 2.0, will *flag* this statement for the following input language levels: DOS/VS COBOL, OS/VS COBOL LANGLVL(1), and OS/VS COBOL LANGLVL(2).

OS/VS COBOL and DOS/VS COBOL allow a nonstandard order for phrases in the OCCURS clause. They allow the DEPENDING ON phrase inserted after or among the ASCENDING/DESCENDING phrases. They also allow the DEPENDING ON phrase after the INDEXED BY phrase. COBOL/370 only allows phrases in the standard order. OCCURS clauses with phrases in nonstandard order are *flagged*.

OCCURS DEPENDING ON clause (variable-length record). CCCA, Release 2.0, will *convert* this statement for the following input language levels: DOS/VS COBOL, OS/VS COBOL LANGLVL(1), and OS/VS COBOL LANGLVL(2).

COBOL statements that result in data transfer to a variable-length receiver that contains its own OCCURS DEPENDING ON (ODO) object behave differently under the ANSI 85 standard. Under the ANSI 68 and ANSI 74 standards, all ODO objects in sending and receiving fields must be set before the statement is executed. The actual lengths of the sender and receiver are calculated just before the execution of the data movement statement. Under the ANSI 85 standard, the maximum length of the variable-length group is used when it is a receiver in some circumstances, whereas the ANSI 68 and ANSI 74 standard always use the actual length. CCCA, Release 2.0, preserves the ANSI 68 and ANSI 74 behavior in the following way. For the following statements,

```
MOVE . . . TO identifier
READ . . . INTO identifier
RETURN . . . INTO identifier
UNSTRING . . . INTO identifier DELIMITER IN identifier
```

if the identifier is a variable-length data item that contains its own ODO object, then reference modification is added to it. For example,

```
MOVE . . . TO identifier
```

is changed to

```
MOVE . . . TO identifier (1:LENGTH OF identifier)
```

For the following statements,

```
RELEASE record-name FROM identifier
REWRITE record-name FROM identifier
WRITE record-name FROM identifier
```

if the identifier is a variable-length data item that contains its own ODO object, the FROM phrase is *removed* from the statement, and a MOVE statement with reference modification is added before the statement. For example,

```
WRITE record-name FROM identifier
```

is changed to

```
MOVE identifier TO record-n me (1:LENGTH OF record-name)
WRITE record-name
```

MOVE CORRESPONDING statements are *flagged* because reference modification is not allowed when the CORRESPONDING phrase is specified.

ON statement. CCCA, Release 2.0, will *convert* and *flag* this statement for the following language levels: DOS/VS COBOL, OS/VS COBOL LANGLVL(1), and OS/VS COBOL LANGLVL(2). It is *removed* from COBOL for MVS & VM (or COBOL/370). This statement will be *converted*. More complex ON statements are *flagged*. The ON statement is not supported by the target languages.

The statement,

```
ON integer
```

imperative statement
is *converted* to

```
ADD 1 TO LCP-ONCTR-nn IF LCP-ONCTR-nn = integer
```

imperative statement.

The statement

```
ON integer-1 until integer 2
```

imperative statement
is *converted* to:

```
ADD 1 TO LCP-ONCTR-nn
  IF LCP-ONCTR-nn > (integer 1 - 1) & < integer-2
```

imperative statement.

A data item with the data name LCP-ONCTR-nn (where nn is a sequence number) is added into the WORKING-STORAGE section with an initial value of zero. More complex ON statements are *flagged*.

OPEN . . . DISP/OPEN . . . LEAVE/OPEN . . . REREAD statements. CCCA, Release 2.0, will *convert* these statements for the following input language levels: OS/VS COBOL LANGLVL(1) and OS/VS COBOL

LANGLVL(2). CCCA, Release 2.0, will *remove* the DISP option, LEAVE option, and REREAD option.

OPEN . . . REVERSED statement. CCCA, Release 2.0, will *flag* this statement for the following input language levels: OS/VS COBOL LANGLVL(1) and OS/VS COBOL LANGLVL(2). You should check whether the file in the OPEN statement has multiple reels. If it does, you will have to make a change to the program because for the target languages this option is only valid for single-reel files. OS/VS COBOL handles single-reel files and, in an undocumented extension, multireel files.

ORGANIZATION clause. CCCA, Release 2.0, will *convert* this clause for the following input language levels: DOS/VS COBOL, OS/VS COBOL LANGLVL(1), and OS/VS COBOL LANGLVL(2). For VSAM files, this clause is *removed*.

OTHERWISE. CCCA, Release 2.0, will *convert* this statement for the following input language levels: DOS/VS COBOL, OS/VS COBOL LANGLVL(1), and OS/VS COBOL LANGLVL(2). OTHERWISE is replaced by ELSE.

PERFORM/ALTER. CCCA, Release 2.0, will *flag* this section for the following input language levels: DOS/VS COBOL, OS/VS COBOL LANGLVL(1), and OS/VS COBOL LANGLVL(2). The section is checked for a priority number less than 49 and for the presence of ALTER. If this is not the case, manual changes may be required if this independent section is performed from outside the section.

PERFORM . . . VARYING . . . AFTER statement. CCCA, Release 2.0, will *flag* this statement for the following input language levels: DOS/VS COBOL, OS/VS COBOL LANGLVL(1), and OS/VS COBOL LANGLVL(2). Under the ANSI 85 standard, the rules for augmenting variables have changed. If there are dependencies between variables of the statement, then the statement may behave differently. All PERFORM . . . VARYING . . . AFTER statements are *flagged*. You should check to see if there are any dependencies between the variables of the statement that will result in different behavior. If there are, you should modify the statement.

In OS/VS COBOL, in a PERFORM statement with the VARYING . . . AFTER phrase, two actions take place when an inner condition tests as TRUE:

- The identifier/index associated with the inner condition is set to its current FROM value.

- The identifier/index associated with the outer condition is augmented by its current BY value.

With such a PERFORM statement in COBOL/370 and COBOL for MVS & VM, the following takes place when an inner condition tests as TRUE:

- The identifier/index associated with the outer condition is augmented by its current BY value.
- The identifier/index associated with the inner condition is set to its current FROM value.

The following example illustrates the differences in execution:

```
PERFORM ABC VARYING X FROM 1 BY 1 UNTIL X > 3
    AFTER Y FROM X BY 1 UNTIL Y > 3
```

In OS/VS COBOL, ABC is executed eight times with the following values:

```
X: 1 1 1 2 2 2 3 3
Y: 1 2 3 1 2 3 2 3
```

In COBOL/370 and COBOL for MVS & VM, ABC is executed six times with the following values:

```
X: 1 1 1 2 2 3
Y: 1 2 3 2 3 3
```

Periods. CCCA, Release 2.0, will *convert* periods for the following input language levels: DOS/VS COBOL, OS/VS COBOL LANGLVL(1), and OS/VS COBOL LANGLVL(2). If there is no period immediately before or immediately after paragraph names or section headers in the PROCEDURE DIVISION, one is inserted.

PICTURE clause scaled integers. CCCA, Release 2.0, will *flag* PICTURE clause scaled integers and provide information for the following input language levels: DOS/VS COBOL, OS/VS COBOL LANGLVL(1).

Scaled integers (i.e., data items that have a *P* as the rightmost symbol in their PICTURE strings) are *flagged*. If the scaled integer is the sending field in a MOVE statement and the receiving field is alphanumeric- or numeric-edited, you will have to *convert* this. If the scaled integer is compared with an alphanumeric- or numeric-edited field, you will have to *convert* this statement. Scaled integers are *flagged*.

Picture P in RELATIVE KEY. CCCA, Release 2.0, will *flag* PICTURE P in RELATIVE KEY for the following input language levels: DOS/VS

COBOL, OS/VS COBOL LANGLVL(1), and OS/VS COBOL LANGLVL(2). This is *flagged*.

PROCESSING MODE clause. CCCA, Release 2.0, will *remove* this clause for the following input language levels: DOS/VS COBOL, OS/VS COBOL LANGLVL(1), and OS/VS COBOL LANGLVL(2). The PROCESSING MODE clause is *removed*.

PROGRAM-ID header. CCCA, Release 2.0, will *convert* the PROGRAM-ID header for the following input language levels: DOS/VS COBOL, OS/VS COBOL LANGLVL(1), and OS/VS COBOL LANGLVL(2). If the PROGRAM-ID header begins in Area B, it is moved to the left so it begins in Area A.

Program name. CCCA, Release 2.0, will *convert* the program name for the following input language levels: DOS/VS COBOL, OS/VS COBOL LANGLVL(1), and OS/VS COBOL LANGLVL(2).

COBOL/370 does not allow a data item to have a data name that is the same as the program name. If there is one in the program, the data name will be suffixed in the same way as data names that are reserved words. In the called subprogram, the name of the program and the argument name in the procedure statement cannot be the same.

READ statement ISAM files. CCCA, Release 2.0, will *convert* READ statement ISAM files for the following input language levels: DOS/VS COBOL, OS/VS COBOL LANGLVL(1), and OS/VS COBOL LANGLVL(2). For randomly accessed indexed (ISAM) files, the following statement is added prior to the READ statement:

```
MOVE nominal-key-name TO record-key-name
```

After the READ statement, the statement

```
MOVE record-key-name TO nominal-key-name
```

is added. You should *convert* the file to VSAM.

READY TRACE statement. CCCA, Release 2.0, will *remove* this statement for the following input language levels: DOS/VS COBOL, OS/VS COBOL LANGLVL(1), and OS/VS COBOL LANGLVL(2).

RECEIVE statement. CCCA, Release 2.0, will *flag* this statement for the following input language levels: OS/VS COBOL LANGLVL(1) and OS/VS COBOL LANGLVL(2). This is a Communications statement. The Communications module is not supported by the target languages, and there is nothing with which it can be replaced. CCCA, Release 2.0, will *flag* it.

RECORD CONTAINS. CCCA, Release 2.0, will *remove* this clause for the following input language levels: DOS/VS COBOL, OS/VS COBOL LANGLVL(1), and OS/VS COBOL LANGLVL(2). The clause is *removed* from the program, except for RECORD CONTAINS 0, which is left in place.

RECORDING MODE clause. CCCA, Release 2.0, will *remove* this clause for the following input language levels: DOS/VS COBOL, OS/VS COBOL LANGLVL(1), and OS/VS COBOL LANGLVL(2). The COBOL/370 compiler will ignore this clause if it is specified for a VSAM file. If the clause is in a file description entry for a VSAM file or a file that is to be *converted* to VSAM, it is *removed*.

REDEFINES clause in FD or SD entry. CCCA, Release 2.0, will *convert* a REDEFINES clause in FD or SD entry for the following input language levels: DOS/VS COBOL, OS/VS COBOL LANGLVL(1), and OS/VS COBOL LANGLVL(2). COBOL/370 does not permit REDEFINES clauses in FD or SD entries. Because they are superfluous, they are *removed*.

REMARKS paragraph. CCCA, Release 2.0, will *convert* a REMARKS paragraph for the following input language levels: DOS/VS COBOL, OS/VS COBOL LANGLVL(1), and OS/VS COBOL LANGLVL(2). It is *removed* from COBOL for MVS & VM (or COBOL/370). CCCA, Release 2.0, fully *converts* this statement by commenting it out with an asterisk (*") inserted in column 7 of the paragraph header and all succeeding lines of the paragraph.

REPORT WRITER statements. CCCA, Release 2.0, will *flag* these statements for the following input language levels: DOS/VS COBOL, OS/VS COBOL LANGLVL(1), and OS/VS COBOL LANGLVL(2). These statements are not supported by COBOL for MVS & VM (or COBOL/370):

- GENERATE
- INITIATE
- REPORT
- TERMINATE
- USE BEFORE REPORTING

If you specify Y for the Report Writer Statement *Flagging* option on the Optional Processing Panel, they will be *flagged*.

RESERVE ALTERNATE AREAS. CCCA, Release 2.0, will *convert* RESERVE ALTERNATE AREAS for the following input language levels: DOS/VS COBOL, OS/VS COBOL LANGLVL(1), and OS/VS COBOL LANGLVL(2). The following changes are performed: from RESERVE NO/n ALTERNATE AREA/AREAS to RESERVE 1/n + 1 AREA/AREAS.

RESERVE AREA/AREAS. CCCA, Release 2.0, will *convert* RESERVE AREAS/AREAS for the following input language levels: DOS/VS COBOL, OS/VS COBOL LANGLVL(1), and OS/VS COBOL LANGLVL(2). The following changes are performed: from ANSI 68 RESERVE n AREA to ANSI 74 RESERVE n+1 AREA/AREAS.

Reserved words. CCCA, Release 2.0, will *convert* reserved words for the following input language levels: DOS/VS COBOL, OS/VS COBOL LANGLVL(1), and OS/VS COBOL LANGLVL(2). A suffix is appended to all user-defined words that are reserved words in the target language. You specify the suffix that you want appended in the RESERVED word suffix field of the Conversion Parameters Panel. The number 74 is the default suffix.

RESET TRACE statement. CCCA, Release 2.0, will *remove* this statement for the following input language levels: DOS/VS COBOL, OS/VS COBOL LANGLVL(1), and OS/VS COBOL LANGLVL(2).

REWRITE statement ISAM files. CCCA, Release 2.0, will *convert* REWRITE statement ISAM files for the following input language levels: DOS/VS COBOL, OS/VS COBOL LANGLVL(1), and OS/VS COBOL LANGLVL(2). For randomly accessed indexed (ISAM) files, the following statement is added prior to the REWRITE statement:

```
MOVE nominal-key-name TO record-key-name
```

After the REWRITE statement, the statement

```
MOVE record-key-name TO nominal-key-name
```

is added. You should *convert* the file to VSAM.

SEARCH ALL. CCCA, Release 2.0, will *flag* this statement for the following input language levels: DOS/VS COBOL and OS/VS COBOL LANGLVL(1).

SAME AREA clause. CCCA, Release 2.0, will *convert* this clause for the following input language levels: DOS/VS COBOL, OS/VS COBOL LANGLVL(1), and OS/VS COBOL LANGLVL(2). SAME AREA is changed to SAME RECORD AREA.

SEARCH... WHEN. CCCA, Release 2.0, will *convert* this statement for the following input language levels: DOS/VS COBOL, OS/VS COBOL LANGLVL(1), and OS/VS COBOL LANGLVL(2).

In DOS/VS COBOL and OS/VS COBOL, the ASCENDING/DESCENDING KEY data item may be specified as either the subject or the object of the WHEN relation condition. In the target languages, it must be specified as the subject. If the key is not the subject, the condition is reversed, so that the subject becomes the object. NEXT SENTENCE is added if no statement is found.

SECURITY paragraph. CCCA, Release 2.0, will *convert* the SECURITY paragraph for the following input language levels: DOS/VS COBOL, OS/VS COBOL LANGLVL(1), and OS/VS COBOL LANGLVL(2). If you specify *Y* for the Obsolete Element Removal option on the Optional Processing Panel, the SECURITY paragraph in the Identification Division is commented out.

SEEK. CCCA, Release 2.0, will *remove* this statement for the following input language levels: DOS/VS COBOL, OS/VS COBOL LANGLVL(1), and OS/VS COBOL LANGLVL(2). CCCA, Release 2.0, *removes* this statement from the program because this is a BDAM file-handling statement. Programs using BDAM files should be *converted* to programs using RRDS VSAM files. This can be done by using the VSAM utility program IDCAMS.

SELECT OPTIONAL. CCCA, Release 2.0, will *remove* this phrase for the following input language levels: DOS/VS COBOL, OS/VS COBOL LANGLVL(1), and OS/VS COBOL LANGLVL(2). The OPTIONAL phrase is *removed* from the program.

SEND statement. CCCA, Release 2.0, will *flag* this statement for the following input language levels: OS/VS COBOL LANGLVL(1) and OS/VS COBOL LANGLVL(2). CCCA, Release 2.0, will *flag* it because this is a Communications statement. The Communications module is not supported by the target languages, and there is nothing with which it can be replaced.

Signed VALUE. CCCA, Release 2.0, will *convert* a signed VALUE for the following input language levels: DOS/VS COBOL, OS/VS COBOL LANGLVL(1), and OS/VS COBOL LANGLVL(2). The sign is *removed* from the value if PIC is unsigned.

SORT-OPTION clause. CCCA, Release 2.0, will *remove* this clause for the following input language level: DOS/VS COBOL. The clause is *removed* from the SD entry.

START . . . USING KEY statement. CCCA, Release 2.0, will *convert* this statement for the following input language levels: DOS/VS COBOL, OS/VS COBOL LANGLVL(1), and OS/VS COBOL LANGLVL(2). The USING KEY clause of the START statement is not supported by the target languages. START statements that specify this clause are *converted* to START . . . KEY statements.

STOP RUN statement. CCCA, Release 2.0, will *convert* this statement for the following input language levels: DOS/VS COBOL, OS/VS COBOL LANGLVL(1), and OS/VS COBOL LANGLVL(2).

Under the ANSI 85 standard, control cannot flow beyond the last line of a called subprogram. The compiler generates an implicit EXIT PROGRAM at the end of each program. Under the ANSI 68 and ANSI 74 standards, control can flow beyond the last line of a called program. When this happens, the program ABENDS. The ANSI 68 and ANSI 74 standard behavior can be preserved under the ANSI 85 standard by adding, at the end of the program, a section with a call to an ABEND macro. If you specify Y for the Call "ILBOABN0" Statement Generation option on the Optional Processing Panel and if EXIT PROGRAM, STOP RUN, or GOBACK is not the last physical statement in the program, a section that includes a CALL to the ABEND macro ILBOABN0 will be inserted at the end of the program.

STRING statement. CCCA, Release 2.0, will *flag* this statement for the following input language levels: OS/VS COBOL LANGLVL(1) and OS/VS COBOL LANGLVL(2). The statement is *flagged* if it has a receiving field with a PICTURE string that consist of A's and B's only. The ANSI 74 standard classes these fields as alphabetic, while the ANSI 85 standard classes them as alphanumeric-edited. You will have to make a change to the program because alphanumeric-edited receiving fields in the STRING statement are not permitted.

The statement is *flagged* if the PROGRAM COLLATING SEQUENCE established in the OBJECT COMPUTER paragraph identifies an alphabet that was defined with the ALSO clause. Under these circumstances, the statement will behave differently under the ANSI 85 standard.

The following string statements,

```
STRING identifier-1 DELIMITED BY identifier-2
INTO identifier-3 WITH POINTER identifier-4 . . .
```

are *flagged* where identifier-1 or identifier-2 is the same as identifier-3 or identifier-4 or where identifier-3 is the same as identifier-4.

> THAN relational operator. CCCA, Release 2.0, will *convert* this relational operator for the following input language levels: DOS/VS COBOL, OS/VS COBOL LANGLVL(1), and OS/VS COBOL LANGLVL(2). THAN is *removed*.

< THAN relational operator. CCCA, Release 2.0, will *convert* this relational operator for the following input language levels: DOS/VS COBOL, OS/VS COBOL LANGLVL(1), and OS/VS COBOL LANGLVL(2). THAN is *removed*.

> THEN relational operator. CCCA, Release 2.0, will *convert* this relational operator for the following input language levels: DOS/VS COBOL, OS/VS COBOL LANGLVL(1), and OS/VS COBOL LANGLVL(2). THEN is *removed*.

< THEN relational operator. CCCA, Release 2.0, will *convert* this relational operator for the following input language levels: DOS/VS COBOL, OS/VS COBOL LANGLVL(1), and OS/VS COBOL LANGLVL(2). THEN relational operator is *removed*.

THEN. CCCA, Release 2.0, will *remove* this statement for the following input language levels: DOS/VS COBOL, OS/VS COBOL LANGLVL(1), and OS/VS COBOL LANGLVL(2). THEN used between statements is *removed*.

TIME-OF-DAY special register. CCCA, Release 2.0, will *convert* this special register for the following input language levels: DOS/VS COBOL, OS/VS COBOL LANGLVL(1), and OS/VS COBOL LANGLVL(2). Whenever TIME-OF-DAY is referenced in the program, it is replaced by code that contains the date from the system and puts it in the format of the TIME-OF-DAY register.

The TIME-OF-DAY register is not supported by the target languages. The fields required for the reformatting are generated in the WORKING-STORAGE section. For CICS programs, the time is retrieved from the system using an EXEC CICS ASKTIME statement. CICS, Release 1.7

or later, is required. For non-CICS programs, the ACCEPT . . . FROM TIME statement is used to obtain the time.

=TO relational operator. CCCA, Release 2.0, will *convert* this relational operator for the following input language levels: DOS/VS COBOL, OS/VS COBOL LANGLVL(1), and OS/VS COBOL LANGLVL(2). TO is *removed*.

TOTALING/TOTALED AREA. CCCA, Release 2.0, will *remove* this option and provide information for the following input language levels: OS/VS COBOL LANGLVL(1), and OS/VS COBOL LANGLVL(2). This option is *removed* from the program. The data name associated with this option is listed at the end of the diagnostic listing.

TRACK-AREA. CCCA, Release 2.0, will *remove* this clause for the following input language levels: DOS/VS COBOL, OS/VS COBOL LANGLVL(1), and OS/VS COBOL LANGLVL(2). The clause is *removed* from the program by CCCA, Release 2.0.

TRACK-LIMIT clause. CCCA, Release 2.0, will *remove* this clause for the following input language levels: OS/VS COBOL LANGLVL(1) and OS/VS COBOL LANGLVL(2). The clause is *removed* from the program by CCCA, Release 2.0.

TRANSFORM statement. CCCA, Release 2.0, will *convert* this statement for the following input language levels: DOS/VS COBOL, OS/VS COBOL LANGLVL(1), and OS/VS COBOL LANGLVL(2). CCCA, Release 2.0, changes TRANSFORM to INSPECT.

UNSTRING statement. CCCA, Release 2.0, will *flag* this statement for the following input language level: OS/VS COBOL LANGLVL(1). The UNSTRING statement is *flagged* if an ALL is specified in the DELIMITED BY phrase.

CCCA, Release 2.0, will *convert* this statement for the following input language level: OS/VS COBOL LANGLVL(2). Insert the word OR between identifiers in the DELIMITED BY PHRASE if it is missing. CCCA, Release 2.0, will *convert* this statement for the following input language level: OS/VS COBOL LANGLVL(2). *Remove* the word IS if it appears in the POINTER phrase.

CCCA, Release 2.0, will *flag* this statement for the following input language levels: OS/VS COBOL LANGLVL(1) and OS/VS COBOL LANGLVL(2). The statement is *flagged* if the PROGRAM COLLATING

SEQUENCE established in the OBJECT COMPUTER paragraph identifies an alphabet that was defined with the ALSO clause. Under these circumstances, the statement will behave differently under the ANSI 85 standard.

UPSI name. CCCA, Release 2.0, will *convert* and *flag* this statement for the following language levels: DOS/VS COBOL, OS/VS COBOL LANGLVL(1), and OS/VS COBOL LANGLVL(2). Condition names are added. UPSI-n is replaced by condition name, for example,

```
LCP-ON-UPSI-n
```

and

```
LCP-OFF-UPSI-n
```

where n is a number from 0 to 7.

USE AFTER STANDARD ... ON ... GIVING. CCCA, Release 2.0, will *remove* this statement and provide information for the following input language levels: DOS/VS COBOL, OS/VS COBOL LANGLVL(1), and OS/VS COBOL LANGLVL(2). The GIVING option is *removed* from the program. A list of GIVING affected data names is printed in the conversion listing.

USE BEFORE STANDARD. CCCA, Release 2.0, will *remove* this statement for the following input language levels: DOS/VS COBOL, OS/VS COBOL LANGLVL(1), and OS/VS COBOL LANGLVL(2). USE BEFORE STANDARD is *removed* from the program.

USE FOR DEBUGGING. CCCA, Release 2.0, will *flag* this statement for the following input language levels: DOS/VS COBOL, OS/VS COBOL LANGLVL(1), and OS/VS COBOL LANGLVL(2). If an identifier following DEBUGGING is a file name, then the statement is *flagged*. If an identifier following DEBUGGING is not a procedure name and the Procedure Name Checking option on the Optional Processing Panel is set to Y, then the statement is *flagged*.

VALUE in 88 level. CCCA, Release 2.0, will *convert* a VALUE in 88 level for the following input language levels: DOS/VS COBOL, OS/VS COBOL LANGLVL(1), and OS/VS COBOL LANGLVL(2). If the value of a level 88 refers to a variable defined with a PICTURE X and the value is not enclosed between quotation marks or apostrophes, quotation marks or apostrophes will be added.

VALUES. CCCA, Release 2.0, will *convert* this statement for the following input language levels: DOS/VS COBOL, OS/VS COBOL LAN-

GLVL(1), and OS/VS COBOL LANGLVL(2). If not used in 88 level, VALUES is changed to VALUE.

VALUE OF clause. CCCA, Release 2.0, will *remove* a VALUE OF clause for the following input language levels: DOS/VS COBOL, OS/VS COBOL LANGLVL(1), and OS/VS COBOL LANGLVL(2). If you specify Y for the Obsolete Element Removal option on the Optional Processing Panel, the VALUE OF clause is *removed* from the FD entry.

WHEN-COMPILED. CCCA, Release 2.0, will *convert* this statement for the following input language levels: DOS/VS COBOL, OS/VS COBOL LANGLVL(1), and OS/VS COBOL LANGLVL(2).

Both COBOL/370 and OS/VS COBOL support the use of the WHEN-COMPILED special register. The rules for using the special register are the same for both compilers. However, the format of the data differs, as shown in Table 6.1.

Wherever WHEN-COMPILED is referenced in the program, code is inserted that changes the data from the register to the old format. The fields required for the reformatting are generated in the WORKING-STORAGE section.

WRITE . . . AFTER POSITIONING n. CCCA, Release 2.0, will *convert* this statement for the following input language levels: DOS/VS COBOL, OS/VS COBOL LANGLVL(1), and OS/VS COBOL LANGLVL(2).

If n is a literal, this is changed to WRITE . . . AFTER lines ADVANCING n LINES. If n is an identifier, SPECIAL-NAMES are generated and a section is added at the end of the program. Note: When compiling the *converted* program with the COBOL for MVS & VM (or COBOL/370) compiler, use the NOADV option. If POSITIONING and ADVANCING are used in the old program, you should review the ADV option.

OS/VS COBOL supports the WRITE statement with the AFTER POSITIONING phrase. COBOL for MVS & VM and COBOL/370 do not. In

Table 6.1 Format of Data: Differences for WHEN-COMPILED

IN OS/VS COBOL, THE FORMAT IS:	IN COBOL FOR MVS & VM (OR COBOL/370), THE FORMAT IS:
hh.mm.ssMMM DD, YYYY	MM/DD/YYhh.mm.ss
(hour.minute.secondMONTH DAY, YEAR)	(MONTH/DAY/YEARhour.minute.second

COBOL for MVS & VM and COBOL/370, you can use the WRITE . . . AFTER ADVANCING statement to receive behavior similar to WRITE . . . AFTER POSITIONING. The following two examples show OS/VS COBOL POSITIONING phrases and the equivalent COBOL for MVS & VM (or COBOL/370) phrases. When using WRITE . . . AFTER ADVANCING with *literals*:

COBOL for MVS & VM

OS/VS COBOL

COBOL/370

```
AFTER POSITIONING 0    AFTER ADVANCING PAGE
AFTER POSITIONING 1    AFTER ADVANCING 1 LINE
AFTER POSITIONING 2    AFTER ADVANCING 2 LINES
AFTER POSITIONING 3    AFTER ADVANCING 3 LINES
```

When using WRITE . . . AFTER ADVANCING with *nonliterals*:

```
WRITE OUTPUT-REC AFTER POSITIONING SKIP-CC.
SKIP-CC
AFTER POSITIONING SKIP-CC 1    AFTER ADVANCING PAGE
AFTER POSITIONING SKIP-CC ' '  AFTER ADVANCING 1 LINE
AFTER POSITIONING SKIP-CC 0    AFTER ADVANCING 2 LINES
AFTER POSITIONING SKIP-CC -    AFTER ADVANCING 3 LINES
```

NOTE: With COBOL for MVS & VM and COBOL/370, channel skipping is only supported with references to SPECIAL-NAMES.

CCCA can automatically *convert* WRITE . . . AFTER POSITIONING statements. For example, given the following statement,

```
WRITE OUTPUT-REC AFTER POSITIONING n.
```

if n is a literal, CCCA would change this to WRITE . . . AFTER ADVANCING n LINES. If n is an identifier, SPECIAL-NAMES are generated and a section is added at the end of the program.

WRITE . . . BEFORE/AFTER ADVANCING mnemonic-name LINE/LINES. CCCA, Release 2.0, will *convert* these for the following input language levels: DOS/VS COBOL, OS/VS COBOL LANGLVL(1), and OS/VS COBOL LANGLVL(2). They are *removed*.

WRITE statement ISAM files. CCCA, Release 2.0, will *convert* this statement for the following input language levels: DOS/VS COBOL, OS/VS COBOL LANGLVL(1), and OS/VS COBOL LANGLVL(2). For randomly accessed indexed (ISAM) files, the following statement is added prior to the WRITE statement:

```
MOVE nominal-key-name TO record-key-name
```

After the WRITE statement, the statement

```
MOVE record-key-name TO nominal-key-name
```

is added. You should *convert* the file to VSAM.

6.3 CCCA Conversions

The following sidebars describe problems we experienced during CCCA conversions and the resolutions we arrived at for those problems.

Copybook Issue

Problem:
The description of the *problem* for this case is as follows: OS/VS COBOL allows COPY statements with associated names; COBOL/370 does not. For example, with the following copy member (PROGM1JN),

```
000100*01 JOB-PROGSTEP-PROCSTEP.
000200 05 JOB-JOB-ID PIC X(8).
000210 05 JOB-PROGRAM-STEP PIC X(8).
000220 05 JOB-PROC-STEP PIC X(8).
```

The *problem* is that the following coding technique is valid in OS/VS COBOL but not valid in COBOL/370:

```
01 JOB-PROGSTEP-PROCSTEP
 COPY PROGM1JN.
```

Sample Text:
```
IBM COBOL 370 Release 4.0 09/15/92
    011800         05   TCR-8-80          PIC X(73).
    011900 01 FILLER REDEFINES TEMP-CHANGE-REC.
    012000         03   TCR-1-72          PIC X(72).
    012100         03   TCR-73-80         PIC X(8).
    012200 01 FILLER REDEFINES TEMP-CHANGE-REC.
    012300         03   TCR-SEQ           PIC X(6).
    012400         03   TCR-SEQ-N REDEFINES TCR-SEQ PIC 9(6).
```

continues

Copybook Issue (Continued)

```
       012500     03  FILLER             PIC X(74).
012600 01 JOB-PROGSTEP-PROCSTEP
COPY PROGM1JN.
   000100*01  JOB-PROGSTEP-PROCSTEP.
   000200     05  JOB-JOB-ID             PIC X(8).
IGYDS1082-E A period was required. A period was assumed before "05".
   000300     05  JOB-PROGRAM-STEP       PIC X(8).
   000400     05  JOB-PROC-STEP          PIC X(8).
```

Sample Text Resolution:

The description of the resolution for this problem is as follows: The program was manually revised by inserting a period (".") before the COPY statement for COBOL/370 compiler as follows:

```
01   JOB-PROGSTEP-PROCSTEP.
                                         COPY PROGM1JN.
```

The majority of COPY problems we experienced during this conversion were this type of COPY statement. According to IBM, however, a number of the problems we had shouldn't have occurred in the old version. IBM suspected we had converted the source code as LANGLVL(2) rather than LANGLVL(1) OS/VS COBOL. There is a major difference in the way COPY statements are processed and converted by CCCA, Release 2.0, depending on the LANGLVL. This didn't seem to solve our problem, however. What we have seen, however, is that the newer release of CCCA (2.1) automatically accounts for this problem.

Copybook Resolution

```
IBM COBOL 370 Release 4.0 09/15/92
   011800        05  TCR-8-80              PIC X(73).
   011900  01  FILLER REDEFINES TEMP-CHANGE-REC.
   012000     03  TCR-1-72              PIC X(72).
   012100     03  TCR-73-80             PIC X(8).
   012200  01  FILLER REDEFINES TEMP-CHANGE-REC.
   012300     03  TCR-SEQ               PIC X(6).
   012400     03  TCR-SEQ-N REDEFINES TCR-SEQ PIC 9(6).
   012500     03  FILLER                PIC X(74).
012700 01 JOB-PROGSTEP-PROCSTEP.
COPY PROGM1JN.
   000100*01  JOB-PROGSTEP-PROCSTEP.
   000200     05  JOB-JOB-ID            PIC X(8).
   000300     05  JOB-PROGRAM-STEP      PIC X(8).
   000400     05  JOB-PROC-STEP         PIC X(8).
```

Upgrading OS/VS COBOL to VS COBOL/370 Using CCCA

Relational Operator Issue

Problem:
The description of the *problem* for this case is as follows: Within the scope of an abbreviated combined relation condition, COBOL/370 does not support relational operators inside parentheses.

Sample Text:
```
     090300        PERFORM 9120-GU-SEQ0EHI1-IMPLODE THRU
008
     090400                9120-EXIT.
009
     090500        PERFORM 9130-GNP-SEQ0EHI1-IMPLODE THRU
009
     090600                9130-EXIT.
009
     090700        PERFORM 4500-CHECK-PARENT-LEVELS THRU
009
     090800                4500-EXIT
009
     090900        UNTIL DB4-STATUS NOT (EQUAL '  ' OR 'GA').
009

IGYPS2093-S "(" was found in a conditional expression.  The "PERFORM" statement
            discarded.

     091000
009
     091100
273700         IF (MI0ASS1-STATUS-CODE NOT    EQUAL '0' AND NOT '1')
02721*2

273800            MOVE 'CANNOT DELETE'
02722*1
273900              TO MO-A030-LINE-MESSAGE (SCREEN-SUB)
02723*1
274000            MOVE 'Y' TO UPDATE-ERRORS-FOUND-SW
02724*1
274100            GO TO 3131-END-DLT-LEVEL01-SUB.
02725*1
274200
02726*1
274300         PERFORM 9161-DLET-MI0ASS1 THRU 9161-END-DLT-MI0ASS1.
02727*2
      5785-ABJ R2.0   - IBM    COBOL CONVERSION AID -
```

continues

Relational Operator Issue *(Continued)*

```
SEQNBR-A 1 B.. ... 2 ... ...    COBOL SOURCE STATEMENTS    ... 6 ... ... 7
.IDENTFC

274400        IF   DB-STATUS IS NOT EQUAL TO SPACES
02728*1
274500             PERFORM 3800-MOVE-MI-TO-MO
02729*1
274600                THRU 3800-END-MOVE-MI-TO-MO
02730*1
274700             MOVE 'DLET FAILED' TO WS-EDIT-MESSAGE
02731*1
274800             MOVE DB-STATUS TO WS-EDIT-STATUS
02732*1
274900             MOVE WS-15-CHARACTER-MESSAGE
02733*1
275000                TO MO-A030-LINE-MESSAGE (SCREEN-SUB)
02734*1
275100             MOVE 'Y' TO UPDATE-ERRORS-FOUND-SW
02735*1
275200        ELSE
02736*1
D NOT '1')           02721*23 271900   ABJ6225 08 BRACKETS MOVED
                                               *MANUAL UPDATE MAY BE
REQUIRED
                     02722*11 272000
                     02723*11 272100
                     02724*11 272200
                     02725*11 272300
                     02726*11 272400
ET-MI0ASS1.          02727*23 272500

  ... 6 ... ... 7 .IDENTFCN OLD/SQ S  MSGID SEV --- D I A G N O S T I C
S ---

                     02728*11 272600
                     02729*11 272700
                     02730*11 272800
                     02731*11 272900
                     02732*11 273000
                     02733*11 273100
                     02734*11 273200
                     02735*11 273300
                     02736*11 273400
```

Resolution:

In COBOL/370, this statement was modified by removing the relational operator from the parentheses as shown in sample text above. The response from IBM

Upgrading OS/VS COBOL to VS COBOL/370 Using CCCA

is that this is a bug with CCCA, Release 2.0, and one IBM has tried to resolve in the past. CCCA, Release 2.0, gets confused when trying to determine where to move the parentheses. CCCA, Release 2.1, has resolved this issue.

Sample Text:
```
090300         PERFORM 9120-GU-SEQ0EHI1-IMPLODE THRU
090400                 9120-EXIT.
090500         PERFORM 9130-GNP-SEQ0EHI1-IMPLODE THRU
090600                 9130-EXIT.
090700         PERFORM 4500-CHECK-PARENT-LEVELS THRU
090800                 4500-EXIT
090900 UNTIL DB4-STATUS NOT EQUAL (' ' OR 'GA').
091000
091100
091200         IF LINK-IS-VALID
091300             MOVE MI-ASSEM-NUMBER-2 (SCREEN-SUB)
091400               TO SSA-SEQ0EHE1-EQUIPMENT-NUMBER
091500             PERFORM 9140-GU-SEQ0EHE1-EXPLODE THRU
009
004577         273500      IF  MI0ASS1-STATUS-CODE NOT  EQUAL ('0' OR '1'
)
004578       1 273600          MOVE 'CANNOT DELETE'
004579       1 273700            TO MO-A030-LINE-MESSAGE (SCREEN-SUB)
004580       1 273800          MOVE 'Y' TO UPDATE-ERRORS-FOUND-SW
004581       1 273900          GO TO 3131-END-DLT-LEVEL01-SUB.
004582         274000
004583         274100      PERFORM 9161-DLET-MI0ASS1 THRU 9161-END-DLET-
MI0ASS1
004584         274200      IF  DB-STATUS IS NOT EQUAL TO SPACES
```

Reserved Word Issue

Problem:

This *problem* is related to a RESERVED WORD in the Comment area. "REMARK" is a COBOL 1985 standard reserved word for a feature not supported by COBOL/370 compiler. If used in a program, it is recognized as a reserved word and flagged with a severe message. The COBOL/370 compiler treats REMARK as a reserved word even in the comment area:

```
    IBM COBOL/370 Release 4.0 09/15/92
      057100*             THERE IS NO COMMENT LINE 2 ON THE INQUIRY.
005
```

continues

Reserved Word Issue (Continued)

```
      057200
005
      057300*    DATE - 11/02/87 TIME - 17.33
005
      057400*    CORRECTED STANDARD VIOLATIONS.  SEVERAL STATEMENTS IN THE   005
      057500*    REMARKS DIDN                                                005
      057600                 'T START IN COL. 12.                            005

IGYDS1089-S "'T START IN COL. 12.                              '" was invalid.
            Scanning was resumed at the next area "A" item, level-num-
ber, or the start of the next clause.


      057700*    DATE - 05/28/88 TIME - 02.06                                005
      057800*    FIX FIRST INQUIRY ON LABOR PLANNING SCREEN WHEN COMING FROM 005
      057900*    THE WORK CONTROL LONG FORM. WAS NOT ALWAYS STARTING WITH THE005
      058000*    FIRST PLANNING SEGMENT.                                     005
      058100*    DATE - 08/03/88 TIME - 17.32                                005
      058200*    FIX PROBLEMS WITH RESCHEDULE PLANNER WR LIST FUNCTION AND   005
      058300*    PLANNERS WITH NO ASSIGNED WRS BEING TREATED AS INVALID.     005
```

Resolution:
In the COBOL/370, this statement was modified as
* REMARKS (Insert "*" on column 7 before "REMARKS")

```
IBM COBOL/370 Release 4.0 09/15/92
      057100*              THERE IS NO COMMENT LINE 2 ON THE INQUIRY.
      057200
      057300*    DATE - 11/02/87 TIME - 17.33                                9992
      057400*    CORRECTED STANDARD VIOLATIONS.  SEVERAL STATEMENTS IN THE
      057500*****  CHANGED DURING COBOL CONVERSION. *********************
      057600*    REMARKS DIDN'T START IN COL. 12.
```

```
          057700***** CHANGED DURING COBOL CONVERSION. ********************
          057800*    DATE - 05/28/88 TIME - 02.06
          057900*    FIX FIRST INQUIRY ON LABOR PLANNING SCREEN WHEN COMING
 FROM
          058000*    THE WORK CONTROL LONG FORM. WAS NOT ALWAYS STARTING
 WITH THE
          058100*    FIRST PLANNING SEGMENT.
          058200*    DATE - 08/03/88 TIME - 17.32
          058300*    FIX PROBLEMS WITH RESCHEDULE PLANNER WR LIST FUNCTION
 AND
          058400*    PLANNERS WITH NO ASSIGNED WRS BEING TREATED AS INVALID.
          058500 ENVIRONMENT DIVISION.
          058600 DATA DIVISION.
```

PERFORM . . . VARYING Issue

Problem:

The *problem* is that the processing of a PERFORM . . . VARYING . . . AFTER statement in COBOL/370 may differ from OS/VS COBOL depending on usage. The rules for PERFORM . . . VARYING have changed from OS/VS COBOL to COBOL/370. In a PERFORM statement with the VARYING . . . AFTER phrase in OS/VS COBOL, two actions take place when an inner condition tests as TRUE:

The identifier/index associated with the inner condition is set to its current FROM value.

The identifier/index associated with the outer condition is augmented by its current BY value.

With such a PERFORM statement in COBOL/370 and COBOL for MVS & VM, the following takes place when an inner condition tests as TRUE:

The identifier/index associated with the outer condition is augmented by its current BY value.

The identifier/index associated with the inner condition is set to its current FROM value.

The following example illustrates the differences in execution:

```
PERFORM ABC VARYING X FROM 1 BY 1 UNTIL X > 3
  AFTER Y FROM X BY 1 UNTIL Y > 3
```

In OS/VS COBOL, ABC is executed eight times with the following values:

```
X: 1 1 1 2 2 2 3 3
Y: 1 2 3 1 2 3 2 3
```

continues

PERFORM . . . VARYING Issue   (Continued)

In COBOL/370 and COBOL for MVS & VM, ABC is executed six times with the following values:

```
X: 1 1 1 2 2 3
Y: 1 2 3 2 3 3
```

Sample Text:

```
054900      PERFORM 1200-LOAD-TABLE              THRU 1200-EXIT      00548
055000          VARYING FIRST-SUB   FROM 1 BY 1                      00549
055100          UNTIL FIRST-SUB IS GREATER THAN 6                    00550
055200          AFTER SEC-SUB FROM 1 BY 1                            00551
055300          UNTIL SEC-SUB IS GREATER THAN 4.                     00552

              00551         ABJ6253 08 RULES FOR AUGMENTING VARIABLES
                                       HAVE CHANGED. IF DEPENDENCIES
                                       BETWEEN VARIABLES EXIST, THEN
                                       *MANUAL UPDATE MAY BE REQUIRED
```

Numeric Comparing with Alphabetic Issue

Problem:
NUMERIC NONINTEGER was compared with SPACES. This comparison is not allowed in COBOL/370. CCCA 2.1 handles this condition.

Sample Text:

```
074200      10 MI-TC-LABOR-DETAIL-AREA.
074300         15 MI-TC-LABOR-DETAIL-LINE OCCURS 12 TIMES.
074400            20 MI-TC-LABOR-DETAIL-ACTION
074500                  PIC X(1).
074600               88 MI-TC-ADD                VALUE 'A'.
074700               88 MI-TC-DELETE             VALUE 'D'.
074800               88 MI-TC-CHANGE             VALUE 'C'.
074900            20 MI-TC-WORK-REQUEST-NUMBER-X.
075000               25 MI-TC-WORK-REQUEST-NUMBER
075100                  PIC 9(7).
075200            20 MI-TC-ELAPSED-TIME-X.
075300               25 MI-TC-ELAPSED-TIME
075400                  PIC 9(3)V9(2).
075500            20 MI-TC-START-TIME-X.
075600               25 MI-TC-START-DIGIT-1
075700                  PIC 9(1).
075800              23 MI-TC-START-DIGITS-2-5-X.
075900                 25 MI-TC-START-DIGITS-2-5
```

Upgrading OS/VS COBOL to VS COBOL/370 Using CCCA

```
076000                           PIC 9(4).
240800      IF FIELDS-ARE-VALID                                    024
```

IGYPA3022-S "MI-TC-ELAPSED-TIME (NUMERIC NONINTEGER)" was compared with "SPACES
        The comparison was discarded.

```
     240900         AND (MI-TC-ELAPSED-TIME (SCREEN-SUB) NOT = SPACES
024
     241000             OR MI-TC-STOP-TIME-X (SCREEN-SUB) NOT = SPACES)
024
1    241100         PERFORM 3640-CHANGE-DETAIL-TIMES
024
1    241200           THRU 3649-END-CHANGE-DETAIL-TIMES
024
1    241300         MOVE SCREEN-SUB TO ADJUSTED-SUB
024
1    241400         PERFORM 3720-DISPLAY-CHANGED-LINE
024
1    241500           THRU 3729-END-DISPLAY-CHANGED-LINE.
024
     241600 3659-END-CHANGE-OUTSIDE-LUNCH.
024
```

Resolution:
Identified condition corrected manually.

DCLGEN Table Declaration Issue

Problem:
DCLGEN's table declaration, which names the table and each of its columns, was not included in the supplied copybook.

Sample Text:
```
3549      352700 11000-GET-MIN-PLANT-XREF.
3550      352800     EXEC SQL
3551      352900         SELECT MIN (PART_NUMBER)
3552      353000             INTO :DCLMI-PART-XREFERENCE.PART-NUMBER
3553      353100                  :PLANT-XREF-IND
3554      353200         FROM    MI_PART_XREFERENCE
3555      353300         WHERE PLANT = :DCLMI-PART-XREFERENCE.PLANT
3556      353400           AND CROSS_REFERENCE
```

continues

DCLGEN Table Declaration Issue (Continued)

```
3557       353500                    = :DCLMI-PART-XREFERENCE.CROSS-REFERENCE
3558       353600         END-EXEC.
3559       353700         CALL 'PROGM0ST' USING SQLCA
3560       353800                          PCOGM0ST-SQLCA.
3561       353900         IF PLANT-XREF-IND NOT = ZERO
3562       354000            MOVE 100 TO SQLCODE.
3563       354100  11000-EXIT.
3564       354200         EXIT.
3565       354300
3566       354400  11010-UPDATE-CROSS-REFERENCE.
LINE 3552 COL 26   UNDEFINED OR UNUSABLE HOST VARIABLE "DCLMI-PART-XREFERENCE"
LINE 3552 COL 48   UNDEFINED OR UNUSABLE HOST VARIABLE "PART-NUMBER"
LINE 3555 COL 31   UNDEFINED OR UNUSABLE HOST VARIABLE "DCLMI-PART-XREFERENCE"
LINE 3555 COL 53   UNDEFINED OR UNUSABLE HOST VARIABLE "PLANT"
LINE 3557 COL 23   UNDEFINED OR UNUSABLE HOST VARIABLE "DCLMI-PART-XREFERENCE"
LINE 3557 COL 45   UNDEFINED OR UNUSABLE HOST VARIABLE "CROSS-REFERENCE"
LINE 3571 COL 53   UNDEFINED OR UNUSABLE HOST VARIABLE "PLANT"
LINE 3573 COL 45   UNDEFINED OR UNUSABLE HOST VARIABLE "CROSS-REFERENCE"
LINE 3587 COL 53   UNDEFINED OR UNUSABLE HOST VARIABLE "PLANT"
LINE 3589 COL 45   UNDEFINED OR UNUSABLE HOST VARIABLE "PART-NUMBER"
LINE 3603 COL 31   UNDEFINED OR UNUSABLE HOST VARIABLE "DCLMI-PRT-DESCRIPTION"
LINE 3603 COL 53   UNDEFINED OR UNUSABLE HOST VARIABLE "PLANT"
LINE 3605 COL 23   UNDEFINED OR UNUSABLE HOST VARIABLE "DCLMI-PRT-DESCRIPTION"
LINE 3605 COL 45   UNDEFINED OR UNUSABLE HOST VARIABLE "PART-NUMBER"
```

Resolution:
Identified condition. Requires manual correction.

6.4 Conclusion

There are enough elements that have changed from COBOL II to COBOL/370 (now known as COBOL for MVS and VM) that we found it beneficial to use a tool to implement consistent fixes. In the next chapter, we'll examine how to use CCCA to migrate from COBOL II to COBOL/370 if you've already migrated off of OS/VS.

CHAPTER 7

Upgrading VS COBOL II to COBOL/370 Using CCCA

CCCA even offers you the ability to convert COBOL II to COBOL/370. This is a benefit to your conversion because some language elements changed between the two versions. And while you could use brute force and just recompile all of your code fixing one issue at a time, if you have the tool it is well worth using it to change out the elements, as we will discuss in this chapter. Also note that even though the conversion and compile steps are usually very clean, the execution behavior may be different, so test carefully.

7.1 Language Elements Converted to COBOL/370

CCCA, Release 2.0, analyzes valid source programs for VS COBOL II, Releases 1, 1.1, 2, 3, and 3.1, or program number 5668-958, and produces COBOL/370 source statements. In addition, CCCA, Release 2.0, indicates which of those old statements are either not supported by the target language (COBOL/370) or are supported in a different manner.

During this migration path, the input COBOL source language level(s) for which the conversion tool will perform COBOL upgrade is one of the following: VS COBOL II, Release 1.0, Release 1.1, or Release 2.0—ANSI 74 standard; VS COBOL II CMPR2, Release 3.0, Release 3.1, or Release 3.2—ANSI 74 standard; and VS COBOL II NOCMPR2, Release 3.0, Release 3.1, or Release 3.2—ANSI 85 standard.

7.2 Language Elements Converted to COBOL/370 from VS COBOL II

The affected commands are presented here in alphabetical order. When you manually upgrade programs, it's best to see upgrade elements in the order in which you will see them in the program. When using a tool (here, CCCA) you will need them to be in alphabetical order so you can find them more rapidly in your run outputs (providing a better reference tool).

ALPHABET clause. CCCA, Release 2.0, will *convert* this statement for the following input language level(s): VS COBOL II, Release 1.0, Release 1.1, or Release 2.0—ANSI 74 standard; or VS COBOL II CMPR2, Release 3.0, Release 3.1, Release 3.2—ANSI 74 standard. CCCA, Release 2.0, will *convert* the clause as follows: The keyword ALPHABET is added in front of the alphabet name within the ALPHABET clause of the SPECIAL-NAMES paragraph.

ALPHABETIC class. CCCA, Release 2.0, will *convert* this statement for the following input language level(s): VS COBOL II, Release 1.0, Release 1.1, or Release 2.0—ANSI 74 standard; or VS COBOL II CMPR2, Release 3.0, Release 3.1, Release 3.2—ANSI 74 standard. CCCA, Release 2.0, will *convert* ALPHABETIC to ALPHABETIC-UPPER.

AUTHOR paragraph. CCCA, Release 2.0, will *convert* this statement for the following input language level(s): VS COBOL II, Release 1.0, Release 1.1, or Release 2.0—ANSI 74 standard; VS COBOL II CMPR2, Release 3.0, Release 3.1, Release 3.2—ANSI 74 standard; VS COBOL II NOCMPR2, Release 3.0, Release 3.1, or Release 3.2—ANSI 85 standard.

The AUTHOR paragraph in the Identification Division is *converted* by commenting out if the Obsolete Element Removal option on the Optional Processing Panel is specified as *Y* (yes).

BLOCK CONTAINS clause. CCCA, Release 2.0, will *convert* this statement for the following input language level(s): VS COBOL II, Release 1.0, Release 1.1, or Release 2.0—ANSI 74 standard; VS COBOL II CMPR2, Release 3.0, Release 3.1, Release 3.2—ANSI 74 standard; VS COBOL II NOCMPR2, Release 3.0, Release 3.1, or Release 3.2—ANSI 85 standard.

CCCA, Release 2.0, will *remove* the clause from VSAM file descriptions if you specify *Y* for the Obsolete Element Removal option on the

Optional Processing Panel. The concept of blocking has no meaning for VSAM files.

CALL identifier statement. CCCA, Release 2.0, will *flag* this statement for the following input language level(s): VS COBOL II, Release 1.0, Release 1.1, or Release 2.0—ANSI 74 standard; and VS COBOL II CMPR2, Release 3.0, Release 3.1, or Release 3.2—ANSI 74 standard.

CCCA, Release 2.0, will *flag* the statement if the identifier has a PICTURE string consisting of characters only. The ANSI 74 standard classes these fields as alphabetic, while the ANSI 85 standard classes them as alphanumeric-edited. You will have to make a change to the program because alphanumeric-edited identifiers are not permitted in the CALL statement.

CALL . . . ON EXCEPTION statement. CCCA, Release 2.0, will *flag* this statement for the following input language level(s): VS COBOL II NOCMPR2, Release 3.0, Release 3.1, or Release 3.2— ANSI 85 standard. The ON EXCEPTION phrase in a VS COBOL II program is not invoked if the program is running under CICS. When an exception condition occurs in a COBOL/370 program running under CICS, the ON EXCEPTION phrase will be invoked if it is specified. CCCA, Release 2.0, will flag the statement if the target language is COBOL/370.

CALL . . . ON OVERFLOW statement. CCCA, Release 2.0, will *flag* this statement for the following input language level(s): VS COBOL II, Release 1.0, Release 1.1, or Release 2.0—ANSI 74 standard; VS COBOL II CMPR2, Release 3.0, Release 3.1, Release 3.2—ANSI 74 standard; VS COBOL II NOCMPR2, Release 3.0, Release 3.1, or Release 3.2—ANSI 85 standard. Under the ANSI 85 standard the ON OVERFLOW phrase executes under more conditions than it does under the ANSI 68 and ANSI 74 standards. When an overflow condition occurs in a COBOL/370 program running under CICS, the ON OVERFLOW phrase will be invoked, if it is specified. CCCA, Release 2.0, will flag the statement if the target language is COBOL/370.

CANCEL statement. CCCA, Release 2.0, will *flag* this statement for the following input language level(s): VS COBOL II, Release 1.0, Release 1.1, or Release 2.0—ANSI 74 standard; and VS COBOL II CMPR2, Release 3.0, Release 3.1, Release 3.2—ANSI 74 standard. The statement is flagged if there is an identifier in the statement with a PICTURE string consisting of A's and B's only. The ANSI 74 standard classes these fields as alphabetic, while the ANSI 85 standard classes them as alphanumeric-edited. You will have to make a change to the program since alphanumeric-edited identifiers are not permitted in the CANCEL statement.

CBL statement. CCCA, Release 2.0, will *convert* this statement for the following input language level(s): VS COBOL II, Release 1.0, Release 1.1, or Release 2.0—ANSI 74 standard; VS COBOL II CMPR2, Release 3.0, Release 3.1, Release 3.2—ANSI 74 standard; and VS COBOL II NOCMPR2, Release 3.0, Release 3.1, or Release 3.2—ANSI 85 standard. If the target language is COBOL/370, all compiler options that COBOL/370 does not support are removed from the statement and where possible are replaced with their COBOL/370 equivalents.

COPY . . . REPLACING statement. CCCA, Release 2.0, will *flag* this statement for the following input language level(s): VS COBOL II, Release 1.0, Release 1.1, or Release 2.0—ANSI 74 standard; and VS COBOL II CMPR2, Release 3.0, Release 3.1, Release 3.2—ANSI 74 standard. If there are lowercase alphabetic characters in operands of the REPLACING phrase that are not in nonnumeric literals, the statement is flagged. Under the ANSI 85 standard, lowercase characters are treated as their uppercase equivalent. You should check to see if this change will result in different text being copied into your program.

If the operands of the REPLACING phrase contain a colon (":") character that is not in a nonnumeric literal, the statement is flagged. Under the ANSI 68 and ANSI 74 standards, the colon (":") is a non-COBOL character. Under the ANSI 85 standard, the colon character is treated as a separator. You should check to see if this change will result in different text being copied into your program. If the operands of the REPLACING phrase contain an ANSI 85 standard non-COBOL character that is not in a nonnumeric literal, the statement is flagged. Under the ANSI 68 and ANSI 74 standards, non-COBOL characters are permitted in the REPLACING option. Under the ANSI 85 standard, non-COBOL characters in the REPLACING phrase are diagnosed. You should remove all non-COBOL characters from the REPLACING phrase and from the copybook.

DATA RECORDS. CCCA, Release 2.0, will *remove* this statement for the following input language level(s): VS COBOL II, Release 1.0, Release 1.1, or Release 2.0—ANSI 74 standard; VS COBOL II CMPR2,

Release 3.0, Release 3.1, Release 3.2—ANSI 74 standard; and VS COBOL II NOCMPR2, Release 3.0, Release 3.1, or Release 3.2—ANSI 85 standard.

If you specify Y for the clause Obsolete Element Removal option on the Optional Processing Panel, the DATA RECORDS clause is removed from the FD entry. The word RECORDS is added if missing when the clause is not removed.

DATE-COMPILED/DATE-WRITTEN paragraphs. CCCA, Release 2.0, will *convert* this statement for the following input language level(s): VS COBOL II, Release 1.0, Release 1.1, or Release 2.0—ANSI 74 standard; VS COBOL II CMPR2, Release 3.0, Release 3.1, Release 3.2—ANSI 74 standard; and VS COBOL II NOCMPR2, Release 3.0, Release 3.1, or Release 3.2—ANSI 85 standard. If you specify Y for the Obsolete Element Removal option on the Optional Processing Panel, these paragraphs in the Identification Division are commented out.

DIVIDE . . . ON SIZE ERROR statement. CCCA, Release 2.0, will *flag* this statement for the following input language level(s): VS COBOL II, Release 1.0, Release 1.1, or Release 2.0—ANSI 74 standard; and VS COBOL II CMPR2, Release 3.0, Release 3.1, Release 3.2—ANSI 74 standard. DIVIDE . . . ON SIZE ERROR statements with multiple receiving fields are flagged because the ON SIZE ERROR phrase will not be executed for intermediate results under the ANSI 85 standard.

ENTER statement. CCCA, Release 2.0, will *remove* this statement for the following input language level(s): VS COBOL II, Release 1.0, Release 1.1, or Release 2.0—ANSI 74 standard; VS COBOL II CMPR2, Release 3.0, Release 3.1, Release 3.2—ANSI 74 standard; and VS COBOL II NOCMPR2, Release 3.0, Release 3.1, or Release 3.2—ANSI 85 standard. If you specify Y for the Obsolete Element Removal option on the Optional Processing Panel, CCCA, Release 2.0, will remove the ENTER statement.

EXIT PROGRAM. CCCA, Release 2.0, will *convert* this statement for the following input language level(s): VS COBOL II, Release 1.0, Release 1.1, or Release 2.0—ANSI 74 standard; and VS COBOL II CMPR2, Release 3.0, Release 3.1, Release 3.2—ANSI 74 standard. Under the ANSI 85 standard, statement control cannot flow beyond the last line of a called subprogram. The compiler generates an implicit EXIT PROGRAM at the end of each program.

The ANSI 68 and ANSI 74 standard behavior can be preserved under the ANSI 85 standard by adding, at the end of the program, a section with a call to an ABEND macro. If you specify Y for the Call "ILBOABN0" Statement Generation option on the Optional Processing Panel and if EXIT PROGRAM, STOP RUN, or GOBACK is not the last physical statement in the program, a section that includes a CALL to the ABEND macro ILBOABN0 will be inserted at the end of the program.

FILE STATUS codes. CCCA, Release 2.0, will *flag* this statement for the following input language level(s): VS COBOL II, Release 1.0, Release 1.1, or Release 2.0—ANSI 74 standard; and VS COBOL II CMPR2, Release 3.0, Release 3.1, Release 3.2—ANSI 74 standard. The file status codes returned under ANSI 85 standard COBOL are different from those returned under ANSI 68 and ANSI 74 standard COBOL. You should check all references to the file status key in the program and update the values of the file status codes where it is required.

GOBACK statement. The input COBOL language level(s) for which CCCA, Release 2.0, will *convert* is VS COBOL II, Release 1.0, Release 1.1, or Release 2.0—ANSI 74 standard; and VS COBOL II CMPR2, Release 3.0, Release 3.1, Release 3.2—ANSI 74 standard.

Under the ANSI 85 standard, control cannot flow beyond the last line of a called subprogram. The compiler generates an implicit EXIT PROGRAM at the end of each program. Under the ANSI 68 and ANSI 74 standard control can flow beyond the last line of a called program. When this happens the program ABENDs. The ANSI 68 and ANSI 74 standard behavior can be preserved under the ANSI 85 standard by adding, at the end of the program, a section with a call to an ABEND macro. If you specify Y for the Call "ILBOABN0" Statement Generation option on the Optional Processing Panel, and if EXIT PROGRAM, STOP RUN, or GOBACK is not the last physical statement in the program a section that includes a CALL to the ABEND macro ILBOABN0 will be inserted at the end of the program.

IDMS. CCCA, Release 2.0, will *flag* this statement for the following input language level(s): VS COBOL II, Release 1.0, Release 1.1, or Release 2.0—ANSI 74 standard; VS COBOL II CMPR2, Release 3.0, Release 3.1, Release 3.2—ANSI 74 standard; and VS COBOL II NOCMPR2, Release 3.0, Release 3.1, or Release 3.2—ANSI 85 standard.

If your programs contain COPY IDMS statements, you should create a dummy copy member called IDMS. The copybook should just have a comment in it.

INSPECT statement. CCCA, Release 2.0, will *flag* this statement for the following input language level(s): VS COBOL II, Release 1.0, Release 1.1, or Release 2.0—ANSI 74 standard; and VS COBOL II CMPR2, Release 3.0, Release 3.1, Release 3.2—ANSI 74 standard. The statement is flagged if the PROGRAM COLLATING SEQUENCE established in the OBJECT COMPUTER paragraph identifies an alphabet that was defined with the ALSO clause to override the standard EBCDIC collating sequence. Under these circumstances, the statement will behave differently under the ANSI 85 standard.

When coded, it affects the INSPECT, STRING, and UNSTRING statements. (It also affects nonnumeric keys in a MERGE or SORT when the COLLATING SEQUENCE is not specified in the SORT or MERGE statement.) The PROGRAM COLLATING SEQUENCE affects nonnumeric comparisons. In OS/VS COBOL, it affects both explicitly coded conditions and implicitly performed conditions (those comparisons that the compiler deems necessary to perform) in INSPECT, STRING, and UNSTRING statements.

In VS COBOL II, the PROGRAM COLLATING SEQUENCE only affects explicitly coded conditions in these statements.

INSTALLATION. CCCA, Release 2.0, will *convert* this statement for the following input language level(s): VS COBOL II, Release 1.0, Release 1.1, or Release 2.0—ANSI 74 standard; VS COBOL II CMPR2, Release 3.0, Release 3.1, Release 3.2—ANSI 74 standard; and VS COBOL II NOCMPR2, Release 3.0, Release 3.1 or Release 3.2—ANSI 85 standard.

If you specify Y for the paragraph Obsolete Element Removal option on the Optional Processing Panel, the INSTALLATION paragraph in the Identification Division is commented out.

LABEL RECORDS. CCCA, Release 2.0, will *remove* this statement for the following input language level(s): VS COBOL II, Release 1.0, Release 1.1, or Release 2.0—ANSI 74 standard; VS COBOL II CMPR2, Release 3.0, Release 3.1, Release 3.2—ANSI 74 standard; and VS COBOL II NOCMPR2, Release 3.0, Release 3.1, or Release 3.2—ANSI 85 standard.

If you specify Y for the clause Obsolete Element Removal option on the Optional Processing Panel, this clause is removed. The word RECORDS is added, if missing, when the clause is not removed.

LABEL RECORDS . . . TOTALING/TOTALED AREA option. CCCA, Release 2.0, will *remove* this statement and provide information for the following input language level(s): VS COBOL II, Release 1.0, Release 1.1, or Release 2.0—ANSI 74 standard; and VS COBOL II CMPR2, Release 3.0, Release 3.1, Release 3.2—ANSI 74 standard.

The LABEL RECORDS . . . TOTALING/TOTALED AREA option is removed from the program. The data name associated with this option is listed at the end of the diagnostic listing.

MEMORY SIZE. CCCA, Release 2.0, will *remove* this statement for the following input language level(s): VS COBOL II, Release 1.0, Release 1.1, or Release 2.0—ANSI 74 standard; VS COBOL II CMPR2, Release 3.0, Release 3.1, Release 3.2—ANSI 74 standard; and VS COBOL II NOCMPR2, Release 3.0, Release 3.1, or Release 3.2—ANSI 85 standard.

If you specify Y for the clause Obsolete Element Removal option on the Optional Processing Panel, the MEMORY SIZE clause of the OBJECT-COMPUTER paragraph is removed.

MULTIPLE FILE TAPE clause. CCCA, Release 2.0, will *remove* this statement for the following input language level(s): VS COBOL II, Release 1.0, Release 1.1, or Release 2.0—ANSI 74 standard; VS COBOL II CMPR2, Release 3.0, Release 3.1, Release 3.2—ANSI 74 standard; and VS COBOL II NOCMPR2, Release 3.0, Release 3.1 or Release 3.2—ANSI 85 standard.

If you specify Y for the clause Obsolete Element Removal option on the Optional Processing Panel, the MULTIPLE FILE TAPE clause is removed from the I-O-CONTROL paragraph.

MULTIPLY . . . ON SIZE ERROR statement. CCCA, Release 2.0, will *flag* this statement for the following input language level(s): VS COBOL II, Release 1.0, Release 1.1, or Release 2.0—ANSI 74 standard; and VS COBOL II CMPR2, Release 3.0, Release 3.1, Release 3.2—ANSI 74 standard. MULTIPLY. . . ON SIZE ERROR statements with multiple receiving fields are flagged because the ON SIZE ERROR phrase will not be executed for intermediate results under the ANSI 85 standard.

For OS/VS COBOL and VS COBOL II with CMPR2, the SIZE ERROR option for the DIVIDE and MULTIPLY statements applies to both intermediate and final results. If your OS/VS COBOL relies upon SIZE ERROR detection for intermediate results, it must be changed or be compiled with the CMPR2 compiler option (see Chapter 4, Section 4.2.1 on behaviors for more on that):

```
01    NUMERICS.
10    NUMERIC-1 PICTURE S9(16).
10 NUMERIC-2      PICTURE S9(16).
10 NUMERIC-3      PICTURE S9(16).
10 NUMERIC-4      PICTURE S9(16).
10 TEMP PICTURE S9(30).
   MULTIPLY NUMERIC-1 BY NUMERIC-2 GIVING NUMERIC-3 NUMERIC-4.
```

should behave like

```
MULTIPLY NUMERIC-1 BY NUMERIC-2 GIVING TEMP
MOVE TEMPORARY TO NUMERIC-3
MOVE TEMPORARY TO NUMERIC-4
```

TEMP is the intermediate result. An intermediate result will have at most thirty digits.

In the preceding example, if NUMERIC-1, NUMERIC-2 , NUMERIC-3, and NUMERIC-4 are all defined as PIC S9(16), NUMERIC-1 will be multiplied by NUMERIC-2, yielding a thirty-two-digit result, which is moved to the thirty-digit intermediate result, TEMP. TEMP is then moved to NUMERIC-3 and NUMERIC-4. A size error may occur if the result exceeds the largest possible value of the result field, during a division by zero, or during an exponential expression.

OCCURS DEPENDING ON clause (variable-length record). CCCA, Release 2.0, will *convert* this statement for the following input language level(s): VS COBOL II, Release 1.0, Release 1.1, or Release 2.0—ANSI 74 standard; and VS COBOL II CMPR2, Release 3.0, Release 3.1, Release 3.2—ANSI 74 standard.

COBOL statements that result in data transfer to a variable-length receiver that contains its own OCCURS DEPENDING ON (ODO) object behave differently under the ANSI 85 standard. Under the ANSI 68 and ANSI 74 standards, all ODO objects in sending and receiving fields must be set before the statement is executed. The actual lengths of the sender and receiver are calculated just before the execution of the data movement statement. Under the ANSI 85 standard, in some circumstances the maximum length of the variable-length group is used when it is a receiver, whereas the ANSI 68 and ANSI 74 standard always use the actual length. CCCA, Release 2.0, preserves the ANSI 68 and ANSI

74 behavior in the following way. For the following statements,

```
MOVE...TO identifier
READ...INTO identifier
RETURN...INTO identifier
UNSTRING...INTO identifier DELIMITER IN identifier
```

If the identifier is a variable-length data item that contains its own ODO object, then reference modification is added to it. For example,

```
MOVE...TO identifier
```

is changed to

```
MOVE...TO identifier (1:LENGTH OF identifier)
```

For the following statements,

```
RELEASE record-name FROM identifier
REWRITE record-name FROM identifier
WRITE record-name FROM identifier
```

If the identifier is a variable-length data item that contains its own ODO object, the FROM phrase is removed from the statement and a MOVE statement with reference modification is added before the statement. For example,

```
WRITE record-name FROM identifier
```

is changed to

```
MOVE identifier TO record-n me (1:LENGTH OF record-name)
WRITE record-name
```

MOVE CORRESPONDING statements are flagged as reference; modification is not allowed when the CORRESPONDING phrase is specified.

PERFORM . . . VARYING . . . AFTER statement. CCCA, Release 2.0, will *flag* this statement for the following input language level(s): VS COBOL II, Release 1.0, Release 1.1, or Release 2.0—ANSI 74 standard; and VS COBOL II CMPR2, Release 3.0, Release 3.1, Release 3.2—ANSI 74 standard. Under the ANSI 85 standard, the rules for augmenting variables have changed. If there are dependencies between variables of the statement, then the statement may behave differently. All PERFORM . . . VARYING . . . AFTER statements are flagged. You should check to see if there are any dependencies between the variables of the statement that will result in different behavior. If there are, you should modify the statement.

PICTURE clause. CCCA, Release 2.0, will *flag* this statement and provide information for the following input language level(s): VS COBOL II, Release 1.0, Release 1.1, or Release 2.0—ANSI 74 standard; and VS

COBOL II CMPR2, Release 3.0, Release 3.1, Release 3.2—ANSI 74 standard. If the scaled integer is compared with an alphanumeric or numeric edited field, you will have to convert this statement. Scaled integers are flagged. If the scaled integer is compared with a nonnumeric field, you will have to convert this statement.

PICTURE P in RELATIVE KEY. CCCA, Release 2.0, will *flag* this statement for the following input language level(s): VS COBOL II, Release 1.0, Release 1.1, or Release 2.0—ANSI 74 standard; and VS COBOL II CMPR2, Release 3.0, Release 3.1, Release 3.2—ANSI 74 standard. PICTURE P in RELATIVE KEY is flagged.

PROCESSING MODE clause. CCCA, Release 2.0, will *remove* this statement for the following input language level(s): VS COBOL II, Release 1.0, Release 1.1, or Release 2.0—ANSI 74 standard; VS COBOL II CMPR2, Release 3.0, Release 3.1, Release 3.2—ANSI 74 standard; and VS COBOL II NOCMPR2, Release 3.0, Release 3.1 or Release 3.2—ANSI 85 standard.

The PROCESSING MODE clause is removed.

RECORD CONTAINS. CCCA, Release 2.0, will *remove* this statement for the following input language level(s): VS COBOL II, Release 1.0, Release 1.1, or Release 2.0—ANSI 74 standard; VS COBOL II CMPR2, Release 3.0, Release 3.1, Release 3.2—ANSI 74 standard; and VS COBOL II NOCMPR2, Release 3.0, Release 3.1 or Release 3.2—ANSI 85 standard.

The RECORD CONTAINS clause is removed from the program, except for RECORD CONTAINS 0, which is left in place.

RECORDING MODE clause. CCCA, Release 2.0, will *remove* this statement for the following input language level(s): VS COBOL II, Release 1.0, Release 1.1, or Release 2.0—ANSI 74 standard; VS COBOL II CMPR2, Release 3.0, Release 3.1, Release 3.2—ANSI 74 standard; and VS COBOL II NOCMPR2, Release 3.0, Release 3.1 or Release 3.2—ANSI 85 standard. COBOL/370 compiler ignores the RECORDING MODE clause if it is specified for a VSAM file. If the clause is in a file description entry for a VSAM file or a file that is to be converted to VSAM it is removed.

SECURITY paragraph. CCCA, Release 2.0, will *convert* this statement for the following input language level(s): VS COBOL II, Release 1.0, Release 1.1, or Release 2.0—ANSI 74 standard; VS COBOL II CMPR2, Release 3.0, Release 3.1, Release 3.2—ANSI 74 standard; and VS COBOL II NOCMPR2, Release 3.0, Release 3.1, or Release 3.2—ANSI 85 standard.

If you specify Y for the Obsolete Element Removal option on the Optional Processing Panel, the SECURITY paragraph in the Identification Division is commented out.

STOP RUN statement. CCCA, Release 2.0, will *convert* this statement for the following input language level(s): VS COBOL II, Release 1.0, Release 1.1, or Release 2.0—ANSI 74 standard; and VS COBOL II CMPR2, Release 3.0, Release 3.1, Release 3.2—ANSI 74 standard.

Under the ANSI 85 standard, control cannot flow beyond the last line of a called subprogram. The compiler generates an implicit EXIT PROGRAM at the end of each program. Under the ANSI 68 and ANSI 74 standards, control can flow beyond the last line of a called program. When this happens the program ABENDs. The ANSI 68 and ANSI 74 standard behavior can be preserved under the ANSI 85 standard by adding, at the end of the program, a section with a call to an ABEND macro. If you specify Y for the Call "ILBOABN0" Statement Generation option on the Optional Processing Panel and if EXIT PROGRAM, STOP RUN, or GOBACK is not the last physical statement in the program, a section that includes a CALL to the ABEND macro ILBOABN0 will be inserted at the end of the program.

STRING statement. CCCA, Release 2.0, will *flag* this statement for the following input language level(s): VS COBOL II, Release 1.0, Release 1.1, or Release 2.0—ANSI 74 standard; and VS COBOL II CMPR2, Release 3.0, Release 3.1, Release 3.2—ANSI 74 standard. The STRING statement is flagged if it has a receiving field with a PICTURE string that consists of A's and B's only. The ANSI 74 standard classes these fields as alphabetic, while the ANSI 85 standard classes them as alphanumeric-edited.

You will have to make a change to the program because alphanumeric-edited receiving fields in the STRING statement are not permitted.

UNSTRING statement. CCCA, Release 2.0, will *flag* this statement for the following input language level(s): VS COBOL II, Release 1.0, Release 1.1, or Release 2.0—ANSI 74 standard; and VS COBOL II CMPR2, Release 3.0, Release 3.1, Release 3.2—ANSI 74 standard. The UNSTRING statement is flagged if the PROGRAM COLLATING SEQUENCE established in the OBJECT COMPUTER paragraph identifies an alphabet that was defined with the ALSO clause.

In these circumstances, the statement will behave differently under the ANSI 85 standard.

UPSI name. CCCA, Release 2.0, will *convert* and *flag* this statement for the following input language level(s): VS COBOL II, Release 1.0, Release 1.1, or Release 2.0—ANSI 74 standard; and VS COBOL II CMPR2, Release 3.0, Release 3.1, Release 3.2—ANSI 74 standard.

Condition names are added. UPSI-n is replaced by condition name, for example, LCP-ON-UPSI-n and LCP-OFF-UPSI-n where n is a number between 0 and 7.

VALUE OF clause. CCCA, Release 2.0, will *remove* this statement for the following input language level(s): VS COBOL II, Release 1.0, Release 1.1, or Release 2.0—ANSI 74 standard; VS COBOL II CMPR2, Release 3.0, Release 3.1, Release 3.2—ANSI 74 standard; and VS COBOL II NOCMPR2, Release 3.0, Release 3.1, or Release 3.2—ANSI 85 standard.

If you specify Y for the Obsolete Element Removal option on the Optional Processing Panel, the VALUE OF clause is removed from the FD entry.

7.3 Migrating from VS COBOL II to COBOL/370

This section presents some observations and lessons we have learned from migrating VS COBOL II to COBOL/370 using CCCA. Some of our issues were defects in the tool, some of which have been corrected in the newest version, 2.1. Some were due to coding styles that had detrimental effects in processing. Also, read the compiler options in Table 7.1.

Table 7.1 Compiler Options (ZWB/NOZWB)

COMPILER OPTIONS (ZWB/NOZWB)	
Detected by:	VS COBOL II and COBOL/370 Programmer's Guide (IBM, 1984, 1990).
Description	With ZWB, the compiler removes the sign from a signed external decimal (DISPLAY) field when comparing this field to an alphanumeric elementary field during execution. If the external decimal item is a scaled item (contains the symbol P in its PICTURE character string), its use in comparisons is not affected by ZWB. Such items always have their sign removed before the comparison is made to the alphanumeric field.
Lesson Learned	ZWB affects how the program runs; the same COBOL source program can give different results, depending on the option setting. ZWB conforms to the COBOL/85 standard.
Warning! Resolution	Use *NOZWB* if you want to test input numeric fields for SPACES.

7.3.1 Periods Issue

If there is no period (".") immediately before or immediately after paragraph names or section headers in the PROCEDURE DIVISION, then COBOL/370 compiler issues return code of 8, which is an error.

Resolution

The description of the resolution for this problem follows. The programs were manually revised by inserting a period (".") immediately before or immediately after paragraph names or section headers in the PROCEDURE DIVISION. We developed the utility program shown in Figure 7.1 to handle the period problem.

```
000100 IDENTIFICATION DIVISION.
000200 PROGRAM-ID.   PERUTIL.
000300 DATE-COMPILED.
000400 ENVIRONMENT DIVISION.
000500 CONFIGURATION SECTION.
000600
000700 SOURCE-COMPUTER.   IBM-370.
000800 OBJECT-COMPUTER.   IBM-370.
000900 INPUT-OUTPUT SECTION.
001000*********************
001100*********************
001200 FILE-CONTROL.
001300*
001400     SELECT INPUT-FILE ASSIGN TO INFILE.
001500     SELECT OUTPUT-FILE ASSIGN TO OUTFILE.
001600
001700 DATA DIVISION.
001800 FILE SECTION.
001900
002000 FD  INPUT-FILE
002100     BLOCK CONTAINS 0 RECORDS
002200     LABEL RECORDS ARE STANDARD
002300     RECORDING MODE IS F.
002400 01  INPUT-REC          PIC X(80).
002500
002600 FD  OUTPUT-FILE
002700     BLOCK CONTAINS 0 RECORDS
002800     LABEL RECORDS ARE STANDARD
002900     RECORDING MODE IS F.
003000 01  OUTPUT-REC         PIC X(80).
003100
003200 WORKING-STORAGE SECTION.
```

Figure 7.1   Code for the utility program to handle the period problem.

```
003300
003400 01  FILLER                      PIC X(40) VALUE
003500          'PERUTIL WORKING STORAGE BEGINS HERE'.
003600
003700 01  WS-FILE-SWITCH              PIC X(01) VALUE 'Y'.
003800     88  MORE-RECS               VALUE 'Y'.
003900     88  NO-MORE-RECS            VALUE 'N'.
004000
004100 01  WS-COBOL-REC.
004200     05  FILLER                  PIC X(06).
004300     05  COBOL-TXT               PIC X(66).
004400     05  FILLER                  PIC X(08).
004500
004600 01  WS-TABLE.
004700     05  WS-TABLE-ENTRY OCCURS 80 TIMES INDEXED BY WS-INDEX.
004800         10  WS-CHAR             PIC X(01).
004900
005000 01  WS-WRITE-REC                PIC X(80).
005100
005200 01  WS-PERIOD-COUNTER           PIC 9(04).
005300
005400 01  WS-CHAR-COUNTER             PIC 9(04).
005500
005600 01  WS-SPACE-COUNTER            PIC 9(04).
005700
005710 01  WS-INDEX-VALUE              PIC 9(04).
005720
005800 01  FILLER                      PIC X(40) VALUE
005900          'PERUTIL WORKING STORAGE ENDS HERE   '.
006000 PROCEDURE DIVISION.
006100     PERFORM U9000-INITIALIZE.
006200     PERFORM U1000-READ.
006300     PERFORM UNTIL NO-MORE-RECS
006400         PERFORM A1000-PROCESS-RECS
006500         PERFORM U1000-READ
006600     END-PERFORM.
006700     WRITE OUTPUT-REC FROM WS-WRITE-REC.
006800     PERFORM U5000-CLOSE.
006900     GOBACK.
007000
007100 A1000-PROCESS-RECS.
007200     IF COBOL-TXT = SPACE
007300         NEXT SENTENCE
007400     ELSE
007500         PERFORM A2000-CHECK-REC.
007600
007700 A2000-CHECK-REC.
007800     MOVE ZERO TO WS-SPACE-COUNTER.
```

continues

```
007900          MOVE ZERO TO WS-CHAR-COUNTER.
008000          INSPECT COBOL-TXT TALLYING WS-SPACE-COUNTER
008100              FOR ALL SPACES.
008200          SUBTRACT WS-SPACE-COUNTER FROM 66 GIVING WS-CHAR-COUNTER.
008300          IF WS-CHAR-COUNTER > 1
008400             IF WS-WRITE-REC > SPACE
008500                MOVE WS-COBOL-REC TO WS-TABLE
008600                PERFORM A3000-CHECK-EJECT
008700                    VARYING WS-INDEX FROM 1 BY 1
008800                    UNTIL WS-INDEX > 80
008900                WRITE OUTPUT-REC FROM WS-WRITE-REC
009000             END-IF
009100             MOVE WS-COBOL-REC TO WS-WRITE-REC
009200          ELSE
009300             MOVE ZERO TO WS-PERIOD-COUNTER
009400             INSPECT COBOL-TXT TALLYING WS-PERIOD-COUNTER
009500                 FOR ALL '.'
009600             IF WS-PERIOD-COUNTER = 1
009700                MOVE '.' TO WS-WRITE-REC(72:1).
009800
009900 A3000-CHECK-EJECT.
010000      IF WS-CHAR(WS-INDEX) = 'E'
010010         SET WS-INDEX-VALUE TO WS-INDEX
010100         IF WS-TABLE(WS-INDEX-VALUE:5) = 'EJECT'
010200            MOVE '.' TO WS-WRITE-REC(72:1).
010300
010400 U1000-READ.
010500      READ INPUT-FILE INTO WS-COBOL-REC
010600      AT END MOVE 'N' TO WS-FILE-SWITCH.
010700
010800 U5000-CLOSE.
010900      CLOSE INPUT-FILE
011000            OUTPUT-FILE.
011100
011200 U9000-INITIALIZE.
011300      OPEN INPUT INPUT-FILE
011400           OUTPUT OUTPUT-FILE.
011500
011600      MOVE SPACE TO WS-WRITE-REC.
011700
```

Figure 7.1 *(Continued)*

7.3.2 Relational Operator Issue

The description of the *problem* for this case follows. Within the scope of an abbreviated combined relation condition, COBOL/370 does *not support relational operators inside parentheses*. See Figure 7.2.

```
        090300       PERFORM 9120-GU-SEQ0EHI1-IMPLODE THRU
008
    090400                9120-EXIT.
009
    090500       PERFORM 9130-GNP-SEQ0EHI1-IMPLODE THRU
009
    090600                9130-EXIT.
009
    090700       PERFORM 4500-CHECK-PARENT-LEVELS THRU
009
    090800                4500-EXIT
009
    090900            UNTIL DB4-STATUS NOT (EQUAL '   ' OR 'GA').
009

IGYPS2093-S "(" was found in a conditional expression.  The "PERFORM" state-
ment
        discarded.


273700    IF (MI0ASS1-STATUS-CODE NOT    EQUAL '0' AND NOT '1')
02721*2

273800       MOVE 'CANNOT DELETE'
02722*1
273900         TO MO-A030-LINE-MESSAGE (SCREEN-SUB)
02723*1
274000       MOVE 'Y' TO UPDATE-ERRORS-FOUND-SW
02724*1
274100       GO TO 3131-END-DLT-LEVEL01-SUB.
02725*1
274200
02726*1
274300    PERFORM 9161-DLET-MI0ASS1 THRU 9161-END-DLT-MI0ASS1.
02727*2
 5785-ABJ R2.0  - IBM    COBOL CONVERSION AID -
SEQNBR-A 1 B.. ... 2 ... ...   COBOL SOURCE STATEMENTS   ... 6 ... ... 7
.IDENTFC

274400    IF  DB-STATUS IS NOT EQUAL TO SPACES
02728*1
274500       PERFORM 3800-MOVE-MI-TO-MO
02729*1
274600          THRU 3800-END-MOVE-MI-TO-MO
02730*1
274700       MOVE 'DLET FAILED' TO WS-EDIT-MESSAGE
02731*1
```

Figure 7.2 Problem with COBOL/370 and the relational operator.   *continues*

```
274800          MOVE DB-STATUS TO WS-EDIT-STATUS
02732*1
274900          MOVE WS-15-CHARACTER-MESSAGE
02733*1
275000              TO MO-A030-LINE-MESSAGE (SCREEN-SUB)
02734*1
275100          MOVE 'Y' TO UPDATE-ERRORS-FOUND-SW
02735*1
275200       ELSE
02736*1
```

Figure 7.2 *(Continued)*

Resolution

In the COBOL/370 source, this statement was manually modified by removing the relational operator from the parentheses as shown in Figure 7.3.

```
Resolution
090300      PERFORM 9120-GU-SEQ0EHI1-IMPLODE THRU
090400           9120-EXIT.
090500      PERFORM 9130-GNP-SEQ0EHI1-IMPLODE THRU
090600           9130-EXIT.
090700      PERFORM 4500-CHECK-PARENT-LEVELS THRU
090800           4500-EXIT
090900           UNTIL DB4-STATUS NOT EQUAL ('  ' OR 'GA').
091000
091100
091200      IF LINK-IS-VALID
091300          MOVE MI-ASSEM-NUMBER-2 (SCREEN-SUB)
091400             TO SSA-SEQ0EHE1-EQUIPMENT-NUMBER
091500          PERFORM 9140-GU-SEQ0EHE1-EXPLODE THRU
009
004577          273500      IF  MI0ASS1-STATUS-CODE NOT  EQUAL ('0' OR '1' )
004578       1  273600          MOVE 'CANNOT DELETE'
004579       1  273700             TO MO-A030-LINE-MESSAGE (SCREEN-SUB)
004580       1  273800          MOVE 'Y' TO UPDATE-ERRORS-FOUND-SW
004581       1  273900          GO TO 3131-END-DLT-LEVEL01-SUB.
004582          274000
004583          274100      PERFORM 9161-DLET-MI0ASS1 THRU 9161-END-DLET-
MI0ASS1
004584          274200      IF  DB-STATUS IS NOT EQUAL TO SPACES
```

Figure 7.3 COBOL/370 code manually modified to remove the relational operator from the parentheses.

7.3.3 PERFORM . . . VARYING Issue

The *problem* is that the processing of PERFORM . . . VARYING . . . AFTER statement in COBOL/370 may differ from OS/VS COBOL depending on usage. The rules for PERFORM . . . VARYING have changed from OS/VS COBOL to COBOL/370. In OS/VS COBOL, in a PERFORM statement with the VARYING . . . AFTER phrase, two actions take place when an inner condition tests as TRUE:

1. The identifier/index associated with the inner condition is set to its current FROM value.
2. The identifier/index associated with the outer condition is augmented by its current BY value.

In COBOL/370 and COBOL for MVS & VM with such a PERFORM statement the following takes place when an inner condition tests as TRUE:

1. The identifier/index associated with the outer condition is augmented by its current BY value.
2. The identifier/index associated with the inner condition is set to its current FROM value.

The following example illustrates the differences in execution:

```
PERFORM ABC VARYING X FROM 1 BY 1 UNTIL X > 3
    AFTER Y FROM X BY 1 UNTIL Y > 3
```

In OS/VS COBOL, ABC is executed eight times with the following values:

```
X: 1 1 1 2 2 2 3 3
Y: 1 2 3 1 2 3 2 3
```

In COBOL/370 and COBOL for MVS & VM, ABC is executed six times with the following values:

```
X: 1 1 1 2 2 3
Y: 1 2 3 2 3 3
```

7.3.4 Numeric Comparing with Alphabetic Issue

In this issue, NUMERIC NONINTEGER is compared with SPACES. This comparison is not allowed in COBOL/370 compiler. See Figure 7.4.

```
074200          10  MI-TC-LABOR-DETAIL-AREA.
074300              15  MI-TC-LABOR-DETAIL-LINE OCCURS 12 TIMES.
074400                  20  MI-TC-LABOR-DETAIL-ACTION
074500                          PIC X(1).
074600                      88  MI-TC-ADD                   VALUE 'A'.
074700                      88  MI-TC-DELETE                VALUE 'D'.
074800                      88  MI-TC-CHANGE                VALUE 'C'.
074900                  20  MI-TC-WORK-REQUEST-NUMBER-X.
075000                      25  MI-TC-WORK-REQUEST-NUMBER
075100                          PIC 9(7).
075200                  20  MI-TC-ELAPSED-TIME-X.
075300                      25  MI-TC-ELAPSED-TIME
075400                          PIC 9(3)V9(2).
075500                  20  MI-TC-START-TIME-X.
075600                      25  MI-TC-START-DIGIT-1
075700                          PIC 9(1).
075800                      23  MI-TC-START-DIGITS-2-5-X.
075900                      25  MI-TC-START-DIGITS-2-5
076000                          PIC 9(4).
240800      IF FIELDS-ARE-VALID                                         024

IGYPA3022-S "MI-TC-ELAPSED-TIME (NUMERIC NONINTEGER)" was compared with
"SPACES"

            The comparison was discarded.

    240900      AND (MI-TC-ELAPSED-TIME (SCREEN-SUB) NOT = SPACES
024
    241000          OR MI-TC-STOP-TIME-X (SCREEN-SUB) NOT = SPACES)
024
  1 241100      PERFORM 3640-CHANGE-DETAIL-TIMES
024
  1 241200         THRU 3649-END-CHANGE-DETAIL-TIMES
024
  1 241300      MOVE SCREEN-SUB TO ADJUSTED-SUB
024
  1 241400      PERFORM 3720-DISPLAY-CHANGED-LINE
024
  1 241500         THRU 3729-END-DISPLAY-CHANGED-LINE.
024
    241600 3659-END-CHANGE-OUTSIDE-LUNCH.
024
```

Figure 7.4 Code showing the numeric comparing with alphabetic issue.

Resolution

We identified the condition, which requires manual remediation, as shown in Figure 7.5.

```
6573    IGYDS0001-W    A blank was missing before character "_" in column 39.    A
bl

                      Same message on line:    6788    8620

6573    IGYDS0027-S    Non-COBOL character(s) were found starting with "_" in
column


007100          ABJ6082     00    NEW   ORGANIZATION IS ADDED
007800          ABJ6181     00    OBSOLETE ELEMENT IS REMOVED
008000          ABJ6177     00    RECORD CLAUSE IS REMOVED
008000          ABJ6181     00    OBSOLETE ELEMENT IS REMOVED
009800          ABJ6181     00    OBSOLETE ELEMENT IS REMOVED
009800          ABJ6119     00    RECORDING MODE CLAUSE REMOVED
009800          ABJ6181     00    OBSOLETE ELEMENT IS REMOVED
```

Figure 7.5 Manual remediation of code for the numeric comparing with alphabetic issue.

7.3.5 Fields Not Defined Issue

The *problem* is that a field was not defined as a data name in the program. This problem is independent of missing copy module problem.

Resolution

We need to identify the missing element and resolve it. This is often a problem when incorrect copybooks are included.

7.4 Conclusion

Issues are going to occur in any migration. Environmental anomalies will creep in. Bad coding practices will finally catch up with you. But you can mitigate much of this by being prepared to put some time in up front to complete the conversion first (rather than just compile). CCCA, we found, performed well and reduced many of the problems we would have otherwise had.

In the next chapter, we'll help you decide if outsourcing your upgrade is right for you and give you some insights into how our factory operated, so you can use our best practices to improve your own upgrade project.

PART THREE

Outsourcing the Upgrade

CHAPTER 8

The Factory Approach

Picture a classic factory with assembly lines, repeating machinery, and consistent quality (versus handmade). That process is what made the Industrial Revolution possible. (Of course, we'd like you to think of the good things made possible by the Industrial Revolution and not its ill side effects.)

Clearly, the benefits of using a well-structured and repeatable process should include the following:

- Higher quality produced
- Reduced completion time
- Predictable results and time frames
- Predictable costs
- Dedicated resources

8.1 The Factory Process

As we occassionally mentioned in the previous 'Do-It-Yourself' sections, you can establish a factory approach of your own by creating a separate group in your firm that only performs the upgrades (see Figure 8.1 for a structural representation of this).

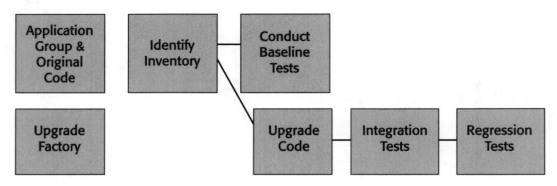

Figure 8.1 The factory process diagram.

Creating the baseline test environment will keep your application group busy enough to justify having a separate group to upgrade the code. The timing here is critical, however. You want the code upgrades to finish when the baseline testing is completed. One benefit of a factory approach is that you will be able to predict when the upgrade will be finished.

8.1.1 When Will the Upgrade Be Finished?

Using CCCA 2.0 and the utilities we developed (such as the automated period fixer and REMARKS section corrector), we upgraded an average of one thousand programs over a calendar period of three weeks, with an FTE (Full-time Equivalent Resource) count of 300 hours. Using CCCA 2.1, we reduced our FTE rate down to 220 hours (same calendar time). That's about 18 minutes per program for CCCA 2.0 and 13.2 for CCCA 2.1. Now, you probably won't have an application with a perfect program count of one thousand programs, so adjust according to your program count as well as for your earning curve and availability.

In the remaining sections of this chapter, we will examine desirable traits for a consulting firm to have when using a factory approach.

8.2 Factory Traits

The dedicated computing and communications technologies of the COBOL upgrade factory should enable it to rapidly deliver successful solutions to your company. If you can, visit the factory's site. In any case, request information regarding the following:

Project Management Methods
- Project management tools (scheduling tools).
- Knowledge repository.
- Reusable elements (test plans, problem-resolution method).
- Experienced project management resources.
- Experienced conversion personnel (knowledge of more than one upgrade tool or evidence of research into better tools).
- Standards.
- References.
- Metrics (number of programs converted from which version to which version, time to complete, number of errors tracked, and so on).
- Ability to handle your unique issues.
- What can't they convert?
- Sample code.
- Their testing methodology.
- Anomaly resolution (bug-fixing) methodology.
- Change management—how does it match yours?
- Ability to take refreshes (if your code changes during the upgrade project).
- Ability to upgrade from each version to the next.

Factory Facilities
- The factory should support R&D and all tool refinements, including tool testing and tool configuration.
- Hours of support.
- Platform.
- Supported tools (both upgrade and configuration management).
- Operating system and version.
- Available compilers.
- Available systems personnel.
- Transfer mechanisms (FTP, cartridge, nine-track, dial-up, and so on).

- Security (SAS 70 available?).
- Amount of DASD.
- Amount of MIPS.

Pricing
- Charges for DASD and MIPS?
- Tool charges or royalty fees.
- Cost per line of code or program? (Ask for a definition of "line of code." Ideally, a line-of-code count will not include blank lines or comments.)
- Time and material plus expenses?

Other Services to Consider
- **On-site packaging.** Unless you have a well-functioning source management tool or procedure in place, you may face challenges obtaining all the necessary components for upgrading. See if your candidates can assist you in identifying the right source modules to upgrade. This assistance could take the form of tools to scan JCL for programs or something that scans programs for copybooks.
- **On-site implementation assistance.** If you are migrating to a new environment or new compiler (new to your shop), you may want help implementing the new compilers or environments (such as LE). The factory's experience may save you some downtime.
- **Customization.** Are you thinking about moving to a new centralized date routine? As long as you are preparing a thorough test environment, now may be a good time to implement a small number of common changes, such as getting rid of your ten current date manipulation routines in favor of a single, more maintainable (and hopefully Y2K-ready) routine. Can your upgrade partner assist you with this? Can they make mass changes?
- **Language or database conversions.** We don't recommend that you try to regression test both database and language upgrade changes simultaneously or language conversions (such as a mixed-language application going from PL/I to COBOL) and language upgrade changes together. But if your upgrade partner has

those capabilities, they should already know your code and environment when it is time to assist with concurrent conversions.

- **On-site test support.** Can your partner supply experienced testers and/or people experienced in arranging tests? Do they have a testing methodology (preferably documented)? Ask for documentation or for a list of the types of information they use to establish a test environment.

- **Documentation.** Ask for support documentation up front to see what sort of help you can count on later. A lack of documentation is a sign of a disorganized company.

8.3 Finding the Right Partner

Now that you know what to look for, how do you find the right partner to work with? Your past experience with outsourcing partners is a good place to start. You can also ask tool vendors if they perform the upgrade or if they partner with another firm who assists them (and why did they choose that particular company to pair with?). You can also try the Internet. Rather than supply you with a list of sites (which change frequently), we'll let you know that we had the best results using the following search elements (together): COBOL MVS OS/VS UPGRADE.

Using the "good traits" we presented in the previous section, you can prepare an appropriate Request for Proposal (RFP) and request that companies who perform these services bid on your project. In your RFP, provide as best you can the following information:

- Scope (number of programs to be upgraded, number of copybooks, lines of code)
- Databases and transaction managers involved
- Current application state description (include language levels)
- Future application state expectation (include language levels)
- Anticipated start and end dates
- Other assistance (see Section 8.2) and documentation required/requested
- Acceptable postimplementation error rates, time limits, and consequences of nonperformance

Before sending out your RFPs, first narrow down your choices to spare yourself the hassle of having to examine twenty proposals. Proposals are usually responded to in one to two weeks. Carefully review any assumptions that are made in the proposal. Are they acceptable? These can become negotiation points for you in later contract negotiations.

8.4 Conclusion

A factory is only as good as its ability to repeat a process in a quality fashion. A good factory has documentation, reliable metrics from past experience, a thorough methodology, a workable project plan, communication mechanisms, the right people, the right tools, and satisfied clients. If your COBOL upgrade project is large, finding assistance through an experienced partner may reduce your cost and effort. Large or small, in-house or outsourced, there is much to learn about good maintenance techniques from a process that develops reusable procedures and stores best-practice and lessons-learned information for future use.

In the following appendixes, we have included some COBOL upgrade reference materials for your review. Good luck!

APPENDIX A

COBOL Language Level Comparison

In this appendix we compare the language elements of OS/VS COBOL and VS COBOL II in Table A.1. If a language element is no longer supported because it is not in the 1985 American National Standard (ANS) or because it's an IBM extension that has been replaced by another language element, we note it as such. Where possible, we also note the replacements for these elements.

For complete descriptions of the two language versions, see the following manuals:

- IBM VS COBOL for OS/VS
- VS COBOL II Application Programming Language Reference

NOTE
1. IBM extensions to the COBOL/85 standard are indicated with an asterisk (*).
2. ISAM and BDAM files are not supported.
3. Some restrictions for OS/VS COBOL under CMS are still restrictions for VS COBOL II under CMS.

Table A.1 A Comparison of OS/VS COBOL, Release 2, with VS COBOL II

LANGUAGE ELEMENT	OS/VS COBOL	VS COBOL II	NOTES
IDENTIFICATION DIVISION:			
AUTHOR paragraph	Yes	Yes	
DATE-COMPILED paragraph	Yes	Yes	
DATE-WRITTEN paragraph	Yes	Yes	
INSTALLATION paragraph	Yes	Yes	
PROGRAM-ID paragraph	Yes	Yes	In VS COBOL II only, COMMON and INITIAL options allowed.
REMARKS paragraph*	Yes	No	Not in the COBOL/ 74 standard; replaced by * (comment line).
SECURITY paragraph	Yes	Yes	
ENVIRONMENT DIVISION:			Optional in VS COBOL II.
Configuration Section:			Optional in VS COBOL II.
OBJECT-COMPUTER	Yes	Yes	OS/VS COBOL accepts paragraph SEGMENT-LIMIT clause, as does VS COBOL II. However, SEGMENT-LIMIT is an obsolete element and is to be deleted from the next revision of the COBOL standard.
SPECIAL-NAMES paragraph	Yes	Yes	Some function-name differences exist: Only OS/VS COBOL accepts Report Writer code. VS COBOL II accepts S03-S05, SYSLST, SYSIPT, and SYSPCH. In OS/VS COBOL, ALPHABET keyword is not allowed. In VS COBOL II, ALPHABET keyword is required; alphabet clause allows STANDARD-2 for the international ISO seven-bit code.
SOURCE-COMPUTER paragraph	Yes	Yes	
Input-Output Section:			
FILE-CONTROL paragraph:			
SELECT clause	Yes	Yes	
ACTUAL KEY clause	Yes	No	IBM extension for BDAM; replaced with VSAM.
ASSIGN clause	Yes	Yes	
ORGANIZATION clause	Yes	Yes	
ACCESS MODE clause	Yes	Yes	

COBOL Language Level Comparison

LANGUAGE ELEMENT	OS/VS COBOL	VS COBOL II	NOTES
RECORD KEY clause	Yes	Yes	
ALTERNATE RECORD KEY clause	Yes	Yes	
NOMINAL KEY clause*	Yes	No	IBM extension for ISAM; replaced with VSAM.
FILE STATUS clause	Yes	Yes	In VS COBOL II, the second status key data item contains more detailed VSAM feedback information. Status key codes are changed and are more specific.
PADDING CHARACTER	No	Yes	In VS COBOL II; for clause sequential files only.
PASSWORD clause*	Yes	Yes	
RECORD DELIMITER	No	Yes	In VS COBOL II; for clause sequential files only.
RESERVE clause	Yes	Yes	VS COBOL II does not accept specification of integer ALTERNATE AREA(S) or NO ALTERNATE AREA(S). Under OS/VS COBOL, specifying the optional word ALTERNATE causes the RESERVE clause to behave as it would under OS/VS COBOL using the LANGLVL(1) option.
TRACK-AREA clause*	Yes	No	IBM extension for ISAM; replaced with VSAM.
TRACK-LIMIT clause*	Yes	No	OS/VS COBOL treats as comment. PROCESSING MODE Yes No OS/VS COBOL treats clause* as comment.
I-O-CONTROL paragraph:			Entries optional in VS COBOL II.
RERUN clause	Yes	Yes	VS COBOL II does not take a checkpoint on the first record.
SAME clause	Yes	Yes	
MULTIPLE FILE TAPE	Yes	Yes	
CONTAINS clause			
APPLY clause*	Yes	Yes	IBM extension to ANSI COBOL/68 standard.

continues

Table A.1 *(Continued)*

LANGUAGE ELEMENT	OS/VS COBOL	VS COBOL II	NOTES
DATA DIVISION:			Optional in VS COBOL II.
File Section:			
File Description entry:			
FD file name	Yes	Yes	
BLOCK CONTAINS clause	Yes	Yes	
CODE-SET clause	Yes	Yes	
DATA RECORDS clause	Yes	Yes	
EXTERNAL clause	No	Yes	In VS COBOL II, allows programs to share files.
LABEL RECORDS clause	Yes	Yes	TOTALING AREA and TOTALED AREA options are not accepted by VS COBOL II.
LINAGE clause	Yes	Yes	
RECORD CONTAINS clause	Yes	Yes	
RECORDING MODE clause*	Yes	Yes	
REPORT clause	Yes	No	VS COBOL II does not support the Report Writer module of the COBOL/74 standard.
VALUE OF clause	Yes	Yes	
Sort/Merge File			
Description entry:			
SD file name	Yes	Yes	
DATA RECORDS clause	Yes	Yes	
LABEL RECORDS clause	Yes	No	
RECORD CONTAINS clause	Yes	Yes	
Data Description entry:			
Data name clause	Yes	Yes	
FILLER clause	Yes	Yes	In VS COBOL II only; optional.
BLANK WHEN ZERO clause	Yes	Yes	
EXTERNAL clause	No	Yes	In VS COBOL II only; level-01 in WORKING-STORAGE SECTION only.
GLOBAL clause	No	Yes	In VS COBOL II, specifies that this file connector is a global name.
JUSTIFIED clause	Yes	Yes	VS COBOL II does not support LANGLVL(1) interpretation of JUSTIFIED clause.

COBOL Language Level Comparison

LANGUAGE ELEMENT	OS/VS COBOL	VS COBOL II	NOTES
OCCURS clause	Yes	Yes	VS COBOL II allows up to seven dimensions. VS COBOL II computes the length of variable-length items at time of reference to the variable-length item, not when the value of the ODO object changes.
PICTURE clause	Yes	Yes	
REDEFINES clause	Yes	Yes	
RENAMES clause	Yes	Yes	
SIGN clause	Yes	Yes	VS COBOL II allows multiple SIGN clauses in a hierarchy.
SYNCHRONIZED clause	Yes	Yes	
USAGE clause	Yes	Yes	OS/VS COBOL does not support BINARY, DISPLAY-1, PACKED-DECIMAL, or POINTER. VS COBOL II supports BINARY, DISPLAY-1, PACKED-DECIMAL, and POINTER; it does not support DISPLAY-ST.
VALUE clause	Yes	Yes	OS/VS COBOL does not support VALUE IS NULL.
WORKING-STORAGE SECTION	Yes	Yes	
LINKAGE SECTION	Yes	Yes	
COMMUNICATION SECTION	Yes	No	VS COBOL II does not support the Communications module of the COBOL/74 standard.
REPORT SECTION	Yes	No	VS COBOL II does not support the Report Writer module of the COBOL/74 standard.
PROCEDURE DIVISION:			Optional in VS COBOL II.
Arithmetic expressions	Yes	Yes	VS COBOL II produces more accurate conversions for floating-point numbers than OS/VS COBOL. As a result, the values produced by VS COBOL II when using floating point may differ from those produced by OS/VS COBOL.
Conditional expressions	Yes	Yes	
Complex conditions	Yes	Yes	

continues

Table A.1 *(Continued)*

LANGUAGE ELEMENT	OS/VS COBOL	VS COBOL II	NOTES
Alphabetic class test	Yes	Yes	In VS COBOL II only: ALPHABETIC class test is true for both uppercase and lowercase letters. ALPHABETIC-UPPER test is true for only uppercase letters. ALPHABETIC-LOWER test is true for only lowercase letters.
DBCS and Kanji class tests	No	Yes	
NOT phrase support	No	Yes	OS/VS COBOL does not allow NOT INVALID KEY, NOT ON SIZE ERROR, NOT ON EXCEPTION, NOT AT END, NOT ON OVERFLOW, and NOT END-OF-PAGE; VS COBOL II allows these phrases.
Reference modification	No	Yes	
Procedure Division Statements:			
ACCEPT statement	Yes	Yes	OS/VS COBOL does not allow mnemonic name in FROM phrase to be declared as SYSIPT; VS COBOL II does.
ACCEPT MESSAGE COUNT	Yes	No	VS COBOL II does not support the statement in the Communications module of the COBOL/74 standard.
ADD statement	Yes	Yes	OS/VS COBOL does not allow the explicit scope terminator END-ADD; VS COBOL II does.
ALTER statement	Yes	Yes	
CALL statement	Yes	Yes	VS COBOL II allows the BY REFERENCE and BY CONTENT phrases, and the explicit scope terminator END-CALL. OS/VS COBOL allows procedure names in the USING option; VS COBOL II does not accept procedure names and nonsequential file names in this option. VS COBOL II allows nested subprograms to be stored separately from the main program.

COBOL Language Level Comparison

LANGUAGE ELEMENT	OS/VS COBOL	VS COBOL II	NOTES
CANCEL statement	Yes	Yes	
CLOSE statement	Yes	Yes	FOR REMOVAL option allowed for sequential I/O but treated as comments. OS/VS COBOL accepts the WITH POSITIONING and DISP options as IBM extensions. VS COBOL II does not.
COMPUTE statement	Yes	Yes	OS/VS COBOL does not allow the explicit scope terminator END-COMPUTE; VS COBOL II does.
CONTINUE statement*	No	Yes	
Debug packets*	Yes	No	IBM extension to ANSI COBOL/68 standard; replaced by USE FOR DEBUGGING declarative.
DELETE statement	Yes	Yes	OS/VS COBOL does not (for I/O) allow the explicit scope terminator END-DELETE; VS COBOL II does.
DISABLE statement	Yes	No	VS COBOL II does not support the Communications module of the COBOL/74 standard.
DISPLAY statement	Yes	Yes	VS COBOL II allows mnemonic name in UPON phrase to be declared as SYSLST, as a DBCS data item, or as a DBCS literal; OS/VS COBOL does not.
DIVIDE statement	Yes	Yes	OS/VS COBOL does not allow the explicit scope terminator END-DIVIDE; VS COBOL II does.
ENABLE statement	Yes	No	VS COBOL II does not support the Communications module of the COBOL/74 standard.
END PROGRAM statement	No	Yes	
ENTRY statement*	Yes	Yes	
EVALUATE statement*	No	Yes	
EXAMINE statement*	Yes	No	Not in the COBOL/74 standard; replaced by the INSPECT statement.

continues

Table A.1 *(Continued)*

LANGUAGE ELEMENT	OS/VS COBOL	VS COBOL II	NOTES
EXHIBIT statement*	Yes	No	Not in the COBOL/74 standard; replaced by the DISPLAY statement.
EXIT statement	Yes	Yes	
EXIT PROGRAM statement	Yes	Yes	
GENERATE statement	Yes	No	VS COBOL II does not support the Report Writer module of the COBOL/74 standard.
GO TO statement	Yes	Yes	
GOBACK statement*	Yes	Yes	
IF statement	Yes	Yes	OS/VS COBOL does not allow the explicit scope terminator END-IF; VS COBOL II does. VS COBOL II replaces the OTHERWISE phrase with ELSE.
INITIALIZE statement	No	Yes	
INITIATE statement	Yes	No	VS COBOL II does not support the Report Writer module of the COBOL/74 standard.
INSPECT statement	Yes	Yes	With CICS, VS COBOL II allows the CONVERTING phrase. OS/VS COBOL does not.
MERGE statement	Yes	Yes	VS COBOL II allows multiple GIVING files.
MOVE statement	Yes	Yes	OS/VS COBOL allows the CURRENT-DATE and TIME-OF-DAY special registers as sending areas. In VS COBOL II, CURRENT-DATE and TIME-OF-DAY are replaced by the DATE and TIME special registers with the ACCEPT statement. VS COBOL II allows you to move numeric-edited fields to numeric-edited or numeric fields.
MULTIPLY statement	Yes	Yes	OS/VS COBOL does not allow the explicit scope terminator END-MULTIPLY; VS COBOL II does.
NOTE statement*	Yes	No	Not in the COBOL/74 standard; replaced by the * symbol in column 7 of source program.
ON statement*	Yes	No	IBM extension to ANSI COBOL/68 standard.

COBOL Language Level Comparison

LANGUAGE ELEMENT	OS/VS COBOL	VS COBOL II	NOTES
OPEN statement	Yes	Yes	OS/VS COBOL accepts the LEAVE, REREAD, or DISP option and allows the REVERSED phrase for multireel files; VS COBOL II does not. VS COBOL II allows OPEN EXTEND for indexed and relative files.
PERFORM statement	Yes	Yes	VS COBOL II allows inline format, explicit scope terminator, and TEST BEFORE and TEST AFTER option (PERFORM WITH TEST BEFORE UNTIL CONDITION imperative statement END-PERFORM).
READ statement	Yes	Yes	OS/VS COBOL does not allow the explicit scope terminator END-READ; VS COBOL II does.
READY TRACE statement*	Yes	No	OS/VS COBOL processes; VS COBOL II checks for proper syntax but otherwise treats as comment.
RECEIVE statement	Yes	No	VS COBOL II does not support the Communications module of the COBOL/74 standard.
RELEASE statement	Yes	Yes	
RESET TRACE statement*	Yes	No	OS/VS COBOL processes; VS COBOL II checks for proper syntax, but otherwise treats as comment.
RETURN statement	Yes	Yes	OS/VS COBOL does not allow the explicit scope terminator END-RETURN; VS COBOL II does.
REWRITE statement	Yes	Yes	OS/VS COBOL does not allow the explicit scope terminator END-REWRITE; VS COBOL II does.
SEARCH statement	Yes	Yes	In OS/VS COBOL, the WHEN phrase condition need not be a data name associated with a data name in the KEY phrase of the table or its subject named in the KEY phrase of the table. In VS COBOL II, it must be. VS COBOL II does not allow the object of the WHEN phrase condition to be an identifier named in the KEY phrase of the table. OS/VS COBOL does not allow the explicit scope terminator END-SEARCH; VS COBOL II does.

continues

Table A.1 *(Continued)*

LANGUAGE ELEMENT	OS/VS COBOL	VS COBOL II	NOTES
SEEK statement	Yes	No	OS/VS COBOL treats as comment.
SEND statement	Yes	No	VS COBOL II does not support the Communications module of the COBOL/74 standard.
SET condition name	No	Yes	
SET statement TRUE	Yes	Yes	
SET ON/OFF statement	Yes		In VS COBOL II, sets external switches.
SET pointer data item*	No	Yes	
SORT statement	Yes	Yes	VS COBOL II allows USING/GIVING for indexed and relative files and multiple GIVING files.
START statement	Yes	Yes	OS/VS COBOL supports the USING phrase; VS COBOL II does not. OS/VS COBOL does not allow the explicit scope terminator END-START; VS COBOL II does.
STOP statement	Yes	Yes	
STRING statement	Yes	Yes	With CICS, OS/VS COBOL neither allows the explicit scope terminator, END-STRING, nor the receiving item to be a group item; VS COBOL II does.
SUBTRACT statement	Yes	Yes	OS/VS COBOL does not allow the explicit scope terminator END-SUBTRACT; VS COBOL II does.
TERMINATE statement	Yes	No	VS COBOL II does not support the Report Writer module of the COBOL/74 standard.
TRANSFORM statement*	Yes	No	IBM extension to the ANSI COBOL/68 standard; replaced by the INSPECT statement.
UNSTRING statement	Yes	Yes	With CICS, OS/VS COBOL does not allow the explicit scope terminator END-UNSTRING; VS COBOL II does. VS COBOL II cannot unstring into numeric-edited items.

COBOL Language Level Comparison

LANGUAGE ELEMENT	OS/VS COBOL	VS COBOL II	NOTES
WRITE statement	Yes	Yes	OS/VS COBOL does not allow the explicit scope terminator END-WRITE; VS COBOL II does. In VS COBOL II, the IBM extension AFTER POSITIONING is replaced by AFTER ADVANCING. In VS COBOL II, you cannot use WRITE for a QSAM file OPEN I-O.
Compiler-directing Statements:			
BASIS statement*	Yes	Yes	
CONTROL statement*	No	Yes	These two statements *CBL statement* are synonymous.
COPY statement	Yes	Yes	OS/VS COBOL supports the COBOL/74 COPY statement and the ANSI COBOL/68 COPY statement with the LANGLVL(1) option. VS COBOL II supports only the COBOL/85 standard COPY. OS/VS COBOL does not allow COPY statements to be nested; VS COBOL II does.
DELETE statement (for programs)*	Yes	Yes	BASIS source.
EJECT statement*	Yes	Yes	IBM extension to ANSI COBOL/68 standard.
ENTER statement	Yes	Yes	Allowed but treated as a comment.
INSERT statement (for programs)*	Yes	Yes	BASIS source.
REPLACE statement	No	Yes	
SERVICE LABEL statement*	No	Yes	
SKIP1/2/3 statements*	Yes	Yes	
TITLE statement*	No	Yes	
USE statement:			
USE AFTER	Yes	Yes	VS COBOL II does not produce an EXCEPTION/ERROR except for the GIVING declarative option; the FILE STATUS clause of the FILE-CONTROL paragraph replaces it.

continues

Table A.1 *(Continued)*

LANGUAGE ELEMENT	OS/VS COBOL	VS COBOL II	NOTES
USE BEFORE	Yes	No	VS COBOL II does not support the Report Writer REPORTING module of the Declarative COBOL/74 standard.
USE AFTER STANDARD labels*	Yes	Yes	Declarative
USE BEFORE STANDARD labels*	Yes	No	Declarative
USE FOR DEBUGGING	Yes	Yes	VS COBOL II supports Declarative level 2 of the COBOL/74 standard Debug module on CICS. OS/VS COBOL does not. Under CICS, VS COBOL II supports level 2 of the COBOL/85 standard Debug module whereas OS/VS does not.
Special Registers:			
ADDRESS OF*	No	Yes	
CURRENT-DATE*	Yes	No	IBM extension to ANSI COBOL/68 standard; replaced by DATE special register with the ACCEPT statement.
DATE	Yes	Yes	
DAY	Yes	Yes	
DAY-OF-WEEK	No	Yes	
DEBUG-ITEM	Yes	Yes	In VS COBOL II, DEBUG-ITEM can be used to display DBCS characters, even though the picture clause for DEBUG-NAME defines single-byte characters.
LENGTH*	No	Yes	
LINAGE-COUNTER	Yes	Yes	
LINE-COUNTER	Yes	No	VS COBOL II does not support the Report Writer module of the COBOL/74 standard.
PAGE-COUNTER	Yes	No	VS COBOL II does not support the Report Writer module of the COBOL/74 standard.
RETURN-CODE*	Yes	Yes	
SHIFT-IN*	No	Yes	In VS COBOL II, used to indicate the end of double-byte character set.

LANGUAGE ELEMENT	OS/VS COBOL	VS COBOL II	NOTES
SHIFT-OUT*	No	Yes	In VS COBOL II, used to indicate the beginning of a double-byte character set.
SORT-CONTROL*	No	Yes	
SORT-CORE-SIZE*	Yes	Yes	In VS COBOL II, this special register is overridden by the corresponding SORT OPTION control statement parameters, which are included in the SORT-CONTROL file.
SORT-FILE-SIZE*	Yes	Yes	In VS COBOL II, this special register is overridden by the corresponding SORT OPTION control statement parameters, which are included in the SORT-CONTROL file.
SORT-MESSAGE*	Yes	Yes	In VS COBOL II, this special register is overridden by the corresponding SORT OPTION control statement parameters, which are included in the SORT-CONTROL file.
SORT-MODE-SIZE*	Yes	Yes	In VS COBOL II, this special register can be overridden by the SMS= control statement in the SORT-CONTROL file.
SORT-RETURN*	Yes	Yes	
TALLY*	Yes	Yes	
TIME	Yes	Yes	
TIME-OF-DAY*	Yes	No	IBM extension to the ANSI COBOL/68 standard; replaced by the TIME special register with the ACCEPT statement.
WHEN-COMPILED*	Yes	Yes	In VS COBOL II, the format of the information in the WHEN-COMPILED special register is the same as that in OS/VS COBOL.

APPENDIX B

A More Advanced Conversion and Compile Reporting Sample

Metrics capturing was very important to the success we enjoyed upgrading COBOL programs. We needed to know how well we and our tools were performing, so we developed a more advanced Conversion and Compile Report than was available from the CCCA tool to capture the following information:

1. Program names
2. Type (OS/VS COBOL or VS COBOL II)
3. BLL
4. DB/2 handled by CCCA
5. IMS, ADABAS, and so on, not handled by CCCA
6. CICS
7. Index problems
8. Copybooks missing
9. Number of conversion errors per program, cluster
10. Number of compile errors per program, cluster
11. Number of manual fixes needed per program, cluster
12. Number or programs going from OS/VS COBOL to VS COBOL II
13. Number of programs going from VS COBOL II to COBOL/370
14. Number of programs going from OS/VS COBOL to COBOL/370

15. Number of programs with Report Writer
16. Number of batch programs
17. Number of copybooks converted
18. Number of programs needing to have database commands commented out, such as ADABAS
19. Time involved in adding and removing comments and in recompiling COBOL programs with ADABAS
20. Documentation of lag time when items, such as copybooks, are reported missing and when they are received
21. Types of errors encountered by class (01 levels, redefines, complex IF, missing period, etc.)

PROGRAM NAME	CONVERSION			COMPILE				
	INIT. CONV. STATUS	CURRENT CONV. STATUS	CURRENT CONV. DATE	INITIAL COMPILE STATUS	INITIAL NO. OF COMPILE ERRORS	CURRENT COMPILE STATUS	CURRENT NO. OF COMPILE ERRORS	CURRENT COMPILE DATE
PROGM30	COMPLETE	COMPLETE	1/11/98	12	21	12	21	1/11/98
PROGM31	COMPLETE	COMPLETE	1/11/98	8	6	8	6	1/11/98
PROGM32	COMPLETE	COMPLETE	1/11/98	8	2	8	2	1/11/98
PROGM33	COMPLETE	COMPLETE	1/11/98	12	15	12	15	1/11/98
PROGM34	COMPLETE	COMPLETE	1/11/98	12	11	12	11	1/11/98
PROGM45	COMPLETE	COMPLETE	1/11/98	0	0	0	0	1/11/98
PROGM80	COMPLETE	COMPLETE	1/11/98	0	0	0	0	1/11/98
PROG145	COMPLETE	COMPLETE	1/11/98	12	95	12	95	1/11/98
PROG270	COMPLETE	COMPLETE	1/11/98	12	8	12	8	1/11/98
PROG400	COMPLETE	COMPLETE	1/11/98	4	0	4	0	1/11/98
PROG915	COMPLETE	COMPLETE	1/11/98	12	7	12	7	1/11/98
PROG065	COMPLETE	COMPLETE	1/11/98	12	46	12	46	1/11/98
PROG070	COMPLETE	COMPLETE	1/11/98	12	18	12	18	1/11/98
PROG075	COMPLETE	COMPLETE	1/11/98	0	0	0	0	1/11/98
PROG800	COMPLETE	COMPLETE	1/11/98	12	69	12	69	1/11/98

A More Advanced Conversion and Compile Reporting Sample

PROGRAM NAME	EST. LEVEL OF EFFORT (MINUTES)	*COBOL UPGRADE	REPORT WRITER	DATABASE A=ADABAS, D=DB/2, B=BOTH, O=OTHER	CICS Y=BLL, O=OTHER, B= BOTH	DATE OPENED	DESCRIPTION OF ISSUES	DATE CLOSED
PROGM30		A			Y			
PROGM31		A			Y			
PROGM32		A			Y			
PROGM33		A						
PROGM34		A	X					
PROGM45		A	X					
PROGM80		A						
PROG145		A	X	A				
PROG270		A						
PROG400		A						
PROG915		A						
PROG065		A						
PROG070		A		A				
PROG075		A		A				
PROG800		A		A				

*A=OS/VS to VSCOBOL II

APPENDIX C

Sample Compile Jobs

The five figures in this chapter illustrate sample compile jobs. Figure C.1 shows a sample compile procedure for COBOL programs that have batch COBOL (VS COBOL II). Figure C.2 shows a sample compile procedure for COBOL programs that have CICS COBOL (VS COBOL II). Figure C.3 shows a sample compile procedure for programs that have CICS/ADABAS COBOL (VS COBOL II). Figure C.4 shows a sample compile procedure for programs that have CICS/DB/2/ADABAS (VS COBOL II). Figure C.5 shows a sample compile procedure for programs that have DB/2/ADABAS COBOL (VS COBOL II).

```
//CO700BAT JOB (CO000P),&PRGM,CLASS=A,MSGCLASS=Z,          00020001
//     NOTIFY=&SYSUID                                      00040000
//JOBLIB   DD DISP=SHR,DSN=CO.CLUSTER.LIB.LOAD             00030000
//****************************************************    00230000
//COMPILE EXEC  PGM=IGYCRCTL,REGION=8192K,                 00240000
// PARM=('RENT,SOURCE,DATA(31),LIB,APOST,TRUNC(BIN)','LANG(UE)')  00250000
//STEPLIB  DD  DSN=SYS1.COB2COMP,DISP=SHR
```

Figure C.1 Sample compile procedure for COBOL programs that have batch COBOL (VS COBOL II).

```
            00270000
//SYSPRINT DD   SYSOUT=*
            00280000
//SYSLIB    DD  DSN=CO.CLUSTER.IN.COPY,DISP=SHR                00290000
//          DD  DSN=SYS7.CICSV4.SDFHCOB,DISP=SHR
            00290000
//          DD  DSN=CO.SYS2.COPYLIB4,DISP=SHR
//SYSUT1    DD  DSN=&&SYSUT1,UNIT=SYSDA,SPACE=(460,(700,300))
            00310000
//SYSUT2    DD  DSN=&&SYSUT2,UNIT=SYSDA,SPACE=(460,(700,300))
            00320000
//SYSUT3    DD  DSN=&&SYSUT3,UNIT=SYSDA,SPACE=(460,(700,300))
            00330000
//SYSUT4    DD  DSN=&&SYSUT4,UNIT=SYSDA,SPACE=(460,(700,300))
            00340000
//SYSUT5    DD  DSN=&&SYSUT5,UNIT=SYSDA,SPACE=(460,(700,300))
            00350000
//SYSUT6    DD  DSN=&&SYSUT6,UNIT=SYSDA,SPACE=(460,(700,300))
            00360000
//SYSUT7    DD  DSN=&&SYSUT7,UNIT=SYSDA,SPACE=(460,(700,300))
            00370000
//SYSLIN    DD  DSN=&&LOADSET,DISP=(MOD,PASS),UNIT=SYSDA,
            00380000
//              SPACE=(TRK,(50,20),RLSE),
            00390000
//              DCB=(DSORG=PS,RECFM=FB,LRECL=80,BLKSIZE=3200)
//SYSIN     DD  DSN=CO.CLUSTER.IN.SOURCE(&PRGM),DISP=SHR       00400000
//*
            00420000
//*****************************************************************
            00900000
//LKED     EXEC PGM=IEWL,PARM='LIST,XREF,LET',
            00910000
//     COND=(5,LT,COMPILE),REGION=512K
            00920000
//SYSLIN    DD  DSN=&&LOADSET,DISP=(OLD,DELETE)
            00940000
//SYSLMOD   DD  DSN=CO.CLUSTER.IN.LOAD.COMPILE(&PRGM),DISP=SHR 00970000
//SYSLIB    DD  DSN=SYS7.CICSV4.SDFHLOAD,DISP=SHR
            00980000
//          DD  DSN=SYS1.SCEELKED,DISP=SHR
            00991000
//          DD  DSN=SYS1.VSCLLIB,DISP=SHR
            00991000
//          DD  DSN=CO.CLUSTER.LIB.LOAD,DISP=SHR               00991000
//          DD  DSN=CO.CLUSTER.IN.LOAD,DISP=SHR                00991000
//          DD  DSN=CO.E010829.SYS1.CALL.LIBRARY,DISP=SHR
            00991000
```

Figure C.1 *Continued*

```
//SYSUT1    DD   UNIT=(SYSDA,SEP=(SYSLIN,SYSLMOD)),              00992000
//               SPACE=(1024,(1500,500),RLSE)                    00993000
//SYSPRINT  DD   SYSOUT=*                                        00994000
//SYSIN     DD   *                                               00995000
//*                                                              00997000
```

Figure C.1 *Continued*

```
//CO29029 JOB (CO000P),FDI0400,CLASS=A,MSGCLASS=Z,
//     NOTIFY=CO290
//*================================================================*
00030000
//TRNSLATE EXEC PGM=DFHECP1$,COND=(4,LT),REGION=4096K,
//       PARM='FE,NOVBREF,NOP,NOSOURCE,SP,COBOL2'
//STEPLIB  DD  DSN=SYS7.CICSV4.SDFHLOAD,DISP=SHR
//SYSPRINT DD  SYSOUT=*
//SYSPUNCH DD  UNIT=SYSDA,DSN=&&SOURCE,DISP=(NEW,PASS),
//             DCB=(BLKSIZE=400,BUFNO=16),SPACE=(CYL,(20,10))
//*SYSIN DD   DSN=CO.MHT2.VSCOBII.SOURCE(KBM6070),DISP=SHR
//SYSIN DD    DSN=CO.CLUSTER.IN.SOURCE.COBOL2(FDI0400),DISP=SHR
//*================================================================*
00030000
//COMPILE EXEC PGM=IGYCRCTL,REGION=8192K,
//*COMPILE EXEC PGM=IGYCRCTL,COND=(0004,LT),REGION=8192K,
//     PARM=('MAP,LIB,NOCMPR2,NOOBJ,SOURCE,NOSEQ,NOOPT,NOADV,RES',
//        'APOST,DATA(24),FLAG(I,I)')
//STEPLIB  DD  DSN=SYS1.COB2COMP,DISP=SHR
//SYSLIB   DD  DSN=CO.CCCA.CLUSTER.OUT.COPY,DISP=SHR
//*SYSLIB  DD  DSN=CO.CCCA.CLUSTER.OUT.COPY,DISP=SHR
//*SYSLIB  DD  DSN=CO.CLUSTER.IN.COPY,DISP=SHR
//         DD  DSN=SYS7.CICSV4.SDFHLOAD,DISP=SHR
//         DD  DSN=CO.SYS2.COPYLIB4,DISP=SHR
//SYSIN    DD  DSN=&&SOURCE,DISP=(OLD,DELETE),DCB=BUFNO=16
//SYSUT1   DD  UNIT=SYSDA,SPACE=(CYL,(10,10)),DCB=BUFNO=16
//SYSUT2   DD  UNIT=SYSDA,SPACE=(CYL,(10,10)),DCB=BUFNO=16
//SYSUT3   DD  UNIT=SYSDA,SPACE=(CYL,(10,10)),DCB=BUFNO=16
//SYSUT4   DD  UNIT=SYSDA,SPACE=(CYL,(10,10)),DCB=BUFNO=16
//SYSUT5   DD  UNIT=SYSDA,SPACE=(CYL,(10,10)),DCB=BUFNO=16
```

Figure C.2 Sample compile procedure for COBOL programs that have CICS COBOL (VS COBOL II).

```
//SYSUT6    DD   UNIT=SYSDA,SPACE=(CYL,(10,10)),DCB=BUFNO=16
//SYSUT7    DD   UNIT=SYSDA,SPACE=(CYL,(10,10)),DCB=BUFNO=16
//SYSPRINT DD    SYSOUT=*
//SYSLIN    DD   UNIT=SYSDA,DSN=&&OBJECT,DISP=(NEW,PASS),
//               SPACE=(TRK,(50,20),RLSE),
//               DCB=(DSORG=PS,RECFM=FB,LRECL=80,BLKSIZE=3200)
//****************************************************************
//LKED      EXEC PGM=IEWL,PARM='LIST,XREF,LET',REGION=1024K,
//               COND=(4,LT,COMPILE)
//SYSUT1    DD   UNIT=SYSDA,SPACE=(TRK,(10,10)),
//               DCB=(BLKSIZE=1024,BUFNO=16)
//SYSLIB    DD   DSN=SYS7.FDI0400V4.SDFHLOAD,DISP=SHR
//          DD   DSN=SYS1.SCEELKED,DISP=SHR
//          DD   DSN=SYS1.DB2V4.SDSNLOAD,DISP=SHR
//          DD   DSN=CO.CLUSTER.IN.LOAD.COMPILE,DISP=SHR
//          DD   DSN=CO.E010829.SYS1.CALL.LIBRARY,DISP=SHR
//          DD   DSN=CO.E10818.SYSFDI0400.LOADLIB,DISP=SHR
//SYSLIN    DD   DSN=SYS7.FDI0400V4.SDFHCOB(DFHEILIC),DISP=SHR
//          DD   DSN=&&OBJECT,DISP=(OLD,DELETE)
//SYSPRINT DD    SYSOUT=*
//SYSIN     DD   *
  LIBRARY RESLIB(AIBTDLI)
//SYSLMOD   DD   DSN=CO.CLUSTER.IN.LOAD(FDI0400IPNP),DISP=SHR
//*
```

Figure C.2 *Continued*

```
//CO525NAT JOB (CO000P),&PRGM,CLASS=A,MSGCLASS=Z,
//     NOTIFY=&SYSUID
//*===============================================================*
00030000
//*    THIS IS TO COMPILE COBOL2/CICS/ADABAS
//*===============================================================*
00030000
//*
00230000
//SQLADA    EXEC PGM=ADASQLC,REGION=2048K
00180000
//STEPLIB   DD DSN=SYS4.ADB.ADA621.SQL171.LOAD,DISP=SHR
00190000
//          DD DSN=SYS4.ADB.ADA621.LOAD,DISP=SHR
00190000
//          DD DSN=CO.E10818.SPN.ADANAT.NEXT.LOAD,DISP=SHR
```

Figure C.3 Sample compile procedure for programs that have CICS/ADABAS COBOL (VS COBOL II).

```
//         DD  DSN=CO.E10818.SPN.ADANAT.CURR.LOAD,DISP=SHR
//DDCARD   DD  DSN=SYS4.ADB.SQL162.SRCE(ADAPARM),                  00200000
//             DISP=SHR                                            00210000
//ADAGLOB  DD  DSN=CO.SPN.ADABAS.PARMLIB(SQLDC),DISP=SHR
//         DD  DSN=CO.SPN.ADABAS.PARMLIB(SQLDICTB),DISP=SHR
//ADAIN    DD  DSN=CO.CLUSTER.IN.SOURCE.ORG(&PRGM),DISP=SHR        00200000
//ADAOUT   DD  DSN=CO.CLUSTER.IN.SOURCE.EXP(&PRGM),DISP=SHR
//*ADAOUT  DD  DSN=&&ADAOUT,DISP=(,PASS),UNIT=SYSDA,
//*           SPACE=(TRK,(30,15),RLSE)
//SYSUT1   DD  DSN=&&TEMP,DISP=(,DELETE),
//             UNIT=SYSDA,SPACE=(CYL,10)
//ADAMES   DD  SYSOUT=*
//SYSOUT   DD  SYSOUT=*
//SYSDBOUT DD  SYSOUT=*
//SYSUDUMP DD  SYSOUT=*
//*
//TRNSLATE EXEC PGM=DFHECP1$,COND=(4,LT),REGION=4096K,
//       PARM='FE,NOVBREF,NOP,NOSOURCE,SP,COBOL2'
//STEPLIB  DD  DSN=SYS7.CICSV4.SDFHLOAD,DISP=SHR
//SYSPRINT DD  SYSOUT=*
//SYSPUNCH DD  UNIT=SYSDA,DSN=&&CICSOUT,DISP=(NEW,PASS),
//             DCB=(BLKSIZE=400,BUFNO=16),SPACE=(CYL,(20,10))
//SYSIN    DD  DSN=CO.CLUSTER.IN.SOURCE.CONV.OUT.COB1(&PRGM),
//             DISP=SHR
//*                                                                00230000
//COMPILE  EXEC  PGM=IGYCRCTL,REGION=8192K,                        00240000
// PARM=('MAP,LIB,NOCMPR2,NOOBJ,SOURCE,NOSEQ,NOOPT,NOADV,RES',     00250000
//       'APOST,DATA(24),FLAG(I,I)')
//STEPLIB  DD  DSN=SYS1.COB2COMP,DISP=SHR                          00270000
//SYSPRINT DD  SYSOUT=*                                            00280000
//SYSLIB   DD  DSN=CO.CLUSTER.IN.COPY,DISP=SHR                     00290000
//         DD  DSN=SYS7.CICSV4.SDFHCOB,DISP=SHR                    00290000
//         DD  DSN=CO.SYS2.COPYLIB4,DISP=SHR
//SYSUT1   DD  DSN=&&SYSUT1,UNIT=SYSDA,SPACE=(460,(700,300))       00310000
//SYSUT2   DD  DSN=&&SYSUT2,UNIT=SYSDA,SPACE=(460,(700,300))       00320000
//SYSUT3   DD  DSN=&&SYSUT3,UNIT=SYSDA,SPACE=(460,(700,300))       00330000
```

Figure C.3 *(continues)*

```
//SYSUT4    DD   DSN=&&SYSUT4,UNIT=SYSDA,SPACE=(460,(700,300))
00340000
//SYSUT5    DD   DSN=&&SYSUT5,UNIT=SYSDA,SPACE=(460,(700,300))
00350000
//SYSUT6    DD   DSN=&&SYSUT6,UNIT=SYSDA,SPACE=(460,(700,300))
00360000
//SYSUT7    DD   DSN=&&SYSUT7,UNIT=SYSDA,SPACE=(460,(700,300))
00370000
//SYSLIN    DD   DSN=&&LOADSET,DISP=(MOD,PASS),UNIT=SYSDA,
00380000
//               SPACE=(TRK,(50,20),RLSE),
00390000
//               DCB=(DSORG=PS,RECFM=FB,LRECL=80,BLKSIZE=3200)
//SYSIN     DD   DSN=&&CICSOUT,DISP=(OLD,PASS)
00400000
//*
//LKED      EXEC PGM=IEWL,PARM='LIST,XREF,LET',REGION=1024K,
//          COND=(4,LT,COMPILE)
//SYSUT1    DD   UNIT=SYSDA,SPACE=(TRK,(10,10)),
//               DCB=(BLKSIZE=1024,BUFNO=16)
//SYSLIB    DD   DSN=SYS7.CICSV4.SDFHLOAD,DISP=SHR
//          DD   DSN=SYS4.ADB.ADA613.LOAD,DISP=SHR
//          DD   DSN=SYS1.SCEELKED,DISP=SHR
//          DD   DSN=CO.CLUSTER.IN.LOAD,DISP=SHR
//          DD   DSN=CO.E010829.SYS1.CALL.LIBRARY,DISP=SHR
//          DD   DSN=CO.E10818.SPN.ADANAT.CURR.LOAD,DISP=SHR
//          DD   DSN=CO.E10818.SYSCICS.LOADLIB,DISP=SHR
//SYSLIN    DD   DSN=SYS7.CICSV4.SDFHCOB(DFHEILIC),DISP=SHR
//          DD   DSN=&&LOADSET,DISP=(OLD,DELETE)
//SYSPRINT  DD   SYSOUT=*
//SYSIN     DD   *
  LIBRARY RESLIB(AIBTDLI)
//SYSLMOD   DD   DSN=CO.CLUSTER.IN.LOAD.COMPILE(&PRGM),DISP=SHR
//*
```

Figure C.3 *Continued*

```
//CO700NAT JOB (CO000P),&PRGM,CLASS=A,MSGCLASS=Z,
00020001
//      NOTIFY=&SYSUID
00040000
//JOBLIB   DD DISP=SHR,DSN=CO.CLUSTER.LIB.LOAD                    00030000
//* - COMPILE JCL SKELETON USED FOR COMPILING BATCH
```

Figure C.4 Sample compile procedure for programs that have CICS/DB/2/ADABAS (VS COBOL II).

```
COB/CICS/DB2/ADABAS00050000
//*================================================================*
00160000
//SQLADA    EXEC PGM=ADASQLC,REGION=2048K
00180000
//STEPLIB   DD DSN=SYS4.ADB.ADA621.SQL171.LOAD,DISP=SHR
00190000
//          DD DSN=SYS4.ADB.ADA621.LOAD,DISP=SHR
00190000
//          DD DSN=CO.E10818.SPN.ADANAT.NEXT.LOAD,DISP=SHR
//          DD DSN=CO.E10818.SPN.ADANAT.CURR.LOAD,DISP=SHR
//DDCARD    DD DSN=SYS4.ADB.SQL162.SRCE(ADAPARM),
00200000
//             DISP=SHR
00210000
//ADAGLOB   DD DSN=CO.SPN.ADABAS.PARMLIB(SQLDC),DISP=SHR
//          DD DSN=CO.SPN.ADABAS.PARMLIB(SQLDICTB),DISP=SHR
//ADAIN     DD DSN=CO.CLUSTER.IN.SOURCE.ORG(&PRGM),                 00200000
//             DISP=SHR
00210000
//ADAOUT    DD DSN=CO.CLUSTER.IN.SOURCE.EXP(&PRGM),DISP=SHR
//*ADAOUT   DD DSN=&&ADAOUT,DISP=(,PASS),UNIT=SYSDA,
//*           SPACE=(TRK,(30,15),RLSE)
//SYSUT1    DD DSN=&&TEMP,DISP=(,DELETE),
//             UNIT=SYSDA,SPACE=(CYL,10)
//ADAMES    DD SYSOUT=*
//SYSOUT    DD SYSOUT=*
//SYSDBOUT  DD SYSOUT=*
//SYSUDUMP  DD SYSOUT=*
//*
//DB2SQL    EXEC PGM=DSNHPC,
00180000
//             PARM='HOST(COBOL),APOST,APOSTSQL',
//             REGION=4096K
//STEPLIB   DD DSN=SYS1.DB2V4.SDSNEXIT,DISP=SHR
00190000
//          DD DSN=SYS1.DB2V4.SDSNLOAD,DISP=SHR
00190000
//DBRMLIB   DD DSN=&&DBRM(&PRGM),UNIT=SYSDA,
//             SPACE=(TRK,(1,1,1)),
//             DISP=(,PASS),DCB=BLKSIZE=6320
//SYSCIN    DD DSN=&&DSNHOUT,DISP=(MOD,PASS),UNIT=SYSDA,
//             DCB=BLKSIZE=23440,SPACE=(23440,(30,15),RLSE)
//SYSLIB    DD DISP=SHR,DSN=CO.CLUSTER.IN.DCLLIB
//          DD DISP=SHR,DSN=CO.CLUSTER.IN.COPY
//          DD DISP=SHR,DSN=CO.E10818.SYS2.PROD.DCLLIB
//          DD DISP=SHR,DSN=CO.SYS2.COPYLIB4
```

Figure C.4 *(continues)*

```
//SYSPRINT  DD  SYSOUT=*
//SYSTERM   DD  SYSOUT=*
//SYSUDUMP  DD  SYSOUT=*
//SYSUT1    DD  SPACE=(23440,(30,15),,,ROUND),UNIT=SYSDA
//SYSUT2    DD  SPACE=(23440,(30,15),,,ROUND),UNIT=SYSDA
//SYSIN     DD  DSN=CO.CLUSTER.IN.SOURCE.EXP(&PRGM),DISP=SHR
//SYSUDUMP  DD  SYSOUT=*
//*
00230000
//TRNSLATE EXEC PGM=DFHECP1$,COND=(4,LT),REGION=4096K,
//     PARM='FE,NOVBREF,NOP,NOSOURCE,SP,COBOL2'
//STEPLIB   DD  DSN=SYS7.CICSV4.SDFHLOAD,DISP=SHR
//SYSPRINT  DD  SYSOUT=*
//SYSPUNCH  DD  UNIT=SYSDA,DSN=&&CICSOUT,DISP=(NEW,PASS),
//             DCB=(BLKSIZE=400,BUFNO=16),SPACE=(CYL,(20,10))
//SYSIN     DD  DSN=&&DSNHOUT,DISP=(OLD,PASS)
//*
00230000
//COMPILE EXEC  PGM=IGYCRCTL,REGION=8192K,
00240000
// PARM=('MAP,LIB,NOCMPR2,NOOBJ,SOURCE,NOSEQ,NOOPT,NOADV,RES',
00250000
//       'APOST,DATA(24),FLAG(I,I)')
//STEPLIB   DD  DSN=SYS1.COB2COMP,DISP=SHR
00270000
//SYSPRINT  DD  SYSOUT=*
00280000
//SYSLIB    DD  DSN=CO.CLUSTER.IN.COPY,DISP=SHR                      00290000
//          DD  DSN=CO.SYS2.COPYLIB4,DISP=SHR
//          DD  DSN=SYS7.CICSV4.SDFHCOB,DISP=SHR
00290000
//SYSUT1    DD  DSN=&&SYSUT1,UNIT=SYSDA,SPACE=(460,(700,300))
00310000
//SYSUT2    DD  DSN=&&SYSUT2,UNIT=SYSDA,SPACE=(460,(700,300))
00320000
//SYSUT3    DD  DSN=&&SYSUT3,UNIT=SYSDA,SPACE=(460,(700,300))
00330000
//SYSUT4    DD  DSN=&&SYSUT4,UNIT=SYSDA,SPACE=(460,(700,300))
00340000
//SYSUT5    DD  DSN=&&SYSUT5,UNIT=SYSDA,SPACE=(460,(700,300))
00350000
//SYSUT6    DD  DSN=&&SYSUT6,UNIT=SYSDA,SPACE=(460,(700,300))
00360000
//SYSUT7    DD  DSN=&&SYSUT7,UNIT=SYSDA,SPACE=(460,(700,300))
00370000
//SYSLIN    DD  DSN=&&LOADSET,DISP=(MOD,PASS),UNIT=SYSDA,
```

Figure C.4 *(continues)*

```
00380000
//              SPACE=(TRK,(50,20),RLSE),
00390000
//              DCB=(DSORG=PS,RECFM=FB,LRECL=80,BLKSIZE=3200)
//SYSIN    DD   DSN=&&CICSOUT,DISP=(OLD,PASS)
00400000
//*
00420000
//LKED   EXEC  PGM=IEWL,PARM='LIST,XREF,LET',
00910000
//       COND=(5,LT,COMPILE),REGION=512K
00920000
//SYSLIN   DD   DSN=SYS7.CICSV4.SDFHCOB(DFHEILIC),DISP=SHR
//         DD   DSN=&&LOADSET,DISP=(OLD,DELETE)
00940000
//SYSLMOD  DD   DSN=CO.CLUSTER.IN.LOAD.COMPILE(&PRGM),DISP=SHR   00970000
//SYSLIB   DD   DSN=SYS1.COB2LIB,DISP=SHR
00991000
//         DD   DSN=SYS4.ADB.ADA613.LOAD,DISP=SHR
//         DD   DSN=CO.E10818.SPN.ADANAT.CURR.LOAD,DISP=SHR
00980000
//         DD   DSN=CO.E10818.SPN.ADANAT.NEXT.LOAD,DISP=SHR
00980000
//         DD   DSN=CO.E10818.SYSCICS.LOADLIB,DISP=SHR
00980000
//         DD   DSN=SYS7.CICSV4.SDFHLOAD,DISP=SHR
00980000
//         DD   DSN=SYS1.DB2V4.SDSNLOAD,DISP=SHR
//         DD   DSN=SYS1.SCEELKED,DISP=SHR
00991000
//         DD   DSN=SYS1.VSCLLIB,DISP=SHR
00991000
//         DD   DSN=CO.CLUSTER.LIB.LOAD,DISP=SHR                 00991000
//         DD   DSN=CO.CLUSTER.IN.LOAD,DISP=SHR                  00991000
//         DD   DSN=CO.E010829.SYS1.CALL.LIBRARY,DISP=SHR
00991000
//SYSUT1   DD   UNIT=(SYSDA,SEP=(SYSLIN,SYSLMOD)),
00992000
//              SPACE=(1024,(1500,500),RLSE)
00993000
//SYSPRINT DD   SYSOUT=*
00994000
//SYSIN    DD   *
00995000
//*
00900000
```

Figure C.4 *Continued*

```
//CO29030  JOB (CO000P),PROG180,CLASS=A,MSGCLASS=Z,
00020001
//     NOTIFY=&SYSUID
00040000
//JOBLIB    DD DISP=SHR,DSN=CO.CLUSTER.LIB.LOAD                  00030000
//****************************************************************
00230000
//SQLADA    EXEC PGM=ADASQLC,REGION=8192K
00180000
//STEPLIB   DD DSN=SYS4.ADB.SQL162.LOAD,DISP=SHR
00190000
//          DD DSN=SYS4.ADB.ADA613.LOAD,DISP=SHR
00190000
//DDCARD    DD DSN=SYS4.ADB.SQL162.SRCE(ADAPARM),DISP=SHR
00200000
//ADAGLOB   DD DSN=CO.SPN.ADABAS.PARMLIB(SQLDB),DISP=SHR
//          DD DSN=CO.SPN.ADABAS.PARMLIB(SQLDICTE),DISP=SHR
//ADAIN DD DSN=CO.CLUSTER.IN.SOURCE.COBOL2(PROG180),
//*ADAIN DD DSN=CO.CLUSTER.IN.SOURCE.COBOL2.CONV(PROG180),
//         DISP=SHR
//ADAOUT    DD DSN=CO.CLUSTER.IN.SOURCE.EXP(PROG180),DISP=OLD
//SYSUT1    DD DSN=&&TEMP,DISP=(,DELETE),
//            UNIT=SYSDA,SPACE=(CYL,10)
//ADAMES    DD SYSOUT=*
//SYSOUT    DD SYSOUT=*
//SYSDBOUT DD SYSOUT=*
//SYSUDUMP DD SYSOUT=*
//****************************************************************
00170000
//DB2SQL    EXEC PGM=DSNHPC,
00180000
//         PARM='HOST(COBOL),APOST,APOSTSQL',
//         REGION=4096K
//STEPLIB   DD DSN=SYS1.DB2V4.SDSNEXIT,DISP=SHR
00190000
//          DD DSN=SYS1.DB2V4.SDSNLOAD,DISP=SHR
00190000
//DBRMLIB   DD DSN=&&DBRM(PROG180),UNIT=SYSDA,
00200000
//            SPACE=(TRK,(1,1,1)),
00210000
//            DISP=(,PASS),DCB=BLKSIZE=6320
//SYSCIN    DD DSN=&&DSNHOUT,DISP=(MOD,PASS),UNIT=SYSDA,
//            DCB=BLKSIZE=23440,SPACE=(23440,(30,15),RLSE)
//SYSLIB    DD DISP=SHR,DSN=CO.E10818.SYS2.PROD.DCLLIB
//          DD DISP=SHR,DSN=CO.SYS2.COPYLIB4
```

Figure C.5 Sample compile procedure for programs that have DB/2/ADABAS COBOL (VS COBOL II).

```
//SYSPRINT DD  SYSOUT=*
//SYSTERM  DD  SYSOUT=*
//SYSUDUMP DD  SYSOUT=*
//SYSUT1   DD  SPACE=(23440,(30,15),,,ROUND),UNIT=SYSDA
//SYSUT2   DD  SPACE=(23440,(30,15),,,ROUND),UNIT=SYSDA
//SYSIN    DD  DSN=CO.CLUSTER.IN.SOURCE.EXP(PROG180),DISP=SHR
//****************************************************************
00230000
//COMPILE EXEC  PGM=IGYCRCTL,REGION=8192K,
00240000
// PARM=('RENT,SOURCE,LIB,APOST,DYNAM,TRUNC(BIN)','LANG(UE)')
00250000
//STEPLIB  DD   DSN=SYS1.COB2COMP,DISP=SHR
00270000
//SYSPRINT DD   SYSOUT=*
00280000
//SYSLIB   DD   DSN=CO.CLUSTER.IN.COPY,DISP=SHR                    00290000
//         DD   DSN=SYS7.CICSV4.SDFHCOB,DISP=SHR
00290000
//         DD   DSN=CO.SYS2.COPYLIB4,DISP=SHR
00290000
//SYSUT1   DD   DSN=&&SYSUT1,UNIT=SYSDA,SPACE=(460,(700,300))
00310000
//SYSUT2   DD   DSN=&&SYSUT2,UNIT=SYSDA,SPACE=(460,(700,300))
00320000
//SYSUT3   DD   DSN=&&SYSUT3,UNIT=SYSDA,SPACE=(460,(700,300))
00330000
//SYSUT4   DD   DSN=&&SYSUT4,UNIT=SYSDA,SPACE=(460,(700,300))
00340000
//SYSUT5   DD   DSN=&&SYSUT5,UNIT=SYSDA,SPACE=(460,(700,300))
00350000
//SYSUT6   DD   DSN=&&SYSUT6,UNIT=SYSDA,SPACE=(460,(700,300))
00360000
//SYSUT7   DD   DSN=&&SYSUT7,UNIT=SYSDA,SPACE=(460,(700,300))
00370000
//SYSLIN   DD   DSN=&&LOADSET,DISP=(MOD,PASS),UNIT=SYSDA,
00380000
//              SPACE=(TRK,(50,20),RLSE),
00390000
//              DCB=(DSORG=PS,RECFM=FB,LRECL=80,BLKSIZE=3200)
//SYSIN    DD   DSN=&&DSNHOUT,DISP=(OLD,PASS)
00400000
//****************************************************************
00900000
//LKED    EXEC  PGM=IEWL,PARM='LIST,XREF,LET',
00910000
//     COND=(5,LT,COMPILE),REGION=512K
00920000
```

Figure C.5 *(continues)*

```
//SYSLIN    DD   DSN=&&LOADSET,DISP=(OLD,DELETE)
00940000
//SYSLMOD   DD   DSN=CO.CLUSTER.IN.LOAD.COMPILE(PROG180),DISP=SHR    00970000
//SYSLIB    DD   DSN=SYS1.COB2LIB,DISP=SHR
00991000
//          DD   DSN=CO.E10818.SYSCICS.LOADLIB,DISP=SHR
00980000
//          DD   DSN=SYS1.SCEELKED,DISP=SHR
00991000
//          DD   DSN=SYS1.VSCLLIB,DISP=SHR
00991000
//          DD   DSN=SYS4.ADB.ADA613.LOAD,DISP=SHR
//          DD   DSN=SYS7.CICSV4.SDFHLOAD,DISP=SHR
00980000
//          DD   DSN=CO.CLUSTER.LIB.LOAD,DISP=SHR                    00991000
//          DD   DSN=CO.CLUSTER.IN.LOAD,DISP=SHR                     00991000
//          DD   DSN=CO.E010829.SYS1.CALL.LIBRARY,DISP=SHR
00991000
//          DD   DSN=CO.E10818.SPN.ADANAT.CURR.LOAD,DISP=SHR
//          DD   DSN=CO.E10818.SPN.ADANAT.NEXT.LOAD,DISP=SHR
00980000
//SYSUT1    DD   UNIT=(SYSDA,SEP=(SYSLIN,SYSLMOD)),
00992000
//               SPACE=(1024,(1500,500),RLSE)
00993000
//SYSPRINT  DD   SYSOUT=*
00994000
//SYSIN     DD   *
00995000
//*
00900000
```

Figure C.5 *Continued*

APPENDIX D

Comparing CCCA Version 2.0 and Version 2.1

You may already have CCCA in your shop. We began with CCCA, Version 2.0, but later upgraded, even though there was a cost associated with doing so (IBM treated it practically as a new product). We then compared the two versions. We present our findings in this appendix.

D.1 CCCA, Release 2.1: New Product Overview

First, the new CCCA version works on OS/390. To conduct the evaluation test, all of the source, copy, map, and DCLGEN libraries were moved from MVS to OS/390. Since the new product was sensitive to language-level selection, it was crucial that we properly configure the new tool to get accurate conversion test results.

D.1.1 Test Description

The following types of programs were selected for testing:

- Batch COBOL
- CICS (with no BLL) COBOL
- CICS (with BLL) COBOL
- CICS DB/2 COBOL
- CICS ADABAS COBOL
- DB/2 COBOL

All the tests were conducted in August 1998 with the following different versions of source COBOL:

- OS/VS COBOL LANGUAGE LEVEL 01
- OS/VS COBOL LANGUAGE LEVEL 02
- VS COBOL II

D.1.2 Evaluation

After we conducted the tests, we reached the following conclusions:

- Significant improvements were made in the new version (Release 2.1).
- Determining the source language element level as OS/VS COBOL LANGUAGE LEVEL 01 or OS/VS COBOL LANGUAGE LEVEL 02 was extremely important for both versions of COBOL upgrades (e.g., COPY statement).
- The way CCCA, Release 2.0, processes copybooks and COPY statements has been greatly improved in the new version of CCCA, Release 2.1.
- A CICS-only upgrade cannot be done using either version of CCCA.
- COBOL programs with ADABAS statements need special attention in both versions.
- In other words, you are still required to exclude unsupported environments by commenting them out before conversion and by removing comments after conversion.

D.1.3 Conclusion

The new tool is simple and easier to use, and its user manual is greatly improved. The new tool also significantly reduces the number of manual fixes. Local support will be provided with the new tool. Remote support (through IBM Australia) was provided for the older tool. We prepared Table D.1 to provide test cases for evaluating the new tool. Table D.2 shows the results that were gained using the new tool, CCCA, Release 2.1. Table D.3 shows the results using the old tool, CCCA, Release 2.0.

Table D.4 shows a comparison result between the old (Release 2.0) and the new tool (Release 2.1).

Table D.1 Test Cases

PROGRAM NAME	CATEGORY
PROGRM01	RULES FOR AUGMENTED VARIABLES CHANGED.
PROGRM02	CICS.
PROGRM03	QUALIFYING INDEX NAME IS NOT SUPPORTED.
PROGRM04	INDEX NAME -SET TO VALUE > MAX NO. OCCUR.
PROGRM05	INDEX NAME -SET TO VALUE > MAX NO. OCCUR.
PROGRM06	CICS - BLL AND DB/2 SQL.
PROGRM07	COPYBOOK ISSUE.
PROGRM08	COPYBOOK ISSUE.
PROGRM09	INDEX NAME -SET TO VALUE > MAX NO. OCCUR.
PROGRM10	CICS - INSUFFICIENT BLL CELLS.
PROGRM11	CICS - BLL AND DB/2 SQL.
PROGRM12	CICS - INFORMATIONAL ERROR.
PROGRM13	CICS - BLL AND DB/2 SQL.
PROGRM14	ISAM.
PROGRM15	RESERVED WORD ISSUE.
PROGRM16	COPYBOOK ISSUE.
PROGRM17	ADABAS.
PROGRM18	REPORT WRITER AND ON CONDITION.
PROGRM19	NO ADABAS.
PROGRM20	MANY MANUAL FIXES REQUIRED.
PROGRM21	COMPARE PACKED DECIMAL AGAINST ALPHABETIC.
PROGRM22	ORGANIZATION IS INDEXED.
PROGRM23	UNSTRING - INDEX.
PROGRM24	TRUNCATES THE VALUE CLAUSE.
PROGRM25	ADABAS.
PROGRM26	RELATIONAL OPERATOR.
PROGRM27	COMPARE DECIMAL AGAINST ALPHABETIC.
PROGRM28	RESERVED WORD ISSUE.
PROGRM29	CCIS - BLL DOES NOT REFERENCE 01.

Table D.2 Test Results from Release 2.1

PROGRAM NAME	ORIGINAL COBOL: OS/VS=1 COBOL II=2	TARGET COBOL: COBOL II=2 COBOL/370=3	CICS: BLL=Y OTHER=O NONE=N BOTH=B	DATABASE: DB/2=D ADABAS=A NONE=N	REPORT WRITER: YES=Y NO=N	ISAM: YES=Y NO=N	NUMBER OF LINES ORIGINAL PROGRAM	NUMBER OF LINES CONVERSION WARNING	NUMBER OF LINES MANUAL CONVERSION REQUIRED	NUMBER OF LINES COMPILED ERROR	NUMBER OF LINES COMPILED SEVERE
PROGRM01	1	2	N	A	N	N	2,859	2	1	0	8
PROGRM02	1	2	O	A	N	N	287	0	0	0	0
PROGRM03	1	2	O	N	N	N	1,085	0	0	0	0
PROGRM04	1	2	O	A	N	N	890	0	0	0	0
PROGRM05	1	2	O	A	N	N	5,351	0	0	0	0
PROGRM06	1	2	Y	N	N	N	1,809	101	0	0	0
PROGRM07	1	2	O	N	N	N	2,608	0	0	0	0
PROGRM08	1	2	Y	D	N	N	1,271	0	0	0	0
PROGRM09	1	3	N	N	N	Y	1373	20	0	0	0
PROGRM10	1	3	N	N	N	N	350	0	0	0	0
PROGRM11	1	2	N	A	N	N	937	3	0	0	0
PROGRM12	1	2	N	N	Y	N	252	0	0	0	0
PROGRM13	1	2	N	N	N	N	308	1	0	0	0
PROGRM14	1	2	N	A	N	N	442	0	0	0	0

Table D.2 (Continued)

PROGRAM NAME	ORIGINAL COBOL: OS/VS=1 COBOL II =2	TARGET COBOL: COBOL II=2 COBOL/370=3	CICS: BLL=Y OTHER=O NONE=N BOTH=B	DATABASE: DB/2 = D ADABAS=A NONE=N	REPORT WRITER: YES=Y NO=N	ISAM: YES=Y NO=N	NUMBER OF LINES ORIGINAL PROGRAM	NUMBER OF LINES CONVERSION WARNING	NUMBER OF LINES MANUAL CONVERSION REQUIRED	NUMBER OF LINES COMPILED ERROR	NUMBER OF LINES COMPILED SEVERE
PROGRM15	1	2	N	N	N	N	1,034	1	7	1	1
PROGRM16	1	2	N	A	N	N	461	0	0	2	1
PROGRM17	1	2	N	A	N	N	18,166	0	0	0	0
PROGRM18	1	2	N	N	N	N	466	0	0	0	1
PROGRM19	1	2	N	A	N	N	1,342	0	0	0	0
PROGRM20	1	3	N	N	N	N	4,678	0	0	1	1
PROGRM21	1	3	N	D	N	N	3,340	0	0	0	0
PROGRM22	1	3	N	N	N	N	6,056	0	0	0	0
PROGRM23	1	2	O	N	N	N	2,443	10	0	0	0
PROGRM24	1	2	N	N	N	Y	1,030	1	0	0	0
PROGRM25	2	3	Y	D	N	N	1,384	0	0	0	0
PROGRM26	1	2	Y	D	N	N	5,292	0	0	0	0
PROGRM27							65,514	139	8	4	12
PROGRM28											
PROGRM29											

Table D.3 Test Results from Release 2.0

PROGRAM NAME	ORIGINAL COBOL: OS/VS=1 COBOL II =2	TARGET COBOL: COBOL II=2 COBOL/370=3	CICS: BLL=Y OTHER=O NONE=N BOTH=B	DATABASE: DB/2 = D ADABAS=A NONE=N	REPORT WRITER: YES=Y NO=N	ISAM: YES=Y NO=N	NUMBER OF LINES ORIGINAL PROGRAM	NUMBER OF LINES CONVERSION WARNING	NUMBER OF LINES MANUAL CONVERSION REQUIRED	NUMBER OF LINES COMPILED ERROR	NUMBER OF LINES COMPILED SEVERE
PROGRM01	1	2	N	A	N	N	2,859	2	1	0	8
PROGRM02	1	2	O	A	N	N	287	0	0	0	0
PROGRM03	1	2	O	N	N	N	1,085	0	0	0	0
PROGRM04	1	2	O	A	N	N	890	0	0	0	0
PROGRM05	1	2	O	A	N	N	5,351	0	0	0	0
PROGRM06	1	2	Y	N	N	N	1,809	101	3	4	0
PROGRM07	1	2	O	N	N	N	2,608	162	0	0	0
PROGRM08	1	2	Y	D	N	N	1,271	0	0	0	0
PROGRM09	1	3	N	N	N	Y	1373	0	0	0	1
PROGRM10	1	3	N	N	N	N	350	0	0	0	0
PROGRM11	1	2	N	A	N	N	937	2	3	0	7
PROGRM12	1	2	N	N	Y	N	252	0	0	0	0
PROGRM13	1	2	N	N	N	N	308	0	0	2	4
PROGRM14	1	2	N	A	N	N	442	0	0	0	6
PROGRM15	1	2	N	N	N	N	1,034	3	0	0	2
PROGRM16	1	2	N	A	N	N	461	0	0	2	1
PROGRM17	1	2	N	A	N	N	18,166	0	0	0	0
PROGRM18	1	2	N	N	N	N	466	0	0	0	1
PROGRM19	1	2	N	A	N	N	1,342	0	0	0	0

Table D.3 (Continued)

PROGRAM NAME	ORIGINAL COBOL: OS/VS=1 COBOL II=2	TARGET COBOL: COBOL II=2 COBOL/370=3	CICS: BLL=Y OTHER=O NONE=N BOTH=B	DATABASE: DB/2=D ADABAS=A NONE=N BOTH=B	REPORT WRITER: YES=Y NO=N	ISAM: YES=Y NO=N	NUMBER OF LINES ORIGINAL PROGRAM	NUMBER OF LINES CONVERSION WARNING	NUMBER OF LINES MANUAL CONVERSION REQUIRED	NUMBER OF LINES COMPILED ERROR	NUMBER OF LINES COMPILED SEVERE
PROGRM20	1	3	N	N	N	N	4,678	1	15	1	1
PROGRM21	1	3	N	D	N	N	3,340	3	0	0	1
PROGRM22	1	3	N	N	N	N	6,056	1	0	0	0
PROGRM23	1	2	O	N	N	N	2,443	10	0	0	0
PROGRM24	1	2	N	N	N	Y	1,030	1	0	0	0
PROGRM25	2	3	Y	D	N	N	1,384	0	0	0	0
PROGRM26	1	2	Y	D	N	N	5,292	0	0	0	0
PROGRM27							65,514	286	22	9	32
PROGRM28											
PROGRM29											

Table D.4 Differences between Release 2.0 and Release 2.1

VERSION/ RELEASE	ORIGINAL COBOL: OS/VS=1 COBOL II=2	TARGET COBOL: COBOL II=2 COBOL/370=3	CICS: BLL=Y OTHER=O NONE=N BOTH=B	DATABASE: DB/2=D ADABAS=A NONE=N BOTH=B	REPORT WRITER: YES=Y NO=N	ISAM: YES=Y NO=N	NUMBER OF LINES ORIGINAL PROGRAM	NUMBER OF LINES CONVERSION WARNING	NUMBER OF LINES MANUAL CONVERSION REQUIRED	NUMBER OF LINES COMPILED ERROR	NUMBER OF LINES COMPILED SEVERE
Release 2.0							65,514	286	22	9	32
Release 2.1							65,514	139	8	4	12
DIFFERENCE								147	14	5	20
IMPROVEMENT								51.4%	63.6%	55.6%	62.5%

Based solely on the written information provided to us, we prepared a comparison of the new and old tools in our evaluation (see Table D.5).

Table D.5 Tool Comparison

EVALUATION CRITERIA	IBM CCCA, VERSION 2, RELEASE 1 (PROGRAM NUMBER 5648-B05)	IBM CCCA, RELEASE 2.0 (PROGRAM NUMBER 5785-ABJ)
WHEN-COMPILED	Automatic conversion.	Automatic conversion.
The option to specify the COBOL compiler of choice, for use by the tool?	YES	YES
Supports ADABAS?	NO	NO
Supports customers locally?	YES (California)	NO (Australia)
Supports PANVALET/ ENDEVOR/LIBRARIAN/ SQL COPY?	YES	YES
Source Languages	DOS/VS COBOL OS/VS COBOL source code or COBOL/74 Standard VS COBOL II (either VS COBOL II, Release 1 and 2, or VS or COBOL II, Release 3 and 4 [CMPR2]) source code.	DOS/VS COBOL OS/VS COBOL source code or COBOL/74 Standard VS COBOL II (either VS COBOL II, Release 1 and 2, or VS or COBOL II, Release 3 and 4 [CMPR2]) source code.
Target Languages	COBOL /85 Standard VS COBOL II, Release 3 or 4 (NOCMPR2) source code IBM COBOL for MVS & VM source code, andCOBOL for OS/390 & VM.	COBOL/85 Standard VS COBOL II, Release 3 or 4, (NOCMPR2) source code IBM COBOL for MVS & VM source code.
SECTION NAME	No error message if name is too long.	No error message if name is too long.
REPORT WRITER (SECTION AND RD). These statements are not supported by the target languages: GENERATE INITIATE REPORT TERMINATE USE BEFORE REPORTING	If you specify *Y* for the Report Writer Statement Flagging option on the Optional Processing Panel, they will be flagged.	If you specify Y for the Report Writer Statement Flagging option on the Optional Processing Panel, they will be flagged.

EVALUATION CRITERIA	IBM CCCA, VERSION 2, RELEASE 1 (PROGRAM NUMBER 5648-B05)	IBM CCCA, RELEASE 2.0 (PROGRAM NUMBER 5785-ABJ)
Removes and/or converts the Base Locator for Linkage (BLL) section mechanism and references?	YES	YES
REMARKS paragraph is converted to comments by inserting an asterisk (*) in column 7 of the paragraph header and all succeeding lines of the paragraph?	Converted for OS/VS COBOL; not for VS COBOL II.	Converted for OS/VS COBOL; not for VS COBOL II
RECORDING MODE clause. The target language compilers ignore this clause if it is specified for a VSAM file. If the clause is in a file description entry for a VSAM file or a file that is to be converted to VSAM, it is removed.	Supposed to be removed automatically. Sometimes it does not remove.	Supposed to be removed automatically. Sometimes it does not remove.
The RECORD CONTAINS XX clause is removed from the program, except for RECORD CONTAINS 0, which is left in place.	YES	YES
PROGRAM XREF - Print program/file report?	YES	YES
Millennium Language Extension (MLE) support?	YES	NO
Optional automatic compile of converted source code?	YES	YES
Operating system	OS/390 and MVS & VM	MVS & VM
Is this product mentioned in the 1991 DATAPRO report?	YES	YES
Are third-party services and education provided for this product?	YES	YES

continues

Table D.5 *(Continued)*

EVALUATION CRITERIA	IBM CCCA, VERSION 2, RELEASE 1 (PROGRAM NUMBER 5648-B05)	IBM CCCA, RELEASE 2.0 (PROGRAM NUMBER 5785-ABJ)
Is the Conversion Aid a menu-driven system?	YES	YES
Hardware	IBM System/370 architecture	IBM System/370 architecture
Flexibility through an open converter design?	YES	YES
First installed	April 1986	April 1986
FILE XREF - Print file/program report?	YES	YES
Eliminates conflicts between user-defined names and words reserved for VS COBOL II?	YES	YES
CURRENT-DATE handling?	YES	YES
COPY XREF - Print program/copy report?	YES	YES
COPY XREF - Print copy/program report?	YES	YES
Converts VS COBOL II to COBOL for MVS & VM?	YES	YES
Converts OS/VS COBOL to VS COBOL II?	YES	YES
Converts OS/VS COBOL to COBOL for MVS & VM?	YES	YES
Converts EXEC CICS commands?	YES	YES
Converts both source programs and copy modules?	YES	YES

Table D.5 (Continued)

EVALUATION CRITERIA	IBM CCCA, VERSION 2, RELEASE 1 (PROGRAM NUMBER 5648-B05)	IBM CCCA, RELEASE 2.0 (PROGRAM NUMBER 5785-ABJ)
Comparing packed decimal data against alphabetic data	Manual translation is required.	Manual translation is required.
CLOSE STATEMENT FOR FILE NAME.	No error message if there is no close statement.	No error message if there is no close statement.
Can we use COBOL Report Writer Precompiler? To perform two functions: (1) to permanently convert Report Writer statements to valid COBOL statements that can be compiled in IBM COBOL for MVS & VM or IBM COBOL for VSE/ESA or (2) to precompile applications containing Report Writer statements so the code will be acceptable to the IBM COBOL for MVS & VM or IBM COBOL for VSE/ESA compiler.	YES	YES
CALL XREF - Print program/call report?	YES	YES
CALL XREF - Print call/program report?	YES	YES
Additional ISPF setup panels for usability?	YES	YES

APPENDIX E

Run-time Issues with CCCA 2.0

E.1 The SYSUT5 Problem

During the conversion step of CCCA, Release 2, we encountered the message, "System Completion Code = 337, Reason Code = 0000000." We learned that this problem will occur when a program contains a table with 168 entries, each entry containing thirty-five characters with initial values.

IBM had had one or two other customers with a similar ABEND. However, IBM was unable to conclusively pinpoint the exact cause of the problem. The problem appears to have something to do with the work file SYSUT5. This file is used by an assembler module that processes converted copybooks and writes them to the output copybook library. In the past, the problem appears to have been space related, but simply allocating more space to the file hasn't fixed the problem. A possible workaround for this would be to comment out the COPY statement for the particular copybook and try the conversion again. Copy the contents of the particular copybook inline into the original program source code and try the conversion again. The authors expanded the space parameter on SYSUT5 and resolved the problem without contacting IBM again. If this doesn't work in your case, you should contact IBM and provide them with the affected original piece of the copybook and the source code.

E.2 Source Program Is Already Converted

When the input COBOL source program is already converted (the language level of input COBOL source equals that of the output COBOL target language), then CCCA will strangely ABEND, without conversion and compile errors.

E.3 Subscript Issue

Here, the problem is that the program references a subscript that is larger than the number of occurrences in the table.

Resolution:

Identified condition.

Response from IBM:

There were many "undocumented features" (bugs) in the old compilers that allowed programmers to get away with suspicious code. While CCCA, Release 2.0, tries to handle some of the more well-known bugs and convert the code accordingly, it is impossible to handle all bugs. This is one such instance. CCCA, Release 2.0, is not designed to correct coding or syntax errors.

The following is an actual piece of code, where the authors had to deal with a unique index problem:

```
000135         012000 01  SORTED-REQ-AREA.
000136         012100     05  REQ-TBL-ENTRY     OCCURS 175 TIMES.
000137         012200         10  REQUEST-NO                  PIC XXX.
000148         013300         10  END-REQ-IND                 PIC X.

000150         013500 01  MASTER-RECORD-AREA.
000151         013600     05  MASTER-FIELD-1.

000618    2    043900             WRITE S-ING-POS-O-R FROM SEL-INGR-
POSITIONS
000619    2    044000             MOVE SPACES TO SEL-INGR-POSITIONS
000620    2    044100             MOVE 'X' TO END-REQ-IND (176)

000620==> IGYPS2073-E Subscript or index literal "176" exceeded the max-
imum occurrence value "175" for the table.  The maximum occurrence value
was assumed.
```

E.4 Large Block Sizes

OS/VS COBOL and VS COBOL II have different block size capacities. We received a tool error when a copybook went over a certain K factor (16K). CCCA ABENDs without conversion and with many compile errors. One of the messages was "Blocksize exceeds 16K."

Solution:

You need to choose language level 2 on the appropriate panel.

E.5 Extra Period

Suppose you get the error code ABJ6036 (Period Added at the End of Paragraph). This means the tool is inserting an extra period (.) in a value clause, which is causing a conversion error with code ABJ6036 and ABJ6075 (****** ERROR FILE NAME ********).

Solution:

Manually remove the period (.) from the converted source and recompile using a separate compile procedure.

E.6 BLL Cell Placement

This conversion error is received when the BLL cell is the second item in the target of the MOVE statement. The documentation implies that the BLL is the first target of the MOVE statement.

Solution:

You need to manually recode the MOVE statement using two lines, one for each data name.

E.7 EXEC SQL Error

This conversion error means DB/2 commands are not recognized and thus generate multiple errors.

Solution:

You need to edit the skeleton JCL and alter it so that the SQL translator is invoked before the CICS translator. Currently, the CICS translator is invoked before the SQL translator.

E.8 Decimal Divide Exception

A Decimal Divide Exception is caused when the divisor is zero.

Condition:

```
IF PEX2-UNIT-RATE = ZERO
        MOVE ZEROS TO PEX2-DEAL-DEAL-UNITS
    ELSE
        COMPUTE PEX2-DEAL-DEAL-UNITS =
                    PEX2-EXPENSE / S110-A-UNIT-RATE.
  2550-EXIT.                    EXIT.
```

Resolution:

This problem is unrelated to COBOL upgrading. This is an existing program bug. To resolve this problem, your company will need to revise the coding as follows:

```
IF S110-A-UNIT-RATE = ZERO
        MOVE ZEROS TO PEX2-DEAL-DEAL-UNITS
    ELSE
        COMPUTE PEX2-DEAL-DEAL-UNITS =
                    PEX2-EXPENSE / S110-A-UNIT-RATE.
  2550-EXIT.                    EXIT.
```

E.9 Default Parameter Setting for Apostrophe (') or Quotation Mark (")

This option (Optional Processing Panel o.3, Option 13) is extremely important. Ensure that you will set this option to "Y" for the apostrophe ('). If you set this option to "Y" for the quotation mark ("), then you will receive an enormous amount of errors during compilation time.

E.10 Copy Replacing Statement Resulting in ABJ6249

In this error, the colon (":") symbol is not being accepted, and we receive conversion error code ABJ6249.

Solution:

The colon problem is a quirk in the COPY Language Conversion Program. It doesn't really check to see what language level CCCA, Release 2.0, is converting from when it encounters a colon in the REPLACING clause of the COPY statement. Hence, message ABJ6249 is valid and is applicable if one were converting from OS/VS COBOL but is not really applicable when converting from VS COBOL II. The easiest way around this problem is to set the return code level message to 00 or 04. You can do this via option 2.10. This will allow the conversion job to invoke the compiler after conversion is complete.

E.11 Hex Value

This error means that the use of the number hexadecimal equivalent for a character is not being accepted.

Solution:

This is a known bug in CCCA, Release 2.0, for which IBM has no fix. We cannot easily fix this bug in the current release because of the way CCCA, Release 2.0, tokenizes the source code. Either upgrade to the new release or simply remove the space CCCA, Release 2.0, creates in the hex literal values.

E.12 Copybook Containing CICS Statements

You may receive compile errors caused when CICS statements are not recognized.

Solution:

This is a CICS preprocessing problem. CCCA, Release 2.0, will quite happily include and convert copybooks that contain original CICS source code (i.e., EXEC CICS . . .). The CICS precompiler, however, does not expand copybooks, so one must assume that the company must put the CICS code through the precompiler before putting it into a copybook. This then gets included in the source code at compile time.

After passing the source code and copybooks containing CICS statements through CCCA, Release 2.0, it's not really practical to do the compile because the code in the converted copybooks must first be passed through the CICS precompiler before it can be used in a copybook for inclusion in the main program. This must be done as a separate exercise. The postconversion compile processing that CCCA, Release 2.0, performs assumes that only COBOL source code will exist in copybooks.

Option 1—Don't bother with postconversion compiles of those programs that have CICS statements in copybooks.

Option 2—Devise a procedure that will identify copybooks that contain CICS statements and after converting these through CCCA, Release 2.0, extract the code from them, pass them through the CICS precompiler, and use the CICS converted code for the postconversion compile.

Option 3—Place the CICS statements contained in the copybooks into the mainline code with appropriate comments.

E.13 Unstring Statement Resulting in ABJ6025

This conversion error occurs when an unstring statement is being rejected by the tool.

Solution:

This will only occur if one assumes that the source code is ANSI 68 level. However, if the same source code is converted as ANSI 74, the message will not occur. Refer to the OS/VS COBOL Language Reference, which explains the difference in the way "Delimited by All" is handled by ANSI 68 and ANSI 74.

E.14 Removal of Brackets ABJ6225

This error occurs when brackets in the source code are being removed by the CCCA, Release 2.0, tool.

Solution:

Looks like a bug. Obviously, CCCA, Release 2.0, shouldn't remove the bracket before the "<-20". IBM believes the problem was encountered once before with another customer, but they were unable to track down the exact cause. Note the message ABJ6225 and modify the brackets manually after the conversion.

E.15 ADABAS (or Any Other Vendor Database)

The OS/VS COBOL conversion (CCCA, Release 2.0) doesn't handle ADABAS commands in COBOL programs. Those commands need to be remarked before upgrading the programs. After the OS/VS COBOL conversion, you need to reactivate all the ADABAS statements in the new VS COBOL II source. We need to allow for more time so we can analyze the numerous compile error messages that are still generated even though the ADABAS statements have been commented out. We used a JCL script to add comment on all the lines, from EXEC ADABAS through END-EXEC, and we later used another JCL to remove the comments after postconversion so we could compile them.

E.16 Value Clause Is Truncated by CCCA, Release 2.0

This conversion error has the following condition and resolution.

Condition:
CCCA truncated the value clause as follows:

```
021100      05  PROGRM63B-IN              PIC  9(007) VALUE 0.
021200      05  PROGRM63C-OUT             PIC  9(007) VALUE 0.
021300      05  PROGRM63D-OUT             PIC  9(007) VALUE 0.
*OLD**      05  KTSGL-REG-TBL-SIZE        PIC  S9(03) COMP-3 VALUE +10
021400      05  KTSGL-REG-TBL-SIZE        PIC  S9(03) COMP-3 VALUE
 +10
021500
*OLD**      05  KTSGL-OH-TBL-SIZE         PIC  S9(03) COMP-3 VALUE +90
021600      05  KTSGL-OH-TBL-SIZE         PIC  S9(03) COMP-3 VALUE +
021700
```

Resolution:

This program requires an action by IBM. The authors have learned from IBM that this problem will be eliminated if you specify that the input COBOL source level is OS/VS COBOL language level 2 when you submit a job using CCCA.

ABOUT THE AUTHORS

YOUNG CHAE has been working with COBOL for the past twenty-nine years. As a programmer, systems analyst, project leader, project manager, and systems manager he has worked for companies in the entertainment; management consulting; automotive; oil and gas; pulp and paper; chemical; food and beverage; and electronics industries in the United States, Japan, and Korea. He is presently a senior consultant for Ernst & Young's Year 2000 projects at the Accelerated Conversion Center (ACC) in Costa Mesa, California. Young received his master's in computer science from Iowa State University, Ames, Iowa.

MR. STEVEN ROGERS has been working with COBOL for the past eighteen years as a programmer, CASE tool analyst, regional IT shop director, and most recently as a senior manager for Ernst & Young LLP, where he works in the Management Consulting Information Technology Group as the conversion manager for their Accelerated Conversion Center Year 2000 factory. He was the founding president of the Los Angeles Micro Focus COBOL User Group in 1991. Steven holds a bachelor's and master's degree in computer science from California State University at Fullerton.

INDEX

\> THAN relational operator, 150, 184
< THAN relational operator, 151, 184
\> THEN relational operator, 45, 151, 184
< THEN relational operator, 45, 151, 184
=TO relational operator, 151, 185

A

ABJ6025, 276
ABJ6225, 276
ABJ6249, 274–275
ACCEPT MESSAGE COUNT statement, 121, 158
ACTUAL KEY clause, 122, 158
ADABAS, 277
Addressability, maintaining, 71
ALPHABET clause, 39, 122–123, 158, 200
ALPHABETIC class, 41, 93, 123, 158–159, 200
Apostrophe, default parameter setting, 274
APPLY CORE-INDEX clause, 123, 159
APPLY CYL-INDEX clause, 123, 159
APPLY CYL-OVERFLOW clause, 123, 159
APPLY EXTENDED-SEARCH clause, 123, 159
APPLY MASTER-INDEX clause, 123–124, 159
APPLY RECORD-OVERFLOW clause, 124, 160
APPLY REORG-CRITERIA clause, 124, 160
APPLY-WRITE ONLY clause, restrictions removed, 41
APPLY WRITE-VERIFY clause, 124, 160
Arithmetic statement, 41–42
ASSIGN clause, 124–125, 160–161
ASSIGN integer system-name, 125, 161
ASSIGN...OR, 125, 161
AUTHOR paragraph, 125, 161, 200

B

Basic direct access method. *See* BDAM
BDAM:
 conversion issues, 62, 64–66
 file-handling migration actions, 65–66
BDAM files, 125, 161–162
BLANK WHEN ZERO clause, 35, 126, 162
BLL cell placement, 273
BLOCK CONTAINS clause, 126, 162, 200–201

C

CALL identifier statement, 126, 162, 201
CALL...ON EXCEPTION statement, 93, 201
CALL...ON OVERFLOW statement, 93, 126, 162–163, 201

CALL statement, 42–43, 126, 163
  dynamic, 70
  static, 70
CALL...USING statement, 126–127, 163
CANCEL statement, 93, 127, 163, 201–202
CBL compiler, directing statement changes, 24–27
CBL statement, 202
CCCA, 259–269
  ADABAS, 277
  BLL cell placement, 273
  conversion problems, 189–198
  converting CICS, 80–81
  copybook containing CICS statements, 275–276
  copy replacing statement resulting in ABJ6249, 274–275
  Decimal Divide Exception, 274
  default parameter setting for ' or ", 274
  errors, 81–83
  evaluation, 260
  EXEC SQL error, 273–274
  extra period, 273
  hex value, 275
  large block sizes, 273
  recommendations, 119–122
  removal of brackets in ABJ6225, 276
  source program already converted, 272
  specifications, 107
  subscript issue, 272
  SYSUT5 problem, 271
  test description, 259–260
  tool-based conversion process, 106–119
    conversion path, 108
    converting and compiling COBOL programs, 112–113
    Easytrieve Plus reporting program, 114–117
    inventory phase, 106–111
    language-level identification, 111–112
    modifying CONTROL file, 114
    postconversion compile jobs, 118–119
    program/file report, 112, 114
    report sample, 117–118
  unstring statement resulting in ABJ6025, 276
  upgrading OS/VS COBOL to
    VS COBOL II, 119–121
    VS COBOL/370, 157–198
  upgrading VS COBOL II to COBOL/370, 199–219
  value clause is truncated, 277
  VSAM problem with, 155
Chained storage areas, accessing, 76–78
Channel skipping, 53
CICS:
  converting statements, 81–83
  manually converting, 69–80
    base addressability considerations, 71
    conversion summary, 72
    DL/I call interface, 72–80
    dynamic CALL statement, 70
    LENGTH OF special register, 70–71
    SERVICE RELOAD statement, 71
    setting compiler options, 80
    setting run-time options, 80
    static CALL statement, 70
    using elements requiring GETMAIN services, 71
  using CCCA to convert, 80–81
CICS statements, CCCA copybook containing, 275–276
CLOSE...REEL/UNIT FOR REMOVAL statement, 43, 127, 163
CLOSE WITH DISP/CLOSE...WITH POSITIONING statements, 43, 127, 164
CMPR2 compiler option, 24–25
COBOL, migrating from COBOL II to, 96–98

Index

COBOL/370, migrating from VS COBOL II, 211–219
COBOL1, language level identification, 111–112
COBOL I, commands, versus COBOL II, 54
COBOL II:
  commands, versus COBOL I, 54
  manual upgrades
    conversion summary workplan, 6
    organizing project, 5–8
  migrating to COBOL, 96–98
  upgrade standards, 7–8
COBOL/370. *See* VS COBOL II, manually upgrading to COBOL/370
Combined abbreviated relation condition, 43
Communications, 66
COMMUNICATIONS SECTION, 127, 164
Compile jobs:
  postconversion, 118–119
  sample, 247–258
Compiler:
  options, 98
  setting options with CICS, 80
COM-REG special register, 36, 127, 164
CONFIGURATION SECTION header, 127–128, 164
Consulting firm:
  finding, 227–228
  traits, 224–227
CONTROL file, modifying, 114
COPY problems, 189–190
COPY...REPLACING statement, 93, 128–130, 164–165, 202
COPY statement, 35–36, 130–132, 165
CURRENCY SIGN, 37, 132, 165
CURRENCY SIGN clause, 39
CURRENT-DATE special register, 37, 132–133, 165–166

D

Data Division, 34–41, 92
DATA RECORDS clause, 133, 166, 202–203
DATE-COMPILED/DATE-WRITTEN headers, 133, 166
DATE-COMPILED/DATE-WRITTEN paragraphs, 133, 166
DATE-COMPILED header, 133, 166
DCLGEN table declaration problem, 197–198
DEBUG card and packet, 133, 166
Debugging declarative valid operands, 27–28
Debugging, source language, 27–28
Decimal Divide Exception, 274
DISABLE statement, 133, 166
DIVIDE...ON SIZE ERROR statement, 94, 134, 167, 203
DL/I call interface, 72–80
  accessing chained storage areas, 76–78
  processing storage areas exceeding 4K, 74–76
  receiving communications area, 73–74
  using OCCURS DEPENDING ON, 78–80

E

Easytrieve Plus reporting program, 114–117
ENABLE statement, 134, 167
ENTER statement, 45, 134, 167, 203
Environment Division, 29–34, 91–92
ERROR declaratives, 134, 167
  GIVING option, 134, 167
EXAMINE, 134, 167
EXEC SQL error, 273–274
EXHIBIT statement, 134, 167
EXIT PROGRAM, 89, 135, 168, 203–204
EXIT PROGRAM statement, 45

F

Factory process, 223–224
Field names, requiring changes, 8
File, obsolete, dealing with, 8
FILE-LIMIT/FILE-LIMITS clauses, 135, 168
FILE STATUS clause, 135, 168
FILE STATUS codes, 135, 168, 204
FOR MULTIPLE REEL/UNIT clause, 135–136, 169
Full-Time Equivalent Resource, 224

G

GETMAIN, 71
GOBACK statement, 45, 89, 136, 169, 204
GREATER THEN relational operator, 136, 169

H

Hex value, 275
High values, 54

I

Identification Division, 28–29, 91
IDMS, 136, 169, 204–205
IF...OTHERWISE statement, 45
IF statement, 136–137, 169–170
Indexes, qualified, 137, 170
INSPECT statement, 25, 94, 137, 170, 205
INSTALLATION, 205
INSTALLATION paragraph, 137, 170
Inventory phase, 106–112
ISAM:
   conversion options and issues, 59–62
   extraction, 62–65
ISAM files, 137–138, 170–171
   conversion options, 60–61
   handling language items affects, 60
ISAM program, conversion, 61–62
IS, optional word, 44

J

JUSTIFIED clause, changes, 36–37
JUSTIFIED RIGHT clause, 138, 171

L

LABEL RECORDS, 205–206
LABEL RECORDS clause, 138, 171
LABEL RECORDS... TOTALING/TOTALED AREA option, 138, 171, 206
Language level:
   comparison, 229–241
   determining, 22–23
Large block sizes, 273
LENGTH OF special register, 70–71
LESS THEN relational operator, 138, 171
Literals, nonnumeric, 138–139, 172
Load module, link-editing, 87–88
Logical operator evaluation, 43–44

M

MEMORY SIZE, 206
MEMORY SIZE clause, 139, 172
MOVE ALL literal, 139, 172
MOVE CORR/CORRESPONDING statement, 139, 172
MOVE statement, 45–46, 140, 172, 172
MULTIPLE FILE TAPE clause, 139, 172, 206
MULTIPLY...ON SIZE ERROR statement, 94–95, 139–140, 172–173, 206–207
MVS, migrating from COBOL II to COBOL, 96–98
MVS COBOL, testing for, 53–54

N

NOMINAL KEY clause, 140–141, 173–174
NOT, 43–44, 141, 174
NOTE statement, 141, 174

NSTD-REELS special register, 141, 174
Numeric comparing with alphabetic issue, 196–197, 217–219

O

OCCURS clause, 141, 174
OCCURS DEPENDING ON, DL/I call interface, 78–80
OCCURS DEPENDING ON clause, 37, 95–96, 141–142, 175–176, 207–208
   value for receiving items, 38–39
ON SIZE ERROR option, 46–47
ON statement, 46, 143, 176
OPEN...DISP/OPEN...LEAVE/OPEN...REREAD statements, 143, 176
OPEN EXTENDED statement, changes, 33
OPEN...REVERSED statement, 143, 176–177
ORGANIZATION clause, 39, 143, 177
OS/VS COBOL:
   commands requiring updates, 24–53
      CBL compiler option, 24–27
      Data Division, 34–41
      Environment Division, 29–34
      Identification Division, 28–29
      Procedure Division, 41–53
      source language debugging changes, 27–28
   migrating to VS COBOL II, 53–54
   problematic elements, 10–12
   sorting, 50
   unsupported commands, 8–10
   upgrading to VS COBOL II, 23
   upgrading to VS COBOL/370 using CCCA, 157–198
      conversion problems, 189–198
      ideal migration path, 157
OTHERWISE, 144, 177

P

PERFORM/ALTER, 144, 177
PERFORM statement:
   changes in VARYING/AFTER options, 47–49
   in independent segments, 26–27
PERFORM VARYING, 25–26
PERFORM...VARYING...AFTER statement, 89–90, 144–145, 177–178, 208
PERFORM...VARYING problem, 195–196, 217
Periods, 145, 178, 212–214
   extra, 273
PICTURE clause, 96, 145, 178, 208–209
   B symbol, 35
PICTURE P in RELATIVE KEY, 145, 178, 209
Postconversion compile jobs, 118–119
Procedure Division, 41–53, 92–96
PROCESSING MODE clause, 145, 178–179, 209
PROGRAM COLLATING SEQUENCE clause, 26
Program/file report, 112, 114
PROGRAM-ID header, 145, 179
Program name, 145–146, 179

Q

Quotation mark, default parameter setting, 274

R

READ statement, 49
   ISAM files, 146, 179
READY TRACE statement, 146, 179
RECEIVE statement, 146, 179
RECORD CONTAINS, 146, 179–180, 209
RECORDING MODE clause, 146, 180, 209

REDEFINES clause, 39, 147, 180
Relational operator:
    evaluation, 43–44
    problem, 191–193, 214–216
REMARKS paragraph, 33, 147, 180
Reporting sample, advanced, 243–245
Report Writer, conversion options and issues, 57–59
Report Writer Precompiler, 59
REPORT WRITER statements, 147, 180
RERUN clause, 49
RESERVE ALTERNATE AREAS, 147, 180–181
RESERVE AREAS, 147, 181
RESERVE clause, changes, 33–34
Reserved words, 12–22, 97, 148, 181
    problems, 193–195
RESET TRACE statement, 148, 181
RETURN statement, 49
REWRITE statement ISAM files, 148, 181

S

SAME AREA clause, 148, 181
SCEELKED, 87
SEARCH ALL, 148, 181
SEARCH statement, 49
SEARCH...WHEN, 148, 182
SECURITY paragraph, 149, 182, 209–210
SEEK, 149, 182
SELECT OPTIONAL, 149, 182
SELECT OPTIONAL clause, 34
SEND statement, 149, 182
SERVICE RELOAD statement, 71
Signed VALUE, 149, 182
SORT, special registers, 49–50
SORT-OPTION clause, 149, 183
Source language, debugging changes, 27–28

Source program, language level, 22–23
SPECIAL-NAMES paragraph, 39
START...USING KEY statement, 50–51, 149, 183
Status key, values, 30–33
STOP RUN statement, 90, 150, 183, 210
STRING statement, 28, 96, 150, 183–184, 210
Subscripts:
    out of range, 28
    problem, 272
SYSUT5 problem, 271

T

THEN, 151, 184
TIME-OF-DAY special register, 151, 184–185
Tool-based upgrades, 101–155
    CCCA for upgrading OS/VS COBOL to VS COBOL II, 119–121
    conversion process with CCCA, 106–119
    selecting tool, 102–106
    VSAM problem with CCCA, 155
TOTALING/TOTALED AREA, 151–152, 185
TRACK-AREA, 152, 185
TRACK-LIMIT clause, 152, 185
TRANSFORM statement, 152, 185

U

UNSTRING statement, 91, 152, 185–186, 210
    subscript evaluation, 51–52
UPSI name, 152–153, 186, 211
UPSI switches, 39–40
USE AFTER STANDARD... ON...GIVING, 153, 186
USE BEFORE STANDARD, 153, 186
USE FOR DEBUGGING, 153, 186

V

VALUE clause
  condition names, 40–41
  truncated, 277
VALUE in 88 level, 153, 186
VALUE OF clause, 153, 187, 211
VALUES, 153, 186–187
VSAM, problem with CCCA, 155
VS COBOL:
  problematic elements, 10–12
  unsupported commands, 8–10
VS COBOL II:
  manually upgrading to COBOL/370, 85–98
    behaviors, 89–90
    Data Division, 92
    Environment Division, 91–92
    Identification Division, 91
    link-editing existing load modules, 87–88
    performance issues, 90–91
    Procedure Division, 92–96
  migrating to COBOL/370, 211–219
    compiler options, 211
    fields not defined, 219
    numeric comparing with alphabetic issue, 217–219
    PERFORM...VARYING problem, 217
    periods issue, 212–214
    relational operator issue, 214–216
  OS/VS COBOL migrating to, 53–54
  sorting, 50
  status key values, 30–33
  unsupported features, 3–5
  upgrading OS/VS COBOL to, 23

W

WHEN-COMPILED, 153–154, 187
Words, changed between reserved and unreserved status, 13–22
WRITE...AFTER POSITIONING, 154, 187–188
WRITE AFTER POSITIONING statement, 52–53
WRITE...BEFORE/AFTER ADVANCING mnemonic-name LINE/LINES, 154, 188
WRITE statement ISAM files, 154, 188–189

Y

Year 2000 compliance, 85

Customer Note: If this book is accompanied by software, please read the following before opening the package.

This software contains files to help you utilize the models described in the accompanying book. By opening the package, you are agreeing to be bound by the following agreement:

This software product is protected by copyright and all rights are reserved by the author, John Wiley & Sons, Inc., or their licensors. You are licensed to use this software as described in the software and the accompanying book. Copying the software for any other purpose may be a violation of the U.S. Copyright Law.

This software product is sold as is without warranty of any kind, either express or implied, including but not limited to the implied warranty of merchantability and fitness for a particular purpose. Neither Wiley nor its dealers or distributors assumes any liability for any alleged or actual damages arising from the use of or the inability to use this software. (Some states do not allow the exclusion of implied warranties, so the exclusion may not apply to you.)

To use this CD-ROM, your system must meet the following requirements:

Platform/Processor/Operating System. Windows 3.1 or higher

RAM. 16MB

Hard Drive Space. 2MB

Peripherals. Microsoft Word 97 (or viewer)